# 마이갓 5 Step 모의고사 공부법

**1** ● **Vocabulary** 필수 단어 암기 & Test
① 단원별 필수 단어 암기 ② 영어 → 한글 Test ③ 한글 → 영어 Test

**2** ● **Text** 지문과 해설
① 전체 지문 해석 ② 페이지별 필기 공간 확보 ③ N회독을 통한 지문 습득

**3** ● **Practice 1** 빈칸 시험 (w/ 문법 힌트)
① 해석 없는 반복 빈칸 시험 ② 문법 힌트를 통한 어법 숙지
③ 주요 문법과 암기 내용 최종 확인

**4** ● **Practice 2** 빈칸 시험 (w/ 해석)
① 주요 내용/어법/어휘 빈칸 ② 한글을 통한 내용 숙지
③ 반복 시험을 통한 빈칸 암기

**5** ● **Quiz** 객관식 예상문제를 콕콕!
① 수능형 객관식 변형문제 ② 100% 자체 제작 변형문제 ③ 빈출 내신 문제 유형 연습

영어 내신의 끝
**마이갓 모의고사** 고1, 2

1 등급을 위한 5단계 노하우
2 모의고사 연도 및 시행월 별 완전정복
3 내신변형 완전정복

영어 내신의 끝
**마이갓 교과서** 고1, 2

1 등급을 위한 10단계 노하우
2 교과서 레슨별 완전정복
3 영어 영역 마스터를 위한 지름길

마이갓 교재
보듬책방 온라인 스토어 (https://smartstore.naver.com/bdbooks)

# 마이갓 10 Step 영어 내신 공부법

## Vocabulary

**필수 단어 암기 & Test**
① 단원별 필수 단어 암기
② 영어 → 한글 Test
③ 한글 → 영어 Test

## Grammar

**단원별 중요 문법과 연습 문제**
① 기초 문법 설명
② 교과서 적용 예시 소개
③ 기초/ Advanced Test

## Text

**지문과 해설**
① 전체 지문 해석
② 페이지별 필기 공간 확보
③ N회독을 통한 지문 습득

## Practice 3

**빈칸 시험 (w/ 해석)**
① 주요 내용/어법/어휘 빈칸
② 한글을 통한 내용 숙지
③ 반복 시험을 통한 빈칸 암기

## Practice 2

**빈칸 시험 (w/ 해석)**
① 주요 내용/어법/어휘 빈칸
② 한글을 통한 내용 숙지
③ 반복 시험을 통한 빈칸 암기

## Practice 1

**어휘 & 어법 선택 시험**
① 시험에 나오는 어법 어휘 공략
② 중요 어법/어휘 선택형 시험
③ 반복 시험을 통한 포인트 숙지

## Quiz

**객관식 예상문제를 콕콕!**
① 수능형 객관식 변형문제
② 100% 자체 제작 변형문제
③ 빈출 내신 문제 유형 연습

## Final Test

**주관식 서술형 예상문제**
① 어순/영작/어법 등
　 주관식 서술형 문제 대비!
② 100% 자체 제작 변형문제

## 전체 영작 연습

**직접 영작 해보기**
① 주어진 단어를 활용한
　 전체 서술형 영작 훈련
② 쓰기를 통한 내용 암기

## 학교 기출 문저

**지문과 해설**
① 단원별 실제 학교 기
　 문제 모음
② 객관식부터 서술형까
　 완벽 커버!

24년 고2
11월 모의고사

# 마이갓

연습과 실전 모두 잡는 내신대비 완벽

| workbook |

보듬영어

# 2024 고2

# 11 <sub>월</sub>

## WORK BOOK

——

**2024년 고2 11월 모의고사 내신대비용 WorkBook & 변형문제**

# CONTENTS

2024 고2 11월 WORK BOOK

보듬영어

| 18 | executive | 집행의, 경영의; 임원, 경영진 | | unexpected | 예기치 않은, 뜻밖의, 갑작스러운 |
|---|---|---|---|---|---|
| | attention | 주의(력), 집중(력), 관심 | | unfolded | 접히지 않은, 펼쳐진 |
| | matter | 문제, 사안, 물질; 문제가 되다, 중요하다 | | reservation | 예약, 보류, 보호구역 |
| | immediate | 즉각적인, 직접의, 인접한 | | locate | ~에 위치하다, (위치를) 찾아내다 |
| | consideration | 고려 (사항), 배려, 숙고 | | make a reservation | 예약하다 |
| | regarding | ~에 관한 | | make a mistake | 실수하다 |
| | apparent | 분명한, 명백한, 겉보기에는 | | deliberately | 의도[계획]적으로, 신중하게 |
| | budget | 예산(안), 운영비; 예산을 세우다 | | ease | 진정시키다; 편함, 용이함 |
| | previously | 전에, 앞서서 | | proceed with | ~을 계속하다 |
| | approve | 찬성하다, 승인하다 | | ruin | 파괴하다, 망치다; 파괴, (-s) 유적, 폐허 |
| | adjustment | 조정, 수정, 적응 | 20 | literate | 교양 있는, 읽고 쓸 수 있는 |
| | in order to V | ~하기 위해, ~하려고 | | critically | 비판적으로, 결정적으로 |
| | emerging | 신흥의, 신생의 | | societal | 사회의, 사회 활동[관습]의 |
| | modification | 변화, 수정, 변경 | | so as to V | ~하도록, ~하기 위해 |
| | initially | 처음에, 초기에 | | inform | (정보를) 알아내다, 알리다, 영향을 주다 |
| | additional | 추가적인, 추가의 | | deal with | ~을 처리[해결]하다, 다루다 |
| | wages | 임금, 노임, 급료 | | complex | 복잡한, 복합의; 복합체, 콤플렉스 |
| | material | 재료, 물질; 물질의, 육체의, 중요한 | | organize | 조직하다, 정리하다, 개최하다 |
| | request | 요청, 요구; 요청[요구]하다 | | navigate | 항해[조종]하다, 길을 찾다, 처리하다 |
| | allocation | 할당, 배당 | | quantify | 수량화하다, 정량하다 |
| | refer to | ~을 언급[참조]하다, 가리키다 | | measure | 측정하다, 평가하다; 척도, 기준, 조치 |
| | attachment | 부착(물), 부속품, 애착 | | estimate | 견적, 평가; 추정하다, 평가하다 |
| | detail | 세부 (항목); 자세히 말하다, 열거하다 | | classify | 분류[구분]하다, 기밀 취급하다 |
| | regard | 간주[주목]하다, 관련있다; 관심, 존경, 관계 | | justify | 정당화하다, 옳음을 증명하다 |
| 19 | approach | 접근하다; 접근(법) | | prove | 입증하다, ~으로 판명되다[드러나다] |

# Voca

| ❶ voca | ❷ text | ❸ [ / ] | ❹ _____ | ❺ quiz 1 | ❻ quiz 2 | ❼ quiz 3 | ❽ quiz 4 | ❾ quiz 5 |

| | | | | | |
|---|---|---|---|---|---|
| | generalize | 일반화하다, 보편화하다 | | instant | 즉각의, 즉석의 |
| | critical | 중요한, 비판적인 | 22 | determine | 결심[결정]하다, 알아내다 |
| | qualitatively | 질적으로 | | mass | 질량, (큰) 덩어리, 집단; 많은, 대량의 |
| | interaction | 상호 작용 | | compare ~ with ... | ~와 ...을 비교하다 |
| | along with | ~와 함께 | | a number of | 많은, 다수의 |
| | context | 상황, 배경, 맥락, 문맥 | | weigh | 무게를 달다, 중요하다, 심사 숙고하다 |
| | so that | 그래서, ~하기 위해서 | | complicate | 복잡하게 하다, 곤란하게 하다 |
| | explicitly | 명시적으로, 분명하게 | | roughly | 대략, 거의, 거칠게 |
| | support | 지지[지원]하다, 부양하다; 지지, 후원 | | involve | 포함[수반]하다, 필요로 하다, 관련시키다 |
| 21 | stingy | 인색한, 적은, 쏘는, 날카로운 | | binary star | 쌍성 |
| | booster | 후원자, 촉진제 | | instance | 사례, 경우 |
| | undoubtedly | 의심할 여지없이, 확실히 | | calculate | 추정하다, 계산[산출]하다 |
| | praiseworthy | 칭찬할 만한 | | in other words | 즉, 다시 말해서 |
| | entirely | 완전히, 전적으로 | | equation | 방정식, 등식, 동일시 |
| | satisfying | 만족스럽게 하는 | | measurement | 측정(치), 측량(치), 치수 |
| | accord | 일치하다, 조화를 이루다; 일치, 협정 | | estimation | 판단, 평가, 견적, 추정, 존중 |
| | generous | 관대한, 너그러운, 푸짐한 | | property | 재산, 부동산, 특성, 속성 |
| | praise | 찬사를 보내다, 칭송하다; 찬사 | | determination | 결정, 결심, 결의 |
| | virtue | 선, 미덕, 가치 | | magnitude | 엄청난 규모, 크기, 중요성, (별의) 광도 |
| | courageous | 용감한, 용기 있는 | 23 | base on | ~에 근거하다 |
| | stable | 안정된, 지속성이 있는; 마구간, 외양간 | | constantly | 지속적으로, 끊임없이 |
| | moral | 도덕적인 | | strive | 노력하다, 애쓰다, 분투하다 |
| | identity | 정체성 | | define | 정의하다, 한계 짓다, 한정하다 |
| | as opposed to | ~이 아니라, ~와는 대조적으로 | | function | 기능하다, 작용하다; 기능, 작용 |
| | impulse | 충동, 자극, 욕구, 추진(력) | | potential | 가능성이 있는, 잠재적인; 가능성, 잠재력 |

## Voca

| | 단어 | 뜻 | | | 단어 | 뜻 |
|---|---|---|---|---|---|---|
| | highs and lows | 기복, 고저 | | | revolutionize | 혁명[대변혁]을 일으키다 |
| | be capable of -ing | ~할 수 있다 | | | disturbing | 불안하게 하는, 충격적인, 불온한 |
| | reliant | 의지하는, 믿고 있는 | | | utter | 말하다, 소리를 내다; 완전한, 순전한 |
| | opposite | 반대(되는 사람[것]); 반대의 | | | lead to | ~을 낳다, ~으로 이어지다 |
| | correspondingly | 상응하여, 부응하여 | | | distinction | 구별, 차이, 특징, 뛰어남, 우수(성) |
| | psychiatrist | 정신과 의사 | | | blur | 모호하게 하다, 흐리게 하다 |
| | attempt | 시도; 시도하다 | | | shift | 변화, 이동, 교대; 바꾸다, 이동하다 |
| | miserable | 비참한, 불쌍한, 괴로운 | | | priority | 우선(권), 우선 사항 |
| | component | (구성) 요소, 성분, 부품; 구성하고 있는 | | | in favor of | ~에 우호적인, ~을 지지하여 |
| | maintain | 유지하다, 주장하다 | | | logical | 논리적인, 필연적인 |
| | neutral | 중립적인, 중립의, 중간의, 공평한 | | | argument | 논쟁, 주장, 논거 |
| | in turn | 결과적으로, 차례차례 | | | temptation | 유혹, 충동 |
| | internal | 내부의, 체내의, 국내의 | | | compel | 강요하다, ~하게 만들다 |
| 24 | sow | (씨를) 뿌리다 | 25 | | respectively | 각각, 각기, 저마다 |
| | adequacy | 타당함, 적당함 | | | surpass | 능가하다, 초월하다 |
| | keep pace with | ~와 보조를 맞추다, ~에 따라가다 | | | anticipate | 예상하다, 기대하다 |
| | itch | 가려움; 가렵다, (~하고 싶어) 못 견디다 | | | exceed | 초과하다 |
| | genuine | 진실한, 진정한, 진짜의 | 26 | | republic | 공화국 |
| | confine | 한정[국한]하다, 가두다; (-s) 경계 | | | be born to V | ~할 운명을 타고 나다 |
| | companion | 친구, 동반자, 동료 | | | immigrant | (타국에서 온) 이주민, 이민자 |
| | spill | 엎지르다, 흘리다; 엎지름, 유출 | | | institute | 기관, 협회; 설립하다, 제정하다 |
| | aspect | 측면, 면, 양상, 관점 | | | elect | 선출하다, 택하다; 선출된 |
| | consumer | 소비자 | | | parliament | 의회, 국회 |
| | electronics | 전자 공학, 전자 기기 | | | adopt | (채)택하다, 선정하다, 취하다 |
| | generation | 세대, 일족, 발생 | | | moderate | 적당한, 온건한; 조정[완화]하다, 완화하다 |

| ❶ voca | ❷ text | ❸ [ / ] | ❹ ＿＿＿ | ❺ quiz 1 | ❻ quiz 2 | ❼ quiz 3 | ❽ quiz 4 | ❾ quiz 5 |
|---|---|---|---|---|---|---|---|---|

|  | stance | 입장, 자세, 태도 |  | finding | 결과, 결론 |
|---|---|---|---|---|---|
|  | progressive | 점진적인, 진보적인 |  | associate ~ with ... | ~을 ...와 결부시키다 |
|  | tirelessly | 지칠 줄 모르고, 끊임없이 |  | completely | 완전히, 충분히 |
|  | expose | 드러내다, 폭로하다, 노출시키다 |  | obviously | 명백하게, 분명히 |
|  | abuse | 남용, 학대; 남용[오용]하다, 학대하다 |  | happen to V | 우연히 ~하다 |
|  | challenging | 힘든, 도전적인 |  | suggest | 제안하다, 암시하다, 시사하다 |
|  | retirement | 퇴직, 은퇴 |  | conversely | 반대로, 역으로 |
|  | continue to V | 계속 ~하다 |  | avoid | 피하다, 막다 |
|  | draft | 초안, 원고, 징병; 초안을 작성하다, 선발하다 |  | stimulus | 자극, 격려, 고무 ((복수형 stimuli)) |
|  | constitution | 헌법, 구조, 설치 |  | unpleasant | 불쾌한, 불편한 |
| 27 | board | 탑승하다; 이사회, 판자, -판 |  | cancer | 암, 악성 종양 |
|  | registration | 등록 (서류), 기재 |  | used to V | ~하곤 했다, ~이었다[했다] |
|  | confirmation | 증거, 확증 |  | A rather than B | B라기 보다는 A |
|  | wrist | 손목, 손재주 |  | saline | 식염수 |
|  | in groups | 떼를 지어, 삼삼오오 |  | whereas | ~에 반하여, 그런데, 그러나 |
|  | designate | 지정하다, 지명하다; 지명된 | 30 | equator | 적도 |
|  | emergency | 긴급, 긴급 상황, 응급 |  | species | (분류상의) 종(種) |
| 28 | consultation | 상담, 협의 |  | breed | 유형, 품종, 혈통; 번식하다, 낳다, 기르다 |
|  | suit | 정장, 소송; 적합하다, (알)맞다 |  | temperate | 온화한, 온건한, 차분한, 절제된 |
|  | employee | 직원, 종업원 |  | polar | 북극[남극]의, 극지의, 양극의 |
|  | company | 친구, 동료, 회사, 교제; 회사의 |  | sharply | 급격히, 날카롭게, 민첩하게 |
|  | booth | 부스, (칸막이를 한) 작은 공간 |  | trigger | 계기, 방아쇠; 유발하다, 쏘다 |
|  | order | 명령[주문]하다, 정돈하다; 명령, 주문, 순서 |  | outcome | 결과(물) |
|  | auditorium | 강당, 청중석 |  | raise | 높이다, 올리다, 기르다, 제기하다; 인상 |
| 29 | conditioned | 조건부의, 길들여진 |  | supply | 공급하다, 주다; 공급 |

## Voca

|   | | | | | |
|---|---|---|---|---|---|
| | reluctant | 꺼리는, 주저하는, 마지못한 | | chemical | 화학적인, 화학의; 화학 물질 |
| | physically | 실제적으로, 신체적으로 | | preparation | 준비, 대비, 조제약 |
| | incapable | 무능한, 할 수 없는 | | vital | 중대한, 활기 있는, 생명의 |
| | shrink | 줄어들다, 움츠러들다, 수축하다 | | succeed | 성공하다, 계승하다, 잇따르다 |
| | exception | 예외(사항), 제외 | | applicable | 들어맞는, 적용[응용]할 수 있는 |
| | nomadic | 유목의, 방랑의 | | in advance | 미리, 사전에 |
| | desert | 버리다, 떠나다; 사막 | | alternative | 대안 |
| | initiate | 시작하다, 입문시키다; 신참 | 32 | pressure | 압력, 압박, 스트레스; 압력을 가하다 |
| | brood | 함께 태어난 새끼들 | | interpretation | 해석, 설명, 이해 |
| | exceptionally | 특별히, 유난히, 예외적으로 | | poet | 시인 |
| | sparrow | 참새 | | set about | 시작하다, 공격하다 |
| | successive | 연속하는, 계속적인, 계승의, 대대의 | | translate | 번역하다, 해석하다, 옮기다 |
| 31 | hinder | 방해하다, 막다 | | on one's own | 혼자, 혼자 힘으로 |
| | resource | 수단, 기지 (-s) 자원, 소질; 자원을 제공하다 | | commentary | 논평, 설명, 해설 |
| | identify | 알아보다, 확인하다, 동일시하다 | | translation | 번역, 통역, 해석 |
| | perform | 수행하다, 행동하다, 공연[연주]하다 | | draw on | ~을 이용하다, ~에 의지하다, 가까워지다 |
| | compulsory | 강제적인, 의무적인, 필수의 | | source | 원천, 근원, (-s) 출처, 정보원 |
| | recognize | 알아보다, 인정[표창]하다, 인식하다 | | consist of | ~으로 구성되다, 이루어져 있다 |
| | simplify | 단순화하다, 간단하게 하다 | | linguistic | 언어의, 언어학의 |
| | performance | 수행, 성과, 성적, 공연 | | arise from | ~에 기인하다, ~에서 발생하다 |
| | conduct | ~을 하다, 지휘하다, (전기 등을) 전도하다; 행동 | | purpose | 목적, 의도; 의도하다 |
| | experiment | 실험, 시험, 시도; 실험하다, 시도하다 | | expectation | 기대, 요구, 예상, 가망 |
| | investigation | 수사, 조사, 연구 | 33 | argue | 논쟁[논의]하다, 주장하다 |
| | have access to | ~에 접근하다 | | logically | 필연적으로, 논리적으로 |
| | laboratory | 실험실; 실험실의 | | consistent | 일관된, 변함없는, 한결같은 |

# Voca

| ❶ voca | ❷ text | ❸ [ / ] | ❹ _____ | ❺ quiz 1 | ❻ quiz 2 | ❼ quiz 3 | ❽ quiz 4 | ❾ quiz 5 |

| | | | | | | |
|---|---|---|---|---|---|---|
| known as | ~으로 알려진 | | | highlight | 집중하다, 강조하다; 가장 중요한 부분 |
| neatly | 깔끔하게, 말쑥하게, 솜씨 있게 | | | spectrum | 범위, 연속체, 스펙트럼 |
| apart from | ~와 별도로, ~을 제외하고 | | | accommodate | 수용하다, 숙박시키다, 적응하다 |
| productive | 생산적인, 다산의 | | | distinct | 구별되는, 분명한, 별개의 |
| loosely | 엉성하게, 느슨하게 | | 34 | perception | 인식, 인지, 지각 |
| belong | 속하다, ~의 것이다 | | | detect | 알아내다, 감지하다, 탐지하다 |
| owing to | ~ 때문에 | | | principle | 원칙, 원리 |
| resemblance | 유사성, 닮음 | | | otherwise | 그렇지 않으면, ~와 다르게 |
| phrase | 구절, (문)구; 말로 표현하다 | | | burning | 불타는, 화급한, 중대한 |
| have in common | 공통점이 있다 | | | vary | 다르다, 바꾸다, 변하다 |
| trait | 특성 | | | strength | 강점, 장점, 힘, 기운 |
| consequently | 결과적으로, 그 결과, 따라서 | | | barely | 거의 ~않게, 가까스로 |
| distinguish A from B | A와 B를 구분[구별]하다 | | | distinguish | 구분[구별]하다, ~을 특징짓다 |
| destined | (~할) 운명에 있는, ~행의 | | 35 | benefit | 이익, 이득; 이익이 되다 |
| agreement | 합의, 동의 | | | individually | 개별적으로, 개인적으로 |
| qualify as | ~으로서 자격을 갖추고 있다[얻다] | | | common | 공통의, 흔한, 평범한 |
| in the first place | 우선, 맨 먼저 | | | traffic jam | 교통 체증, 교통 정체 |
| figure out | 산출[계산]하다, 알아내다 | | | overuse | 남용; 남용하다 |
| border | 국경, 경계, 가장자리; 접경하다 | | | lessen | (크기, 양 등이) 줄다, 감소시키다 |
| edge | 이점, 우위, 모서리, 끝, 가장자리, 날 | | | expand | 확장[확대]하다, 부연[확충]하다 |
| stretch | 잡아 늘이다, 쭉 펴다; 뻗침, 확장 | | | in isolation | 고립된 상태로, 별개로 |
| flexible | 융통성이 있는, 유연한, 탄력적인 | | | fellow | 사나이, 동료, 친구; 동료의 |
| boundary | 경계(선), 한계, 범위 | | | compete | 다투다, 겨루다, 경쟁하다 |
| be worth -ing | ~할 가치가 있다 | | | individual | 개인; 개인의, 개별적인, 독특한 |
| exceptional | 탁월한, 뛰어난, 보기 드문 | | | destruction | 파괴, 파멸, 멸망 |

| | | | | | |
|---|---|---|---|---|---|
| | degeneration | 퇴화, 쇠퇴, 타락 | | serve as | ~의 역할을 하다 |
| | regenerate | 재건하다, 재생하다, 갱생시키다 | | unnecessary | 불필요한, 쓸데없는 |
| 36 | theoretically | 이론상, 이론적으로는 | | seek to V | ~하고자 하다, 시도하다 |
| | capacity | 용량, 수용력, 능력 | | facilitate | 촉진[조장]하다, 용이하게 하다 |
| | theoretical | 이론의, 이론상의 | | cognitive | 인지의, 인식의 |
| | offset | 상쇄하다 | 37 | adhere | 충실하다 |
| | associate with | ~와 어울리다, 관련시키다 | | experimental | 실험의, 실험적인, 경험적인 |
| | retrieve | 상기하다 | | illuminate | 밝히다 |
| | as a result | 그 결과 | | predictable | 예측[예상] 가능한 |
| | efficient | 유능한, 능률적인, 효율적인 | | feature | 특징, 특집, 용모; 특집으로 하다, 특집으로 삼다 |
| | strategy | 전략, 전술, 계획, 방법 | | conceal | 감추다, 숨기다 |
| | dependent on | ~에 의존하는 | | evidence | 증거, 징후 |
| | shortcut | 지름길, 손쉬운 방법 | | explanation | 설명, 해명, 변명 |
| | observe | 관찰하다, 준수하다, (의견 등을) 말하다 | | chronology | 연대순 배열, 연대기 |
| | visual | 시각의, 눈에 보이는 | | construct | 건설하다, 구성[조립]하다 |
| | variable | 다양한, 변하기 쉬운, 가변(성)의; 변수 | | framework | 하부 구조, 체계, 뼈대, 틀 |
| | depending on | ~에 따라 | | systematically | 체계적으로, 조직적으로 |
| | point of view | 관점, 견해, 전망, 경치 | | meaningful | 의미 있는, 중요한 |
| | contextual | 전후 관계의, 문맥상의 | | subject | 주제, 과목, 대상; 지배하다, 복종시키다 |
| | underlying | 근원적인 | | in particular | 특히, 특별히 |
| | general | (육군) 원수, 장군; 일반적인 | | sort | 분류하다, 구분하다; 종류 |
| | allow for | ~을 감안[참고]하다 | | inspire | 영감을 주다, 고무시키다, 격려하다 |
| | recognition | 인식, 인정, 표창 | | analyze | 분석하다, 분해하다 |
| | diverse | 다양한, 여러 가지의 | | neglect | 무시[방치]하다; 소홀, 무시 |
| | circumstance | 상황, 정황, 환경 | | contribution | (원인) 제공, 기여, 기고, 분담금 |

| ❶ voca | ❷ text | ❸ [ / ] | ❹ _____ | ❺ quiz 1 | ❻ quiz 2 | ❼ quiz 3 | ❽ quiz 4 | ❾ quiz 5 |

|    |    |    |    |    |    |
|----|----|----|----|----|----|
|    | treat | 대우하다, 다루다, 치료하다; 대접 | | eager | 갈망[열망]하는, 열심인 |
|    | interpretive | 설명을 위한, 해석의 | | identification | 동일시, 공감 |
|    | straightforward | 솔직한, 직접의, 수월한, 간단한 | | discourage | 의욕을 꺾다, 단념시키다, 훼방하다 |
|    | include | 포함하다, 포괄하다 | | keen | 예리한, 예민한, 열망하는 |
|    | limitation | 제한, 한계 | | injustice | 불평등, 부정 |
|    | misunderstanding | 오해, 착오, 불화 | | be credited with | ~을 가진[한] 것으로 믿어지다 |
| 38 | encounter | 접하다, 마주치다; 마주침, (뜻밖의) 만남 | | revulsion | 혐오감 |
|    | contrary | 반대의, 적합치 않은, 불리한; 정반대 | | slavery | 노예 제도, 노예의 신분 |
|    | claim | 주장[요구]하다, 차지하다; 요구, 주장 | | civil war | 내전 |
|    | literature | 문학, 문예, 문헌 | 39 | morally | 도덕적으로 |
|    | theorist | 이론가, 공론가 | | in spite of | ~에도 불구하고 |
|    | encourage | 장려[격려]하다, 촉구하다 | | instinct | 본능 |
|    | solitary | 혼자의, 외로운, 고립된 | | existence | 생활, 존재, 생존 |
|    | reflection | 반영, 반사, 숙고, 반성 | | hence | 그러므로, 따라서, 지금부터 |
|    | engage with | ~와 관계를 맺다, ~와 맞물리다 | | morality | 도덕률, 도덕 |
|    | counter | 반대의; 계산대; 대응하다 | | liberty | 자유, 해방 |
|    | appreciation | 평가, 인정, 이해, 감탄, 감사 | | application | 신청(서), 지원(서), 적용, 응용 프로그램 |
|    | complexity | 복잡성, 복잡함 | | sovereign | 주권을 가진, 독립의; 주권국, 군주 |
|    | acceptance | 수락, 승인, 용인 | | namely | 즉, 다시 말해 |
|    | promote | 촉진[장려]하다, 홍보하다, 진급시키다 | | emerge | 나오다, 나타나다, 드러나다 |
|    | questioning | 의문을 제기하는 | | nasty | 못된, 심술궂은, 더러운, 불쾌한 |
|    | authority | 권위, 권한, 당국, 기관 | | brutish | 잔인한 |
|    | arrangement | 배열, 배치 | | indeed | 실제로, 사실 |
|    | do harm | 해가 되다, 손해를 끼치다 | | antisocial | 반사회적인, 비사교적인 |
|    | credit ~ with ... | ~가 ...하다고 믿다, ~가 ...의 공로를 인정받다 | | selfishness | 이기적임, 이기심 |

| | ❶ voca | ❷ text | ❸ [ / ] | ❹ _____ | ❺ quiz 1 | ❻ quiz 2 | ❼ quiz 3 | ❽ quiz 4 | ❾ quiz 5 |

| | | | | | | |
|---|---|---|---|---|---|
| | phenomenon | 현상, 사건, 비범한 인물 ((복수형 phenomena)) | | undergo | 겪다, 경험하다, 견디다 |
| | mutual | 상호 간의, 서로의, 공통의 | | to make things worse | 설상가상으로, 엎친 데 덮친 격으로 |
| | affection | 애정, 애착 | | mutation | 돌연변이, 변화 |
| | assemble | 모으다, 조립하다 | | damage | 피해, 손상, 손해; 손해를 입히다 |
| 40 | perceive | 인식하다, 지각하다 | | responsible for | ~에 책임이 있는 |
| | participant | 참여자, 참가자 | | accelerate | 가속하다, 촉진하다 |
| | figure | 생각[계산]하다; 수치, 숫자, 인물, 모양 | | noticeable | 주목할 만한, 두드러진 |
| | depict | 묘사하다, 그리다 | | effect | 결과, 영향, 효과; 초래하다, 이루다 |
| | object | ~에 반대하다; 목표, 대상, 물체 | | distort | 비틀다, 일그러뜨리다, 왜곡하다 |
| | particular | 특정한, 개개의; 사항, 상세 | | result in | 그 결과 ~이 되다, ~을 야기하다 |
| | symbolic | 상징적인, 표상하는 | | iris | 홍채 |
| | make out | 알아내다, 이해하다, (잘)해 나가다, 성공하다 | | be due to | ~ 때문이다 |
| | be associated with | ~과 관련되다 | | multiply | 곱하다, 크게 증가하다 |
| | imply | 넌지시 나타내다, 암시하다, 수반하다 | | patch | 헝겊 조각, 좁은 땅, 구역; 덧대다 |
| | association | 연관(성), 연상, 협회 | | affected | 가장된, 꾸민, 감염된 |
| | object to | ~에 반대하다 | | simultaneously | 동시에, 일제히 |
| | perceptual | 지각의, 인지의 | | lie in | ~에 있다 |
| 41~42 | chromosome | 염색체 | | tissue | (생물) 조직, 화장지 |
| | accumulate | 축적하다 | | differentiated | 차별화된 |
| | be similar to | ~와 유사하다 | | early on | 초기에, 곧 |
| | alteration | 변화, 변경, 바꾸기 | | inherited | 유전된, 상속한, 물려받은 |
| | medieval | 중세의, 중세풍의 | 43~45 | on schedule | 예정대로 |
| | accidentally | 잘못하여, 우연히 | | swing | 흔들(리)다, 진동하다; 흔들기, 그네 |
| | stack | 더미, 다량, (-s) 서고; 쌓다, 쌓아 올리다 | | run into | 우연히 만나다, 부딪히다, 이르다 |
| | acquire | 얻다, 습득하다 | | submit | 제출하다, 복종시키다 |

# Voca Test

영 〉 한

| ❶ voca | ❷ text | ❸ [ / ] | ❹ _____ | ❺ quiz 1 | ❻ quiz 2 | ❼ quiz 3 | ❽ quiz 4 | ❾ quiz 5 |
|---|---|---|---|---|---|---|---|---|
| greet | 인사하다, 맞이하다 | | | | | | | |
| haste | 서두름, 급함, 성급 | | | | | | | |
| furiously | 미친 듯이, 맹렬히 | | | | | | | |
| browse through | 처음부터 끝까지 둘러[훑어]보다 | | | | | | | |
| only to V | 그 결과는 ~뿐, 단지 ~하기 위해 | | | | | | | |
| manage to | (힘든 일을) 간신히 해내다 | | | | | | | |
| to one's surprise | 놀랍게도 | | | | | | | |
| messy | 정리[정돈]되어 있지 않은, 지저분한 | | | | | | | |
| reschedule | 일정을 변경하다 | | | | | | | |
| solution | 해결(책), 용액 | | | | | | | |
| spread | 펴다, 퍼뜨리다, 퍼지다; 확장, 유포, 보급 | | | | | | | |
| hand in | 제출하다, 내다 | | | | | | | |
| satisfaction | 만족, 충족 | | | | | | | |
| from then on | 그 이래로, 그때부터 (쭉) | | | | | | | |
| routine | 일상적인; 일과, 습관적인 동작 | | | | | | | |
| embrace | 포옹하다, 수용하다; 포옹, 수용 | | | | | | | |
| unpredictable | 예측할 수 없는, 예측이 불가능한 | | | | | | | |
| | | | | | | | | |
| | | | | | | | | |
| | | | | | | | | |
| | | | | | | | | |
| | | | | | | | | |
| | | | | | | | | |
| | | | | | | | | |
| | | | | | | | | |

# Voca Test

영 › 한

| | ❶ voca | ❷ text | ❸ [ / ] | ❹ ____ | ❺ quiz 1 | ❻ quiz 2 | ❼ quiz 3 | ❽ quiz 4 | ❾ quiz 5 |
|---|---|---|---|---|---|---|---|---|---|
| 18 | executive | | | | unexpected | | | | |
| | attention | | | | unfolded | | | | |
| | matter | | | | reservation | | | | |
| | immediate | | | | locate | | | | |
| | consideration | | | | make a reservation | | | | |
| | regarding | | | | make a mistake | | | | |
| | apparent | | | | deliberately | | | | |
| | budget | | | | ease | | | | |
| | previously | | | | proceed with | | | | |
| | approve | | | | ruin | | | | |
| | adjustment | | | 20 | literate | | | | |
| | in order to V | | | | critically | | | | |
| | emerging | | | | societal | | | | |
| | modification | | | | so as to V | | | | |
| | initially | | | | inform | | | | |
| | additional | | | | deal with | | | | |
| | wages | | | | complex | | | | |
| | material | | | | organize | | | | |
| | request | | | | navigate | | | | |
| | allocation | | | | quantify | | | | |
| | refer to | | | | measure | | | | |
| | attachment | | | | estimate | | | | |
| | detail | | | | classify | | | | |
| | regard | | | | justify | | | | |
| 19 | approach | | | | prove | | | | |

# Voca Test

| ❶ voca | ❷ text | ❸ [ / ] | ❹ _____ | ❺ quiz 1 | ❻ quiz 2 | ❼ quiz 3 | ❽ quiz 4 | ❾ quiz 5 |
| --- | --- | --- | --- | --- | --- | --- | --- | --- |

| | | | | | |
| --- | --- | --- | --- | --- | --- |
| | generalize | | | instant | |
| | critical | | 22 | determine | |
| | qualitatively | | | mass | |
| | interaction | | | compare ~ with ... | |
| | along with | | | a number of | |
| | context | | | weigh | |
| | so that | | | complicate | |
| | explicitly | | | roughly | |
| | support | | | involve | |
| 21 | stingy | | | binary star | |
| | booster | | | instance | |
| | undoubtedly | | | calculate | |
| | praiseworthy | | | in other words | |
| | entirely | | | equation | |
| | satisfying | | | measurement | |
| | accord | | | estimation | |
| | generous | | | property | |
| | praise | | | determination | |
| | virtue | | | magnitude | |
| | courageous | | 23 | base on | |
| | stable | | | constantly | |
| | moral | | | strive | |
| | identity | | | define | |
| | as opposed to | | | function | |
| | impulse | | | potential | |

## Voca Test

영 › 한

| ❶ voca | ❷ text | ❸ [ / ] | ❹ ____ | ❺ quiz 1 | ❻ quiz 2 | ❼ quiz 3 | ❽ quiz 4 | ❾ quiz 5 |
|---|---|---|---|---|---|---|---|---|

| | | | | | |
|---|---|---|---|---|---|
| | highs and lows | | | revolutionize | |
| | be capable of -ing | | | disturbing | |
| | reliant | | | utter | |
| | opposite | | | lead to | |
| | correspondingly | | | distinction | |
| | psychiatrist | | | blur | |
| | attempt | | | shift | |
| | miserable | | | priority | |
| | component | | | in favor of | |
| | maintain | | | logical | |
| | neutral | | | argument | |
| | in turn | | | temptation | |
| | internal | | | compel | |
| 24 | sow | | 25 | respectively | |
| | adequacy | | | surpass | |
| | keep pace with | | | anticipate | |
| | itch | | | exceed | |
| | genuine | | 26 | republic | |
| | confine | | | be born to V | |
| | companion | | | immigrant | |
| | spill | | | institute | |
| | aspect | | | elect | |
| | consumer | | | parliament | |
| | electronics | | | adopt | |
| | generation | | | moderate | |

# Voca Tes

영 ⟩ 한

| | ❶ voca | ❷ text | ❸ [ / ] | ❹ _____ | ❺ quiz 1 | ❻ quiz 2 | ❼ quiz 3 | ❽ quiz 4 | ❾ quiz 5 |
|---|---|---|---|---|---|---|---|---|---|
| | stance | | | finding | | | | | |
| | progressive | | | associate ~ with ... | | | | | |
| | tirelessly | | | completely | | | | | |
| | expose | | | obviously | | | | | |
| | abuse | | | happen to V | | | | | |
| | challenging | | | suggest | | | | | |
| | retirement | | | conversely | | | | | |
| | continue to V | | | avoid | | | | | |
| | draft | | | stimulus | | | | | |
| | constitution | | | unpleasant | | | | | |
| 27 | board | | | cancer | | | | | |
| | registration | | | used to V | | | | | |
| | confirmation | | | A rather than B | | | | | |
| | wrist | | | saline | | | | | |
| | in groups | | | whereas | | | | | |
| | designate | | 30 | equator | | | | | |
| | emergency | | | species | | | | | |
| 28 | consultation | | | breed | | | | | |
| | suit | | | temperate | | | | | |
| | employee | | | polar | | | | | |
| | company | | | sharply | | | | | |
| | booth | | | trigger | | | | | |
| | order | | | outcome | | | | | |
| | auditorium | | | raise | | | | | |
| 29 | conditioned | | | supply | | | | | |

# Voca Test

영 ● 한

| | ❶ voca | ❷ text | ❸ [ / ] | ❹ ____ | ❺ quiz 1 | ❻ quiz 2 | ❼ quiz 3 | ❽ quiz 4 | ❾ quiz 5 |
|---|---|---|---|---|---|---|---|---|---|

| | | | | | |
|---|---|---|---|---|---|
| | reluctant | | | chemical | |
| | physically | | | preparation | |
| | incapable | | | vital | |
| | shrink | | | succeed | |
| | exception | | | applicable | |
| | nomadic | | | in advance | |
| | desert | | | alternative | |
| | initiate | | 32 | pressure | |
| | brood | | | interpretation | |
| | exceptionally | | | poet | |
| | sparrow | | | set about | |
| | successive | | | translate | |
| 31 | hinder | | | on one's own | |
| | resource | | | commentary | |
| | identify | | | translation | |
| | perform | | | draw on | |
| | compulsory | | | source | |
| | recognize | | | consist of | |
| | simplify | | | linguistic | |
| | performance | | | arise from | |
| | conduct | | | purpose | |
| | experiment | | | expectation | |
| | investigation | | 33 | argue | |
| | have access to | | | logically | |
| | laboratory | | | consistent | |

| | | | | |
|---|---|---|---|---|
| known as | | | highlight | |
| neatly | | | spectrum | |
| apart from | | | accommodate | |
| productive | | | distinct | |
| loosely | | 34 | perception | |
| belong | | | detect | |
| owing to | | | principle | |
| resemblance | | | otherwise | |
| phrase | | | burning | |
| have in common | | | vary | |
| trait | | | strength | |
| consequently | | | barely | |
| distinguish A from B | | | distinguish | |
| destined | | 35 | benefit | |
| agreement | | | individually | |
| qualify as | | | common | |
| in the first place | | | traffic jam | |
| figure out | | | overuse | |
| border | | | lessen | |
| edge | | | expand | |
| stretch | | | in isolation | |
| flexible | | | fellow | |
| boundary | | | compete | |
| be worth -ing | | | individual | |
| exceptional | | | destruction | |

# Voca Test

영 한

| | | | | | | | | |
|---|---|---|---|---|---|---|---|---|
| | degeneration | | | | serve as | | | |
| | regenerate | | | | unnecessary | | | |
| 36 | theoretically | | | | seek to V | | | |
| | capacity | | | | facilitate | | | |
| | theoretical | | | | cognitive | | | |
| | offset | | | 37 | adhere | | | |
| | associate with | | | | experimental | | | |
| | retrieve | | | | illuminate | | | |
| | as a result | | | | predictable | | | |
| | efficient | | | | feature | | | |
| | strategy | | | | conceal | | | |
| | dependent on | | | | evidence | | | |
| | shortcut | | | | explanation | | | |
| | observe | | | | chronology | | | |
| | visual | | | | construct | | | |
| | variable | | | | framework | | | |
| | depending on | | | | systematically | | | |
| | point of view | | | | meaningful | | | |
| | contextual | | | | subject | | | |
| | underlying | | | | in particular | | | |
| | general | | | | sort | | | |
| | allow for | | | | inspire | | | |
| | recognition | | | | analyze | | | |
| | diverse | | | | neglect | | | |
| | circumstance | | | | contribution | | | |

# Voca Test

영 ▷ 한

| ❶ voca | ❷ text | ❸ [ / ] | ❹ ___ | ❺ quiz 1 | ❻ quiz 2 | ❼ quiz 3 | ❽ quiz 4 | ❾ quiz 5 |
|---|---|---|---|---|---|---|---|---|
| | treat | | | | eager | | | |
| | interpretive | | | | identification | | | |
| | straightforward | | | | discourage | | | |
| | include | | | | keen | | | |
| | limitation | | | | injustice | | | |
| | misunderstanding | | | | be credited with | | | |
| 38 | encounter | | | | revulsion | | | |
| | contrary | | | | slavery | | | |
| | claim | | | | civil war | | | |
| | literature | | | 39 | morally | | | |
| | theorist | | | | in spite of | | | |
| | encourage | | | | instinct | | | |
| | solitary | | | | existence | | | |
| | reflection | | | | hence | | | |
| | engage with | | | | morality | | | |
| | counter | | | | liberty | | | |
| | appreciation | | | | application | | | |
| | complexity | | | | sovereign | | | |
| | acceptance | | | | namely | | | |
| | promote | | | | emerge | | | |
| | questioning | | | | nasty | | | |
| | authority | | | | brutish | | | |
| | arrangement | | | | indeed | | | |
| | do harm | | | | antisocial | | | |
| | credit ~ with ... | | | | selfishness | | | |

# Voca Test

| | | | | | | |
|---|---|---|---|---|---|---|
| | phenomenon | | | undergo | | |
| | mutual | | | to make things worse | | |
| | affection | | | mutation | | |
| | assemble | | | damage | | |
| 40 | perceive | | | responsible for | | |
| | participant | | | accelerate | | |
| | figure | | | noticeable | | |
| | depict | | | effect | | |
| | object | | | distort | | |
| | particular | | | result in | | |
| | symbolic | | | iris | | |
| | make out | | | be due to | | |
| | be associated with | | | multiply | | |
| | imply | | | patch | | |
| | association | | | affected | | |
| | object to | | | simultaneously | | |
| | perceptual | | | lie in | | |
| 41~42 | chromosome | | | tissue | | |
| | accumulate | | | differentiated | | |
| | be similar to | | | early on | | |
| | alteration | | | inherited | | |
| | medieval | 43~45 | | on schedule | | |
| | accidentally | | | swing | | |
| | stack | | | run into | | |
| | acquire | | | submit | | |

# Voca Test

영 〉 한

| ❶ voca | ❷ text | ❸ [ / ] | ❹ _____ | ❺ quiz 1 | ❻ quiz 2 | ❼ quiz 3 | ❽ quiz 4 | ❾ quiz 5 |
|---|---|---|---|---|---|---|---|---|
| greet | | | | | | | | |
| haste | | | | | | | | |
| furiously | | | | | | | | |
| browse through | | | | | | | | |
| only to V | | | | | | | | |
| manage to | | | | | | | | |
| to one's surprise | | | | | | | | |
| messy | | | | | | | | |
| reschedule | | | | | | | | |
| solution | | | | | | | | |
| spread | | | | | | | | |
| hand in | | | | | | | | |
| satisfaction | | | | | | | | |
| from then on | | | | | | | | |
| routine | | | | | | | | |
| embrace | | | | | | | | |
| unpredictable | | | | | | | | |
| | | | | | | | | |
| | | | | | | | | |
| | | | | | | | | |
| | | | | | | | | |
| | | | | | | | | |
| | | | | | | | | |

# Voca Test

| ❶ voca | ❷ text | ❸ [ / ] | ❹ _____ | ❺ quiz 1 | ❻ quiz 2 | ❼ quiz 3 | ❽ quiz 4 | ❾ quiz 5 |
|---|---|---|---|---|---|---|---|---|
| 18 | | | 집행의, 경영의; 임원, 경영진 | | | 예기치 않은, 뜻밖의, 갑작스러운 | | |
| | | | 주의(력), 집중(력), 관심 | | | 접히지 않은, 펼쳐진 | | |
| | | | 문제, 사안, 물질; 문제가 되다, 중요하다 | | | 예약, 보류, 보호구역 | | |
| | | | 즉각적인, 직접의, 인접한 | | | ~에 위치하다, (위치를) 찾아내다 | | |
| | | | 고려 (사항), 배려, 숙고 | | | 예약하다 | | |
| | | | ~에 관한 | | | 실수하다 | | |
| | | | 분명한, 명백한, 겉보기에는 | | | 의도[계획]적으로, 신중하게 | | |
| | | | 예산(안), 운영비; 예산을 세우다 | | | 진정시키다; 편함, 용이함 | | |
| | | | 전에, 앞서서 | | | ~을 계속하다 | | |
| | | | 찬성하다, 승인하다 | | | 파괴하다, 망치다; 파괴, (-s) 유적, 폐허 | | |
| | | | 조정, 수정, 적응 | 20 | | 교양 있는, 읽고 쓸 수 있는 | | |
| | | | ~하기 위해, ~하려고 | | | 비판적으로, 결정적으로 | | |
| | | | 신흥의, 신생의 | | | 사회의, 사회 활동[관습]의 | | |
| | | | 변화, 수정, 변경 | | | ~하도록, ~하기 위해 | | |
| | | | 처음에, 초기에 | | | (정보를) 알아내다, 알리다, 영향을 주다 | | |
| | | | 추가적인, 추가의 | | | ~을 처리[해결]하다, 다루다 | | |
| | | | 임금, 노임, 급료 | | | 복잡한, 복합의; 복합체, 콤플렉스 | | |
| | | | 재료, 물질; 물질의, 육체의, 중요한 | | | 조직하다, 정리하다, 개최하다 | | |
| | | | 요청, 요구; 요청[요구]하다 | | | 항해[조종]하다, 길을 찾다, 처리하다 | | |
| | | | 할당, 배당 | | | 수량화하다, 정량하다 | | |
| | | | ~을 언급[참조]하다, 가리키다 | | | 측정하다, 평가하다; 척도, 기준, 조치 | | |
| | | | 부착(물), 부속품, 애착 | | | 견적, 평가; 추정하다, 평가하다 | | |
| | | | 세부 (항목); 자세히 말하다, 열거하다 | | | 분류[구분]하다, 기밀 취급하다 | | |
| | | | 간주[주목]하다, 관련있다; 관심, 존경, 관계 | | | 정당화하다, 옳음을 증명하다 | | |
| 19 | | | 접근하다; 접근(법) | | | 입증하다, ~으로 판명되다[드러나다] | | |

# Voca Test

| ❶ voca | ❷ text | ❸ [ / ] | ❹ _____ | ❺ quiz 1 | ❻ quiz 2 | ❼ quiz 3 | ❽ quiz 4 | ❾ quiz 5 |
|---|---|---|---|---|---|---|---|---|
| | | 일반화하다, 보편화하다 | | | | 즉각의, 즉석의 | | |
| | | 중요한, 비판적인 | 22 | | | 결심[결정]하다, 알아내다 | | |
| | | 질적으로 | | | | 질량, (큰) 덩어리, 집단; 많은, 대량의 | | |
| | | 상호 작용 | | | | ~와 ...을 비교하다 | | |
| | | ~와 함께 | | | | 많은, 다수의 | | |
| | | 상황, 배경, 맥락, 문맥 | | | | 무게를 달다, 중요하다, 심사숙고하다 | | |
| | | 그래서, ~하기 위해서 | | | | 복잡하게 하다, 곤란하게 하다 | | |
| | | 명시적으로, 분명하게 | | | | 대략, 거의, 거칠게 | | |
| | | 지지[지원]하다, 부양하다; 지지, 후원 | | | | 포함[수반]하다, 필요로 하다, 관련시키다 | | |
| 21 | | 인색한, 적은, 쏘는, 날카로운 | | | | 쌍성 | | |
| | | 후원자, 촉진제 | | | | 사례, 경우 | | |
| | | 의심할 여지없이, 확실히 | | | | 추정하다, 계산[산출]하다 | | |
| | | 칭찬할 만한 | | | | 즉, 다시 말해서 | | |
| | | 완전히, 전적으로 | | | | 방정식, 등식, 동일시 | | |
| | | 만족스럽게 하는 | | | | 측정(치), 측량(치), 치수 | | |
| | | 일치하다, 조화를 이루다; 일치, 협정 | | | | 판단, 평가, 견적, 추정, 존중 | | |
| | | 관대한, 너그러운, 푸짐한 | | | | 재산, 부동산, 특성, 속성 | | |
| | | 찬사를 보내다, 칭송하다; 찬사 | | | | 결정, 결심, 결의 | | |
| | | 선, 미덕, 가치 | | | | 엄청난 규모, 크기, 중요성, (별의) 광도 | | |
| | | 용감한, 용기 있는 | 23 | | | ~에 근거하다 | | |
| | | 안정된, 지속성이 있는; 마구간, 외양간 | | | | 지속적으로, 끊임없이 | | |
| | | 도덕적인 | | | | 노력하다, 애쓰다, 분투하다 | | |
| | | 정체성 | | | | 정의하다, 한계 짓다, 한정하다 | | |
| | | ~이 아니라, ~와는 대조적으로 | | | | 기능하다, 작용하다; 기능, 작용 | | |
| | | 충동, 자극, 욕구, 추진(력) | | | | 가능성이 있는, 잠재적인; 가능성, 잠재력 | | |

# Voca Test

| ① voca | ② text | ③ [ / ] | ④ ____ | ⑤ quiz 1 | ⑥ quiz 2 | ⑦ quiz 3 | ⑧ quiz 4 | ⑨ quiz 5 |
|---|---|---|---|---|---|---|---|---|
| | | | 기복, 고저 | | | 혁명[대변혁]을 일으키다 | | |
| | | | ~할 수 있다 | | | 불안하게 하는, 충격적인, 불온한 | | |
| | | | 의지하는, 믿고 있는 | | | 말하다, 소리를 내다; 완전한, 순전한 | | |
| | | | 반대(되는 사람[것]); 반대의 | | | ~을 낳다, ~으로 이어지다 | | |
| | | | 상응하여, 부응하여 | | | 구별, 차이, 특징, 뛰어남, 우수(성) | | |
| | | | 정신과 의사 | | | 모호하게 하다, 흐리게 하다 | | |
| | | | 시도; 시도하다 | | | 변화, 이동, 교대; 바꾸다, 이동하다 | | |
| | | | 비참한, 불쌍한, 괴로운 | | | 우선(권), 우선 사항 | | |
| | | | (구성) 요소, 성분, 부품; 구성하고 있는 | | | ~에 우호적인, ~을 지지하여 | | |
| | | | 유지하다, 주장하다 | | | 논리적인, 필연적인 | | |
| | | | 중립적인, 중립의, 중간의, 공평한 | | | 논쟁, 주장, 논거 | | |
| | | | 결과적으로, 차례차례 | | | 유혹, 충동 | | |
| | | | 내부의, 체내의, 국내의 | | | 강요하다, ~하게 만들다 | | |
| 24 | | | (씨를) 뿌리다 | | 25 | 각각, 각기, 저마다 | | |
| | | | 타당함, 적당함 | | | 능가하다, 초월하다 | | |
| | | | ~와 보조를 맞추다, ~에 따라가다 | | | 예상하다, 기대하다 | | |
| | | | 가려움; 가렵다, (~하고 싶어) 못 견디다 | | | 초과하다 | | |
| | | | 진실한, 진정한, 진짜의 | | 26 | 공화국 | | |
| | | | 한정[국한]하다, 가두다; (-s) 경계 | | | ~할 운명을 타고 나다 | | |
| | | | 친구, 동반자, 동료 | | | (타국에서 온) 이주민, 이민자 | | |
| | | | 엎지르다, 흘리다; 엎지름, 유출 | | | 기관, 협회; 설립하다, 제정하다 | | |
| | | | 측면, 면, 양상, 관점 | | | 선출하다, 택하다; 선출된 | | |
| | | | 소비자 | | | 의회, 국회 | | |
| | | | 전자 공학, 전자 기기 | | | (채)택하다, 선정하다, 취하다 | | |
| | | | 세대, 일족, 발생 | | | 적당한, 온건한; 조정[완화]하다, 완화하다 | | |

# Voca Test

| ❶ voca | ❷ text | ❸ [ / ] | ❹ _____ | ❺ quiz 1 | ❻ quiz 2 | ❼ quiz 3 | ❽ quiz 4 | ❾ quiz 5 |
|---|---|---|---|---|---|---|---|---|
| | | 입장, 자세, 태도 | | | 결과, 결론 | | | |
| | | 점진적인, 진보적인 | | | ~을 …와 결부시키다 | | | |
| | | 지칠 줄 모르고, 끊임없이 | | | 완전히, 충분히 | | | |
| | | 드러내다, 폭로하다, 노출시키다 | | | 명백하게, 분명히 | | | |
| | | 남용, 학대; 남용[오용]하다, 학대하다 | | | 우연히 ~하다 | | | |
| | | 힘든, 도전적인 | | | 제안하다, 암시하다, 시사하다 | | | |
| | | 퇴직, 은퇴 | | | 반대로, 역으로 | | | |
| | | 계속 ~하다 | | | 피하다, 막다 | | | |
| | | 초안, 원고, 징병; 초안을 작성하다, 선발하다 | | | 자극, 격려, 고무 ((복수형 stimuli)) | | | |
| | | 헌법, 구조, 설치 | | | 불쾌한, 불편한 | | | |
| 27 | | 탑승하다; 이사회, 판자, -판 | | | 암, 악성 종양 | | | |
| | | 등록 (서류), 기재 | | | ~하곤 했다, ~이었다[했다] | | | |
| | | 증거, 확증 | | | B라기 보다는 A | | | |
| | | 손목, 손재주 | | | 식염수 | | | |
| | | 떼를 지어, 삼삼오오 | | | ~에 반하여, 그런데, 그러나 | | | |
| | | 지정하다, 지명하다; 지명된 | 30 | | 적도 | | | |
| | | 긴급, 긴급 상황, 응급 | | | (분류상의) 종(種) | | | |
| 28 | | 상담, 협의 | | | 유형, 품종, 혈통; 번식하다, 낳다, 기르다 | | | |
| | | 정장, 소송; 적합하다, (알)맞다 | | | 온화한, 온건한, 차분한, 절제된 | | | |
| | | 직원, 종업원 | | | 북극[남극]의, 극지의, 양극의 | | | |
| | | 친구, 동료, 회사, 교제; 회사의 | | | 급격히, 날카롭게, 민첩하게 | | | |
| | | 부스, (칸막이를 한) 작은 공간 | | | 계기, 방아쇠; 유발하다, 쏘다 | | | |
| | | 명령[주문]하다, 정돈하다; 명령, 주문, 순서 | | | 결과(물) | | | |
| | | 강당, 청중석 | | | 높이다, 올리다, 기르다, 제기하다; 인상 | | | |
| 29 | | 조건부의, 길들여진 | | | 공급하다, 주다; 공급 | | | |

Voca Test

| ❶ voca | ❷ text | ❸ [ / ] | ❹ _____ | ❺ quiz 1 | ❻ quiz 2 | ❼ quiz 3 | ❽ quiz 4 | ❾ quiz 5 |
|---|---|---|---|---|---|---|---|---|
| | | 꺼리는, 주저하는, 마지못한 | | | 화학적인, 화학의; 화학 물질 | | | |
| | | 실제적으로, 신체적으로 | | | 준비, 대비, 조제약 | | | |
| | | 무능한, 할 수 없는 | | | 중대한, 활기 있는, 생명의 | | | |
| | | 줄어들다, 움츠러들다, 수축하다 | | | 성공하다, 계승하다, 잇따르다 | | | |
| | | 예외(사항), 제외 | | | 들어맞는, 적용[응용]할 수 있는 | | | |
| | | 유목의, 방랑의 | | | 미리, 사전에 | | | |
| | | 버리다, 떠나다; 사막 | | | 대안 | | | |
| | | 시작하다, 입문시키다; 신참 | 32 | | 압력, 압박, 스트레스; 압력을 가하다 | | | |
| | | 함께 태어난 새끼들 | | | 해석, 설명, 이해 | | | |
| | | 특별히, 유난히, 예외적으로 | | | 시인 | | | |
| | | 참새 | | | 시작하다, 공격하다 | | | |
| | | 연속하는, 계속적인, 계승의, 대대의 | | | 번역하다, 해석하다, 옮기다 | | | |
| 31 | | 방해하다, 막다 | | | 혼자, 혼자 힘으로 | | | |
| | | 수단, 기지 (-s) 자원, 소질; 자원을 제공하다 | | | 논평, 설명, 해설 | | | |
| | | 알아보다, 확인하다, 동일시하다 | | | 번역, 통역, 해석 | | | |
| | | 수행하다, 행동하다, 공연[연주]하다 | | | ~을 이용하다, ~에 의지하다, 가까워지다 | | | |
| | | 강제적인, 의무적인, 필수의 | | | 원천, 근원, (-s) 출처, 정보원 | | | |
| | | 알아보다, 인정[표창]하다, 인식하다 | | | ~으로 구성되다, 이루어져 있다 | | | |
| | | 단순화하다, 간단하게 하다 | | | 언어의, 언어학의 | | | |
| | | 수행, 성과, 성적, 공연 | | | ~에 기인하다, ~에서 발생하다 | | | |
| | | ~을 하다, 지휘하다, (전기 등을) 전도하다; 행동 | | | 목적, 의도; 의도하다 | | | |
| | | 실험, 시험, 시도; 실험하다, 시도하다 | | | 기대, 요구, 예상, 가망 | | | |
| | | 수사, 조사, 연구 | 33 | | 논쟁[논의]하다, 주장하다 | | | |
| | | ~에 접근하다 | | | 필연적으로, 논리적으로 | | | |
| | | 실험실; 실험실의 | | | 일관된, 변함없는, 한결같은 | | | |

# Voca Test

| ❶ voca | ❷ text | ❸ [ / ] | ❹ _____ | ❺ quiz 1 | ❻ quiz 2 | ❼ quiz 3 | ❽ quiz 4 | ❾ quiz 5 |
|---|---|---|---|---|---|---|---|---|
| | | ~으로 알려진 | | | | 집중하다, 강조하다; 가장 중요한 부분 | | |
| | | 깔끔하게, 말쑥하게, 솜씨 있게 | | | | 범위, 연속체, 스펙트럼 | | |
| | | ~와 별도로, ~을 제외하고 | | | | 수용하다, 숙박시키다, 적응하다 | | |
| | | 생산적인, 다산의 | | | | 구별되는, 분명한, 별개의 | | |
| | | 엉성하게, 느슨하게 | 34 | | | 인식, 인지, 지각 | | |
| | | 속하다, ~의 것이다 | | | | 알아내다, 감지하다, 탐지하다 | | |
| | | ~ 때문에 | | | | 원칙, 원리 | | |
| | | 유사성, 닮음 | | | | 그렇지 않으면, ~와 다르게 | | |
| | | 구절, (문)구; 말로 표현하다 | | | | 불타는, 화급한, 중대한 | | |
| | | 공통점이 있다 | | | | 다르다, 바꾸다, 변하다 | | |
| | | 특성 | | | | 강점, 장점, 힘, 기운 | | |
| | | 결과적으로, 그 결과, 따라서 | | | | 거의 ~않게, 가까스로 | | |
| | | A와 B를 구분[구별]하다 | | | | 구분[구별]하다, ~을 특징짓다 | | |
| | | (~할) 운명에 있는, ~행의 | 35 | | | 이익, 이득; 이익이 되다 | | |
| | | 합의, 동의 | | | | 개별적으로, 개인적으로 | | |
| | | ~으로서 자격을 갖추고 있다[얻다] | | | | 공통의, 흔한, 평범한 | | |
| | | 우선, 맨 먼저 | | | | 교통 체증, 교통 정체 | | |
| | | 산출[계산]하다, 알아내다 | | | | 남용; 남용하다 | | |
| | | 국경, 경계, 가장자리; 접경하다 | | | | (크기, 양 등이) 줄다, 감소시키다 | | |
| | | 이점, 우위, 모서리, 끝, 가장자리, 날 | | | | 확장[확대]하다, 부연[확충]하다 | | |
| | | 잡아 늘이다, 쭉 펴다; 뻗침, 확장 | | | | 고립된 상태로, 별개로 | | |
| | | 융통성이 있는, 유연한, 탄력적인 | | | | 사나이, 동료, 친구; 동료의 | | |
| | | 경계(선), 한계, 범위 | | | | 다투다, 겨루다, 경쟁하다 | | |
| | | ~할 가치가 있다 | | | | 개인; 개인의, 개별적인, 독특한 | | |
| | | 탁월한, 뛰어난, 보기 드문 | | | | 파괴, 파멸, 멸망 | | |

# Voca Test

| ❶ voca | ❷ text | ❸ [ / ] | ❹ ____ | ❺ quiz 1 | ❻ quiz 2 | ❼ quiz 3 | ❽ quiz 4 | ❾ quiz 5 |
|---|---|---|---|---|---|---|---|---|
| | | 퇴화, 쇠퇴, 타락 | | | | ~의 역할을 하다 | | |
| | | 재건하다, 재생하다, 갱생시키다 | | | | 불필요한, 쓸데없는 | | |
| 36 | | 이론상, 이론적으로는 | | | | ~하고자 하다, 시도하다 | | |
| | | 용량, 수용력, 능력 | | | | 촉진[조장]하다, 용이하게 하다 | | |
| | | 이론의, 이론상의 | | | | 인지의, 인식의 | | |
| | | 상쇄하다 | 37 | | | 충실하다 | | |
| | | ~와 어울리다, 관련시키다 | | | | 실험의, 실험적인, 경험적인 | | |
| | | 상기하다 | | | | 밝히다 | | |
| | | 그 결과 | | | | 예측[예상] 가능한 | | |
| | | 유능한, 능률적인, 효율적인 | | | | 특징, 특집, 용모; 특집으로 하다, 특집으로 삼다 | | |
| | | 전략, 전술, 계획, 방법 | | | | 감추다, 숨기다 | | |
| | | ~에 의존하는 | | | | 증거, 징후 | | |
| | | 지름길, 손쉬운 방법 | | | | 설명, 해명, 변명 | | |
| | | 관찰하다, 준수하다, (의견 등을) 말하다 | | | | 연대순 배열, 연대기 | | |
| | | 시각의, 눈에 보이는 | | | | 건설하다, 구성[조립]하다 | | |
| | | 다양한, 변하기 쉬운, 가변(성)의; 변수 | | | | 하부 구조, 체계, 뼈대, 틀 | | |
| | | ~에 따라 | | | | 체계적으로, 조직적으로 | | |
| | | 관점, 견해, 전망, 경치 | | | | 의미 있는, 중요한 | | |
| | | 전후 관계의, 문맥상의 | | | | 주제, 과목, 대상; 지배하다, 복종시키다 | | |
| | | 근원적인 | | | | 특히, 특별히 | | |
| | | (육군) 원수, 장군; 일반적인 | | | | 분류하다, 구분하다; 종류 | | |
| | | ~을 감안[참고]하다 | | | | 영감을 주다, 고무시키다, 격려하다 | | |
| | | 인식, 인정, 표창 | | | | 분석하다, 분해하다 | | |
| | | 다양한, 여러 가지의 | | | | 무시[방치]하다; 소홀, 무시 | | |
| | | 상황, 정황, 환경 | | | | (원인) 제공, 기여, 기고, 분담금 | | |

# Voca Test

| ❶ voca | ❷ text | ❸ [ / ] | ❹ ____ | ❺ quiz 1 | ❻ quiz 2 | ❼ quiz 3 | ❽ quiz 4 | ❾ quiz 5 |
|---|---|---|---|---|---|---|---|---|
| 38 | | | 대우하다, 다루다, 치료하다; 대접 | | | | 갈망[열망]하는, 열심인 | |
| | | | 설명을 위한, 해석의 | | | | 동일시, 공감 | |
| | | | 솔직한, 직접의, 수월한, 간단한 | | | | 의욕을 꺾다, 단념시키다, 훼방하다 | |
| | | | 포함하다, 포괄하다 | | | | 예리한, 예민한, 열망하는 | |
| | | | 제한, 한계 | | | | 불평등, 부정 | |
| | | | 오해, 착오, 불화 | | | | ~을 가진[한] 것으로 믿어지다 | |
| | | | 접하다, 마주치다; 마주침, (뜻밖의) 만남 | | | | 혐오감 | |
| | | | 반대의, 적합치 않은, 불리한; 정반대 | | | | 노예 제도, 노예의 신분 | |
| | | | 주장[요구]하다, 차지하다; 요구, 주장 | | | | 내전 | |
| | | | 문학, 문예, 문헌 | 39 | | | 도덕적으로 | |
| | | | 이론가, 공론가 | | | | ~에도 불구하고 | |
| | | | 장려[격려]하다, 촉구하다 | | | | 본능 | |
| | | | 혼자의, 외로운, 고립된 | | | | 생활, 존재, 생존 | |
| | | | 반영, 반사, 숙고, 반성 | | | | 그러므로, 따라서, 지금부터 | |
| | | | ~와 관계를 맺다, ~와 맞물리다 | | | | 도덕률, 도덕 | |
| | | | 반대의; 계산대; 대응하다 | | | | 자유, 해방 | |
| | | | 평가, 인정, 이해, 감탄, 감사 | | | | 신청(서), 지원(서), 적용, 응용 프로그램 | |
| | | | 복잡성, 복잡함 | | | | 주권을 가진, 독립의; 주권국, 군주 | |
| | | | 수락, 승인, 용인 | | | | 즉, 다시 말해 | |
| | | | 촉진[장려]하다, 홍보하다, 진급시키다 | | | | 나오다, 나타나다, 드러나다 | |
| | | | 의문을 제기하는 | | | | 못된, 심술궂은, 더러운, 불쾌한 | |
| | | | 권위, 권한, 당국, 기관 | | | | 잔인한 | |
| | | | 배열, 배치 | | | | 실제로, 사실 | |
| | | | 해가 되다, 손해를 끼치다 | | | | 반사회적인, 비사교적인 | |
| | | | ~가 ...하다고 믿다, ~가 ...의 공로를 인정받다 | | | | 이기적임, 이기심 | |

## Voca Test

| ❶ voca | ❷ text | ❸ [ / ] | ❹ _____ | ❺ quiz 1 | ❻ quiz 2 | ❼ quiz 3 | ❽ quiz 4 | ❾ quiz 5 |
|---|---|---|---|---|---|---|---|---|
| | | 현상, 사건, 비범한 인물 ((복수형 phenomena)) | | | | 겪다, 경험하다, 견디다 | | |
| | | 상호 간의, 서로의, 공통의 | | | | 설상가상으로, 엎친 데 덮친 격으로 | | |
| | | 애정, 애착 | | | | 돌연변이, 변화 | | |
| | | 모으다, 조립하다 | | | | 피해, 손상, 손해; 손해를 입히다 | | |
| 40 | | 인식하다, 지각하다 | | | | ~에 책임이 있는 | | |
| | | 참여자, 참가자 | | | | 가속하다, 촉진하다 | | |
| | | 생각[계산]하다; 수치, 숫자, 인물, 모양 | | | | 주목할 만한, 두드러진 | | |
| | | 묘사하다, 그리다 | | | | 결과, 영향, 효과; 초래하다, 이루다 | | |
| | | ~에 반대하다; 목표, 대상, 물체 | | | | 비틀다, 일그러뜨리다, 왜곡하다 | | |
| | | 특정한, 개개의; 사항, 상세 | | | | 그 결과 ~이 되다, ~을 야기하다 | | |
| | | 상징적인, 표상하는 | | | | 홍채 | | |
| | | 알아내다, 이해하다, (잘)해나가다, 성공하다 | | | | ~ 때문이다 | | |
| | | ~과 관련되다 | | | | 곱하다, 크게 증가하다 | | |
| | | 넌지시 나타내다, 암시하다, 수반하다 | | | | 헝겊 조각, 좁은 땅, 구역; 덧대다 | | |
| | | 연관(성), 연상, 협회 | | | | 가장된, 꾸민, 감염된 | | |
| | | ~에 반대하다 | | | | 동시에, 일제히 | | |
| | | 지각의, 인지의 | | | | ~에 있다 | | |
| 41~42 | | 염색체 | | | | (생물) 조직, 화장지 | | |
| | | 축적하다 | | | | 차별화된 | | |
| | | ~와 유사하다 | | | | 초기에, 곧 | | |
| | | 변화, 변경, 바꾸기 | | | | 유전된, 상속한, 물려받은 | | |
| | | 중세의, 중세풍의 | 43~45 | | | 예정대로 | | |
| | | 잘못하여, 우연히 | | | | 흔들(리)다, 진동하다; 흔들기, 그네 | | |
| | | 더미, 다량, (-s) 서고; 쌓다, 쌓아 올리다 | | | | 우연히 만나다, 부딪히다, 이르다 | | |
| | | 얻다, 습득하다 | | | | 제출하다, 복종시키다 | | |

# Voca Test

| ❶ voca | ❷ text | ❸ [ / ] | ❹ _____ | ❺ quiz 1 | ❻ quiz 2 | ❼ quiz 3 | ❽ quiz 4 | ❾ quiz 5 |
|--------|--------|---------|---------|----------|----------|----------|----------|----------|
| | | 인사하다, 맞이하다 | | | | |
| | | 서두름, 급함, 성급 | | | | |
| | | 미친 듯이, 맹렬히 | | | | |
| | | 처음부터 끝까지 둘러[훑어]보다 | | | | |
| | | 그 결과는 ~뿐, 단지 ~하기 위해 | | | | |
| | | (힘든 일을) 간신히 해내다 | | | | |
| | | 놀랍게도 | | | | |
| | | 정리[정돈]되어 있지 않은, 지저분한 | | | | |
| | | 일정을 변경하다 | | | | |
| | | 해결(책), 용액 | | | | |
| | | 펴다, 퍼뜨리다, 퍼지다; 확장, 유포, 보급 | | | | |
| | | 제출하다, 내다 | | | | |
| | | 만족, 충족 | | | | |
| | | 그 이래로, 그때부터 (쭉) | | | | |
| | | 일상적인; 일과, 습관적인 동작 | | | | |
| | | 포옹하다, 수용하다; 포옹, 수용 | | | | |
| | | 예측할 수 없는, 예측이 불가능한 | | | | |
| | | | | | | |
| | | | | | | |
| | | | | | | |
| | | | | | | |
| | | | | | | |
| | | | | | | |

# 2024 고2 11월 모의고사

❶ voca  ❷ text  ❸ [ / ]  ❹ _____  ❺ quiz 1  ❻ quiz 2  ❼ quiz 3  ❽ quiz 4  ❾ quiz 5

## 18 목적

❶ Dear Executive Manager Schulz,

Schulz 부장님께

It is a week before the internship program starts.

인턴십 프로그램을 시작하기 일주일 전입니다.

❷ I am writing to bring your attention to a matter that requires immediate consideration regarding the issue my department has.

저희 부서의 사안과 관련하여 즉각적인 고려가 필요한 문제에 대해 당신의 관심을 환기하기 위해 이 글을 씁니다.

❸ As the coordinator, it is becoming apparent to me that the budget, previously approved by your department, needs some adjustments in order to meet the emerging modifications.

업무 담당자로서 최근 생겨난 수정 사항을 충족시키기 위해서, 이전에 당신의 부서로부터 승인받은 예산은 약간의 조정이 필요함이 분명해지고 있습니다.

❹ Since my department has hired three more interns than planned initially, the most expensive need is for additional funding to cover their wages, training costs, and materials.

우리 부서에서 처음에 계획됐던 것보다 세 명의 인턴을 더 고용했기 때문에, 가장 비용이 많이 드는 부족한 부분은 그들의 임금, 훈련 비용, 물품들을 다루기 위한 추가적인 자금입니다.

❺ I kindly request an additional budget allocation for these expenses.

이 비용들을 위해 추가적인 예산 배당을 정중하게 요청합니다.

❻ Please refer to the attachment for details.

자세한 사항은 첨부물을 참고해 주세요.

❼ Thank you for your attention. Best regards, Matt Perry

당신의 관심에 감사드립니다. Matt Perry 드림

# 19 심경

❶ Katie approached the hotel front desk to check-in but an unexpected event unfolded.

Katie는 체크인을 하기 위해 호텔 안내 데스크에 다가갔으나 예상하지 못한 사건이 전개되었다.

❷ The receptionist couldn't find her reservation under the name 'Katie'.

접수 담당자는 'Katie'라는 이름으로 된 예약을 찾을 수 없었다.

❸ "I'm sorry, but I can't seem to locate a reservation under that name," the receptionist said.

"죄송하지만, 그 이름으로 된 예약을 찾을 수 없는 것 같습니다."라고 접수 담당자가 말했다.

❹ "No way, I definitely made a reservation on the phone," Katie said, puzzled.

"말도 안 돼요, 저는 분명히 전화로 예약했어요."라고 Katie가 어리둥절해하며 말했다.

❺ The receptionist asked, "Can you tell me your phone number?" and Katie told it to him, thinking 'What happened? Did I make a mistake?' "Just a moment," the receptionist said, typing deliberately on the keyboard. "I found it! It seems there was a small misspelling. Your reservation is under 'K-A-T-Y'," the receptionist explained.

접수 담당자가 "당신의 전화번호를 말해 주실 수 있을까요?"라고 물어보았고, Katie가 '무슨 일이지? 내가 실수를 저질렀나?'라고 생각하며 전화번호를 그에게 알려 주었다. "잠시만요."라고 접수 담당자가 키보드를 신중하게 치면서 말했다. "알 아냈습니다! 작은 오타가 있었던 것 같습니다. 당신의 예약은 'K-A-T-Y'로 되어 있어요."라고 접수 담당자가 설명했다.

❻ With a sense of ease, Katie watched her reservation appearing on the screen.

편안한 기분으로 Katie는 그녀의 예약이 화면에 나타나는 것을 지켜봤다.

❼ With her heart slowing to a gentle rhythm, she proceeded with her check-in, thinking that a simple misspelling might have ruined her plans.

그녀의 심장이 완만한 리듬으로 느려지면서, 그녀는 단순한 오타가 그녀의 계획들을 망쳤을지도 모른다고 생각하며 체크인을 진행했다.

## 20 요지

❶ To be mathematically literate means to be able to think critically about societal issues on which mathematics has bearing so as to make informed decisions about how to solve these problems.

수학적 문해력이 있다는 것은 수학과 관련된 사회적 이슈에 대해 이러한 문제들을 어떻게 해결할지에 대한 정보에 입각한 결정을 하기 위해서 비판적으로 생각할 수 있다는 것을 의미한다.

❷ Dealing with such complex problems through interdisciplinary approaches, mirroring real-world problems requires innovative ways of planning and organizing mathematical teaching methods.

범교과적인 접근법을 통해 그러한 복잡한 문제들을 다루는 과정에서 실생활 문제들을 반영하는 것은 수학적 교수 방법을 계획하고 조직하는 혁신적인 방법들을 요구한다.

❸ Navigating our world means being able to quantify, measure, estimate, classify, compare, find patterns, conjecture, justify, prove, and generalize within critical thinking and when using critical thinking.

우리의 세계를 탐색한다는 것은 비판적 사고 안에서 그리고 비판적 사고를 사용할 때 수량화하고, 측정하고, 추산하고, 분류하고, 비교하고, 패턴을 찾고, 추측하고, 근거를 제시하고, 증명하고, 일반화할 수 있다는 것을 의미한다.

❹ Therefore, making decisions, even qualitatively, is not possible without using mathematics and critical thinking.

그러므로, 수학과 비판적 사고를 사용하지 않고 의사 결정을 하는 것은 질적인 경우에라도 가능하지 않다.

❺ Thus, teaching mathematics should be done in interaction with critical thinking along with a decision-making process.

따라서, 수학을 가르치는 것은 의사 결정 과정과 함께 비판적 사고와의 상호 작용 안에서 이루어져야 한다.

❻ They can be developed into the mathematical context, so that there is no excuse to not explicitly support students to develop them.

그것들은 수학적인 맥락 안에서 발전될 수 있고, 학생들이 그것들을 발전시킬 수 있도록 명시적으로 도움을 주지 않을 경우 변명의 여지가 없다.

# 21 주장

❶ Imagine that your usually stingy friend delights in buying you a Christmas present after taking a generosity booster.

평소에 인색한 여러분의 친구가 관대함 효능촉진제를 먹고 난 이후에 여러분에게 크리스마스 선물을 사 주며 매우 기뻐한다고 상상해 보라.

❷ How would you feel? Undoubtedly, there is something praiseworthy about the action.

여러분은 어떻게 느끼겠는가? 의심할 여지없이, 그 행동에는 칭찬할 만한 점이 있다.

❸ You'd be pleased to receive the gift. You'd say 'thank you', and mean it. But his change of heart is not entirely satisfying. According to Zagzebski, an American philosopher, he is not really generous.

여러분은 선물을 받아서 기뻐할 것이다. 여러분은 '고마워'라고 말하고, 그것은 진심일 것이다. 하지만 그의 마음의 변화는 완전히 만족스럽지는 않다. 미국의 철학자인 Zagzebski에 따르면, 그는 진정으로 관대한 것이 아니다.

❹ When we praise someone's character, we use words for various virtues: 'generous', 'kind', 'courageous', etc. A person who gives one gift isn't generous.

우리가 누군가의 인품을 칭찬할 때 '관대한,' '친절한,' '용기있는' 등 다양한 미덕에 대한 단어를 사용한다. 선물을 하나 준 사람이 관대한 것은 아니다.

❺ Instead, generosity is a stable part of a person's 'moral identity', an emotional habit that is part of who you are.

대신에, 관대함은 누군가의 '도덕적 정체성'의 안정된 일부인데 그것은 여러분의 모습의 일부인 정서적 습관이다.

❻ Thus virtues, as opposed to nontypical impulse, are the result of your personal history.

따라서 미덕은, 비전형적인 충동과는 달리, 여러분 개인 역사의 결과이다.

❼ They are part of who you are, as they are part of how your character was formed. Instant virtue is therefore impossible. Popping a pill cannot make you a better person.

그것들이 여러분의 인품이 형성되었던 방식의 일부이기 때문에 그것들은 여러분의 모습 중 일부이다. 그러므로 즉각적인 미덕은 있을 수 없다. 약 한 알을 먹는 것이 여러분을 더 나은 사람으로 만들 수는 없다.

## 22 의미

❶ To determine the mass of my bowling ball, I might put it onto a balance and compare it with a known mass, such as a number of metal cubes each weighing 1, 10, or 100 grams.

볼링공 질량을 측정하기 위해, 나는 그것을 저울에 올려놓고 각 1g, 10g, 또는 100g이 나가는 여러 개의 금속 큐브 같은 이미 알고 있는 질량과 그것을 비교할 수 있다.

❷ Things get much more complicated if I want to know the mass of a distant star.

만약 내가 먼 별의 질량을 알고 싶다면 상황은 훨씬 더 복잡해진다.

❸ How do I measure it? We can roughly say that measuring the mass of a star involves various theories.

나는 어떻게 그것을 측정할까? 우리는 별의 질량을 측정하는 것은 다양한 이론을 포함한다고 대략적으로 말할 수 있다.

❹ If we want to measure the mass of a binary star, we first determine a center of mass between the two stars, then their distance from that center which we can then use, together with a value for the period and a certain instance of Kepler's Third Law, to calculate the mass.

우리가 쌍성의 질량을 측정하기를 원한다면, 질량을 계산하기 위해 우리는 먼저 두 별들 사이의 질량 중심을, 그 다음에 우리가 그제서야 사용할 수 있는 그 중심으로부터 떨어진 그것들의 거리를 공전 주기의 값과 케플러 제3 법칙의 특정한 사례를 가지고 측정한다.

❺ In other words, in order to "measure" the star mass, we measure other quantities and use those values, together with certain equations, to calculate the mass.

다시 말해서, 별의 질량을 '측정'하기 위해서 우리는 다양한 수치들을 측정하고 그 값들을 특정 방정식들과 함께 사용하여 질량을 계산한다.

❻ Measurement is not a simple and unmediated estimation of independently existing properties, but a determination of certain magnitudes before the background of a number of accepted theories.

측정은 독립적으로 존재하는 값들의 단순하고 중재되지 않은 측정이 아니라, 이미 정립된 여러 이론들을 바탕으로 특정 크기들을 계산하는 것이다.

# 23 주제

❶ Based on discoveries in neuroscience, pain and pleasure are formed and processed in the same area of the brain.

뇌 과학의 발견들에 따르면, 고통과 쾌락은 뇌의 같은 영역에서 형성되고 처리된다.

❷ Our bodies constantly strive for homeostasis, which is defined as the balance of bodily functions.

우리 몸은 끊임없이 항상성을 추구하는데, 그것은 몸의 기능들의 균형이라고 정의된다.

❸ Without the body's effective compensatory mechanisms, which may cushion potential highs and lows, we would not be capable of surviving.

잠재적인 변동을 완화시킬 수 있는 몸의 효과적인 보상 기제가 없다면 우리는 생존할 수 없을 것이다.

❹ Pleasure and pain are like two sides of the same coin; they seem to work together and are heavily reliant on one another and keep balance.

쾌락과 고통은 동일한 동전의 두 면과 같아서 그들은 함께 작동하는 것 같으며 서로 상당히 의존하고 있고 균형을 유지한다.

❺ If you imagine pleasure and pain as the two opposite points on a scale, you can easily understand that as one of the two points rises, the other must correspondingly fall.

만약에 여러분이 쾌락과 고통을 저울 위의 두 반대 지점으로 상상한다면, 여러분은 두 지점 중 한 지점이 올라가면 다른 한 지점이 상응하여 틀림없이 내려갈 것임을 쉽게 이해할 수 있을 것이다.

❻ We've all heard the expression, "No pain, no gain." Well, according to psychiatrist Dr. Anna Lembke, there may be some truth to these words. She says that our attempts to escape being miserable are in fact making us even more miserable.

우리는 '고통 없이는, 얻는 것도 없다.' 자, 정신과 의사인 Dr. Anna Lembke에 따르면, 이 말에는 어느 정도의 진실이 있을 수 있다. 그녀는 우리가 비참함에서 벗어나려는 우리의 시도가 사실 우리를 훨씬 더 비참하게 만들고 있다고 말한다.

❼ This is because pain is actually an essential component of our ability to maintain a neutral state, and allowing it will in turn reset our internal scale back to balance.

이는 고통이 실제로 중립적인 상태를 유지하기 위한 우리 능력의 필수적인 구성 요소이기 때문이고, 그것을 허용하는 것은 결과적으로 우리의 내부 저울을 균형 상태로 다시 맞출 것이다.

## 24 제목

**❶** Manufacturers masterfully sow seeds of doubt about the adequacy of our current devices.

생산자들은 노련하게 우리의 현재 기기들의 적절성에 대한 의심의 씨앗을 뿌린다.

**❷** Suddenly, the phone that was your lifeline a year ago is now a museum piece, unable to keep pace with your digital demands.

갑자기, 1년 전의 당신의 목숨줄이었던 휴대폰이 지금은 당신의 디지털 수요를 따라가지 못하는, 시대에 뒤떨어진 것이 되었다.

**❸** And thus, the itch to upgrade begins, often before there's a genuine need. This cycle isn't just confined to our digital  companions. It spills over into almost every aspect of consumer electronics, from the self-driving car to the smart fridge.

그래서 종종 진짜 필요가 있기 이전에 업그레이드에 대한 욕구가 시작된다. 이러한 순환은 단지 우리의 디지털 용품에 국한되지 않는다. 이것은 자율 주행 자동차부터 스마트 냉장고에 이르기까지 소비자 전자 기기들의 거의 모든 영역까지 번져나간다.

**❹** Every product seems to be on an unstoppable march towards the next version, the next generation that promises to revolutionize your life.

모든 제품은 다음 버전, 즉, 당신의 삶에 변혁을 일으키겠다는 약속을 하는 다음 세대를 향한 멈출 수 없는 행진을 하는 것으로 보인다.

**❺** What's fascinating, or perhaps disturbing, is the utter efficacy of this cycle in shaping our desires. It's not so much that we want the newest device; we're led to believe we need it.

흥미로운 점, 또는 어쩌면 당황스러운 점은 우리의 욕구를 형성하는 이 순환의 절대적인 효과이다. 우리가 가장 최신 기기를 원하는 것이 아니라, 우리가 그것을 원한다고 믿도록 유도된 것이다.

**❻** The distinction between want and need blurs, shifting our financial priorities in favor of staying current with trends. For all the logical arguments against this ceaseless upgrading, the temptation remains compelling.

최신 트렌드를 유지하는 것을 선호하는 쪽으로 우리의 재정적인 우선순위를 바꾸면서, 원하는 것과 필요한 것 사이의 구분이 흐릿해진다. 이런 끊임없는 업그레이드를 하는 것에 대한 논리적인 논쟁에도 불구하고, 매력은 여전히 강력하다.

# 29 어법

❶ Conditioned Place Preference is a way of finding out what animals want.

조건부 장소 선호도는 동물들이 무엇을 원하는지 알아내는 하나의 방법이다.

❷ Researchers train them to associate one place with an experience such as food or a loud noise and another place with something completely different, usually where nothing happens.

연구자들은 그것들이 한 장소를 음식이나 시끄러운 소리와 같은 경험과 연관시키고 또 다른 장소를 완벽히 다른 어떤 것과 연관시키도록 훈련시키는데 대개 그곳에서는 아무것도 일어나지 않는다.

❸ The two places are made obviously different to make it as easy as possible for the animal to associate each place with what happened to it there.

그 두 장소는 그 동물이 각 장소를 거기에서 그것에게 일어난 일과 연관시키는 것을 가능한 한 쉽게 만들기 위해 명백히 다르게 만들어진다.

❹ The animal's preference for being in one place or another is measured both before and after its experiences in the two places.

한 장소나 다른 장소에 있는 것에 대한 그 동물의 선호도는 두 장소에서 경험하기 전과 후에 모두 측정된다.

❺ If there is a shift in where the animal chooses to spend its time for the reward, this suggests that it liked the experience and is trying to repeat it.

만약 동물이 보상을 위해 어디에서 시간을 보내기로 선택하는지에 변화가 있다면, 이것은 그것이 그 경험을 좋아했고 그것을 반복하려고 노력하는 중이라는 것을 시사한다.

❻ Conversely, if it now avoids the place the stimulus appeared and starts to prefer the place it did not experience it, then this suggests that it found the stimulus unpleasant.

반대로, 만약 그것이 이제 자극이 나타났던 장소를 피하고 그것이 그것을 경험하지 않았던 장소를 선호하기 시작한다면, 그러면 이것은 그것이 그 자극을 불쾌하게 느꼈다는 것을 시사한다.

❼ For example, mice with cancer show a preference for the place where they have been given morphine, a drug used to relieve pain, rather than where they have received saline whereas healthy mice developed no such preference. This suggests that the mice with cancer wanted the morphine.

예를 들어, 암에 걸린 쥐가 식염수를 받아 왔던 곳보다 통증을 완화시키는 데 사용되는 약인 모르핀이 주어졌던 장소에 대한 선호를 보여 준 반면, 건강한 쥐는 그러한 선호가 생기지 않았다. 이것은 암에 걸린 쥐가 그 모르핀을 원했음을 시사한다.

## 30 어휘

❶ Near the equator, many species of bird breed all year round.

적도 근처에서, 새의 많은 종들은 일 년 내내 번식한다.

❷ But in temperate and polar regions, the breeding seasons of birds are often sharply defined. They are triggered mainly by changes in day length.

하지만 온대와 극지방에서는 새들의 번식기들이 대개 뚜렷하게 정해진다. 그것들은 주로 낮의 길이의 변화에 의해 촉발된다.

❸ If all goes well, the outcome is that birds raise their young when the food supply is at its peak.

만약에 모든 것이 잘 진행된다면, 결과는 새들이 먹이 공급이 최고조에 이를 때 새끼들을 기르는 것이다.

❹ Most birds are not simply reluctant to breed at other times but they are also physically incapable of doing so. This is because their reproductive system shrinks, which helps flying birds save weight.

대부분의 새들은 다른 때에 번식하기를 단지 꺼리는 것뿐만 아니라 또한 신체적으로 그렇게 할 수 없는 것이다. 이것은 왜냐하면 그들의 번식 기관이 줄어들기 때문이고, 이 사실은 나는 새들이 몸무게를 줄일 수 있도록 도와준다.

❺ The main exception to this rule are nomadic desert species. These can initiate their breeding cycle within days of rain. It's for making the most of the sudden breeding opportunity.

유목성 사막 종은 이 규칙의 주요 예외이다. 이들은 비가 오는 날들에 번식 주기를 시작할 수 있다. 그것은 갑작스러운 번식 기회를 최대한으로 활용하기 위한 것이다.

❻ Also, different species divide the breeding season up in different ways. Most seabirds raise a single brood. In warm regions, however, songbirds may raise several families in a few months.

또한, 다른 종들은 번식기간을 다른 방식으로 나눈다. 대부분의 바닷새들은 한 무리의 함께 태어난 새끼를 기른다. 그러나, 따뜻한 지역에서는, 명금(鳴禽)들이 몇 달 안에 여러 자녀들을 기를 수도 있다.

❼ In an exceptionally good year, a pair of House Sparrows, a kind of songbird, can raise successive broods through a marathon reproductive effort.

유난히 좋은 해에는 명금(鳴禽)의 한 종류인 참새 한 쌍은 마라톤과 같은 번식 노력을 통해 잇따라 태어난 여러 무리의 함께 태어난 새끼들을 기를 수 있다.

# 31 빈칸

❶ One factor that may hinder creativity is unawareness of the resources required in each activity in students' learning.

창의성을 방해할 수도 있는 한 가지 요소는 학생들의 학습에서 각 활동에 요구되는 자원에 대한 인식이 없다는 것이다.

❷ Often students are unable to identify the resources they need to perform the task required of them.

종종 학생들은 그들에게 요구되는 과제를 수행하는 데 필요한 자원들을 식별할 수 없다.

❸ Different resources may be compulsory for specific learning tasks, and recognizing them may simplify the activity's performance.

여러 가지의 자원들이 특정 학습 과제들에 대해 필수적일 수 있어서 그것들을 인식하는 것은 활동의 수행을 평이하게 해 줄 수도 있다.

❹ For example, it may be that students desire to conduct some experiments in their projects.

예를 들어, 학생들이 프로젝트에서 어떤 실험을 수행하기를 원할 수도 있다.

❺ There must be a prior investigation of whether the students will have access to the laboratory, equipment, and chemicals required for the experiment.

학생들이 실험에 요구되는 실험실, 장비, 그리고 화학 물질에 접근할 수 있을지 여부에 대한 사전 조사가 있어야 한다.

❻ It means preparation is vital for the students to succeed, and it may be about human and financial resources such as laboratory technicians, money to purchase chemicals, and equipment for their learning where applicable.

그것은 학생들이 성공하기 위해 준비가 필수적이라는 것을 의미하며, 그들의 학습을 위해 적용할 수 있는 경우에 그것은 실험실 기술자, 화학 물질 구입 자금, 그리고 장비와 같은 인적 그리고 재정적 자원에 대한 것일 수도 있다.

❼ Even if some of the resources required for a task may not be available, identifying them in advance may help students' creativity. It may even lead to changing the topic, finding alternative resources, and other means.

과제에 요구되는 자원들 중 일부가 이용 가능하지 않을 수도 있지만, 사전에 그것들을 식별하는 것은 학생들의 창의성에 도움이 될 수도 있다. 그것은 심지어 주제 변경, 대체 자원들 찾기, 그리고 다른 방법으로 이어질 수도 있다.

## 32 빈칸

❶ All translators feel some pressure from the community of readers for whom they are doing their work. And all translators arrive at their interpretations in dialogue with other people.

모든 번역가들은 그들이 대상으로 작업하고 있는 독자들의 공동체로부터 약간의 압박을 느낀다. 그리고 모든 번역가들은 다른 사람들과의 대화에서 그들의 해석에 도달한다.

❷ The English poet Alexander Pope had pretty good Greek, but when he set about translating Homer's *Iliad* in the early 18th century he was not on his own.

영국의 시인 알렉산더 포프는 그리스어를 꽤 잘했지만, 18세기 초에 호머의 'Iliad'를 번역하는 것에 대해 착수했을 때 그는 혼자 한 것이 아니었다.

❸ He had Greek commentaries to refer to, and translations that had already been done in English, Latin, and French — and of course he had dictionaries. Translators always draw on more than one source text.

그는 참고할 그리스어 해설과 이미 영어, 라틴어, 프랑스어로 된 번역본을 가지고 있었고, 물론 사전도 가지고 있었다. 번역가들은 항상 한 가지 이상의 원문을 활용한다.

❹ Even when the scene of translation consists of just one person with a pen, paper, and the book that is being translated, or even when it is just one person translating orally for another, that person's linguistic knowledge arises from lots of other texts and other conversations.

심지어 번역 현장이 하나의 펜, 종이, 그리고 번역 중인 책을 가진 단 한 사람으로 구성되어 있거나, 한 사람이 다른 사람을 위해 구두로 번역 중일 때에도, 그 사람의 언어적 지식은 많은 다른 텍스트와 다른 대화에서 발생한다.

❺ And then his or her idea of the translation's purpose will be influenced by the expectations of the person or people it is for. In both these senses every translation is a crowd translation.

그러고 나서 번역의 목적에 대한 그 또는 그녀의 생각은 이것의 대상이 되는 사람 또는 사람들의 기대에 의해 영향을 받는다. 이 두 가지 의미에서 모든 번역은 군중 번역이다.

# 33 빈칸

❶ Some people argue that there is a single, logically consistent concept known as reading that can be neatly set apart from everything else people do with books.

몇몇 사람들은 사람들이 책을 가지고 하는 모든 다른 행동들로부터 깔끔하게 분리될 수 있는, 읽기로 알려진 유일하고 논리적으로 일관성 있는 개념이 있다고 주장한다.

❷ Is reading really that simple? The most productive way to think about reading is as a loosely related set of behaviors that belong together owing to family resemblances, as Ludwig Wittgenstein used the phrase, without having in common a single defining trait.

읽기는 정말로 그렇게 단순할까? 읽기에 대해 생각하는 가장 생산적인 방식은 하나의 명백한 특성을 공통적으로 가지지 않은 채 Ludwig Wittgenstein이 그 어구를 사용한 것처럼 가족 유사성 때문에 함께 속하게 되는 헐겁게 연결된 행동의 묶음으로서이다.

❸ Consequently, efforts to distinguish reading from nonreading are destined to fail because there is no agreement on what qualifies as reading in the first place.

결론적으로, 읽기와 읽기가 아닌 것을 구분하려는 노력은 실패로 돌아가는데, 왜냐하면 애초에 무엇이 읽기로서의 자격을 주는가에 대한 동의가 없기 때문이다.

❹ The more one tries to figure out where the border lies between reading and not-reading, the more edge cases will be found to stretch the term's flexible boundaries.

읽기와 읽기가 아닌 것 사이의 경계가 어디에 있는가를 알려고 하면 할수록, 더욱 많은 특이 사례들이 그 용어의 유연한 경계를 확장하고 있다는 것이 밝혀질 것이다.

❺ Thus, it is worth attempting to collect together these exceptional forms of reading into a single forum, one highlighting the challenges faced by anyone wishing to establish the boundaries where reading begins and ends.

그러므로, 이러한 예외적인 읽기의 형태들을 모두 함께 하나의 토론의 장으로 모으려는 시도는 해 볼 가치가 있으며, 그 토론의 장은 어디서 읽기가 시작되고 끝나는가에 대한 경계를 정하기를 원하는 누구나에 의해 마주하게 될 어려움들을 돋보이게 한다.

❻ The attempt moves toward an understanding of reading as a spectrum that is expansive enough to accommodate the distinct reading activities.

그러한 시도는 별개의 읽기 활동들을 다 수용할 만큼 충분히 광범위한 스펙트럼으로서 읽기를 이해하는 것으로 발전한다.

# 34 빈칸

❶ Weber's law concerns the perception of difference between two stimuli.

베버의 법칙은 두 자극 사이의 차이에 대한 감지에 관한 것이다.

❷ It suggests that we might not be able to detect a 1-mm difference when we are looking at lines 466 mm and 467 mm in length, but we may be able to detect a 1-mm difference when we are comparing a line 2 mm long with one 3 mm long.

이것은 우리가 466mm와 467mm 길이인 선들을 볼 때 1mm의 차이를 감지할 수 없지만, 우리가 2mm 길이와 3mm 길이인 선을 비교할 때는 1mm의 차이를 감지할 수 있을지도 모른다는 것을 암시한다.

❸ Another example of this principle is that we can detect 1 candle when it is lit in an otherwise dark room.

이 원리의 또 다른 예는 촛불이 켜지지 않았으면 어두웠을 방안에 하나의 촛불이 켜졌을 때 이것을 감지할 수 있다는 것이다.

❹ But when 1 candle is lit in a room in which 100 candles are already burning, we may not notice the light from this candle.

그러나 100개의 촛불이 이미 타고 있는 방에 하나의 촛불이 켜졌을 때, 우리는 이 촛불의 빛을 알아차리지 못할지도 모른다.

❺ Therefore, the Just-noticeable difference (JND) varies as a function of the strength of the signals. For example, the JND is greater for very loud noises than it is for much more quiet sounds.

그러므로, 겨우 알아차릴 수 있는 차이 (JND)는 신호의 세기에 대한 함수에 의해 달라진다. 예를 들어, JND는 훨씬 더 작은 소리에 대한 것보다 매우 큰 소음에 대해 더 크다.

❻ When a sound is very weak, we can tell that another sound is louder, even if it is barely louder. When a sound is very loud, to tell that another sound is even louder, it has to be much louder.

한 소리가 매우 약할 때, 우리는 그것이 간신히 더 클지라도, 또 다른 소리가 더 크다는 것을 구분할 수 있다. 어떤 소리가 매우 클 때, 다른 소리가 훨씬 더 크다는 것을 구분하기 위해서는, 그 소리는 훨씬 더 커야 한다.

❼ Thus, Weber's law means that it is harder to distinguish between two samples when those samples are larger or stronger levels of the stimuli.

그러므로, 베버의 법칙은 그 표본들이 자극의 수준이 더 크거나 강할 때 두 표본을 구별하기가 더 어렵다는 것을 의미한다.

# 35 무관

❶ Any new resource (e.g a new airport, a new mall) always opens with people benefiting individually by sharing a common resource (e.g the city or state budget).

어떤 새로운 자원(예를 들어, 새로운 공항, 새로운 쇼핑센터)은 항상 공동의 자원(예를 들어, 시 또는 주 예산)을 공유함으로써 사람들이 개별적으로 이익을 얻으면서 시작된다.

❷ Soon, at some point, the amount of traffic grows too large for the "commons" to support.

곧, 어느 시점에서, 교통량은 '공유지'가 견디기에 너무 커진다.

❸ Traffic jams, overcrowding, and overuse lessen the benefits of the common resource for everyone — the tragedy of the commons!

교통 체증, 과밀, 그리고 과도한 사용은 모두를 위한 공유 자원의 혜택을 줄이는데, 이것은 즉 공유지의 비극이다!

❹ If the new resource cannot be expanded or provided with additional space, it becomes a problem, and you cannot solve the problem on your own, in isolation from your fellow drivers or walkers or competing users.

만약 새로운 자원이 확장될 수 없거나 추가적인 공간이 제공될 수 없다면, 이것은 문제가 되고, 여러분은 여러분의 동료 운전자나 보행자 또는 경쟁 사용자들로부터 고립된 상태로 혼자서 문제를 해결할 수 없다.

❺ The total activity on this new resource keeps increasing, and so does individual activity; but if the dynamic of common use and overuse continues too long, both begin to fall after a peak, leading to a crash.

이 새로운 자원에 대한 총활동은 계속 증가하고, 개인 활동도 증가한다. 그러나 만약 공동 사용과 과도한 사용의 역학이 너무 오래 지속되면, 둘 다 정점 이후에 떨어지기 시작하고, 몰락으로 이어진다.

❻ What makes the "tragedy of commons" tragic is the crash dynamic —the destruction or degeneration of the common resource's ability to regenerate itself.

'공유지의 비극'을 더 비극적이게 만드는 것은 몰락 역학, 즉 그 스스로를 재생산할 수 있는 공동 자원의 능력의 파괴 또는 퇴보이다.

## 36 순서

❶ Theoretically, our brain would have the capacity to store all experiences throughout life, reaching the quality of a DVD.

이론적으로는 우리의 뇌는 DVD의 품질에 도달할 정도로, 삶의 모든 경험들을 저장할 수 있는 수용력을 가지고 있을 것이다.

❷ However, this theoretical capacity is offset by the energy demand associated with the process of storing and retrieving information in memory.

그러나, 이 이론상의 수용력은 기억에 정보를 저장하고 상기하는 과정과 관련된 에너지 수요로 인해 상쇄된다.

❸ As a result, the brain develops efficient strategies, becoming dependent on shortcuts.

그 결과, 뇌는 효율적인 전략들을 수립하고, 지름길에 의존하게 된다.

❹ When we observe a face, the visual image captured by the eyes is highly variable, depending on the point of view, lighting conditions and other contextual factors.

우리가 얼굴을 관찰할 때, 눈에 의해 포착되는 시각적 이미지는 시점, 조명 조건 및 기타 상황적 요인들에 따라 매우 다양하다.

❺ Nevertheless, we are able to recognize the face as the same, maintaining the underlying identity. The brain, rather than focusing on the details of visualization, creates and stores general patterns that allow for consistent recognition across diverse circumstances.

그럼에도 불구하고, 우리는 근본적인 정체성을 유지하면서 얼굴을 같은 것으로 인식할 수 있다. 뇌는 시각화의 세부 사항에 집중하기보다 다양한 상황들에서 일관된 인식을 가능하게 하는 일반적인 패턴을 생성하고 저장한다.

❻ This ability to match what we see with general visual memory patterns serves as an effective mechanism for optimizing brain performance and saving energy.

우리가 보는 것과 일반적인 시각 기억 패턴을 일치시키는 이 능력은 뇌의 수행을 최적화하고 에너지를 절약하는 효과적인 기제로 작용한다.

❼ The brain, being naturally against unnecessary effort, constantly seeks to simplify and generalize information to facilitate the cognitive process.

불필요한 노력에 자연스럽게 대항하는 뇌는 인지 과정을 돕기 위해서 끊임없이 정보를 단순화하고 일반화하는 것을 추구한다.

# 37 순서

❶ Where scientific research is concerned, explanatory tales are expected to adhere closely to experimental data and to illuminate the regular and predictable features of experience.

과학 연구에 관해서는, 설명하는 이야기들이 실험의 데이터에 엄밀히 충실할 것으로 기대되고 경험의 규칙적이고 예측 가능한 특징들을 밝힐 것으로 기대된다.

❷ However, this paradigm sometimes conceals the fact that theories are deeply loaded with creative elements that shape the construction of research projects and the interpretations of evidence.

그러나, 이러한 패러다임은 때때로 이론들이 연구 프로젝트의 구성과 증거의 해석을 형성하는 창의적인 요소들로 철저히 채워져 있다는 사실을 감춘다.

❸ Scientific explanations do not just relate a chronology of facts. They construct frameworks for systematically chosen data in order to provide a consistent and meaningful explanation of what is observed.

과학적 설명들은 단순히 사실들의 연대기를 말하는 것은 아니다. 그것들은 관찰된 것에 대한 일관적이고 의미 있는 설명을 제공하기 위해 체계적으로 선택된 데이터에 대한 틀을 구축한다.

❹ Such constructions lead us to imagine specific kinds of subject matter in particular sorts of relations, and the storylines they inspire will prove more effective for analyzing some features of experience over others.

그러한 구성들은 우리가 특정한 유형의 관계에서 구체적인 종류의 주제를 상상하도록 하며, 그것들이 고취하는 줄거리는 다른 것들보다 경험의 일부 특징을 분석하는 데 더 효과적일 것으로 판명될 것이다.

❺ When we neglect the creative contributions of such scientific imagination and treat models and interpretive explanations as straightforward facts — even worse, as facts including all of reality — we can blind ourselves to the limitations of a given model and fail to note its potential for misunderstanding a situation to which it ill applies.

우리가 그러한 과학적 상상의 창의적 기여를 무시하고 모델과 해석적 설명을 단순한 사실, 훨씬 더 심하게는 현실을 전부 포괄하는 사실로 간주할 때, 우리는 주어진 모델의 한계에 대해 우리 스스로를 눈멀게 하며 그것이 잘못 적용되는 상황에 대해 오해할 가능성을 알아차리지 못할 수 있다.

# 38 삽입

❶ We encounter contrary claims about the relation of literature to action.

우리는 문학과 행동의 관계에 대한 상반된 주장들과 마주한다.

❷ Theorists have maintained that literature encourages solitary reading and reflection as the way to engage with the world and thus counters the social and political activities that might produce social change.

이론가들은 문학이 세상과 관계를 맺는 방법으로써 고독한 독서와 성찰을 장려하고 따라서 사회 변화를 일으킬 수 있을지도 모르는 사회적이고 정치적인 활동들에 거스른다고 주장해 왔다.

❸ At best it encourages detachment or appreciation of complexity, and at worst passivity and acceptance of what is.

기껏해야 이것은 단절 또는 복잡성에 대한 인정을, 최악의 경우 수동성과 있는 그대로에 대한 수용을 조장한다.

❹ But on the other hand, literature has historically been seen as dangerous: it promotes the questioning of authority and social arrangements.

그러나 다른 한편으로, 문학은 역사적으로 권위와 사회적 합의에 대한 의문을 제기하는 것을 조장하므로 위험하다고 여겨져 왔다.

❺ Plato banned poets from his ideal republic because they could only do harm, and novels have long been credited with making people dissatisfied with their lives and eager for something new.

플라톤은 그들이 해를 끼치는 것만 할 수 있기 때문에 그의 이상적인 공화국으로부터 시인들을 추방했고, 소설은 사람들이 그들의 삶에 불만을 품게 만들고 새로운 무언가를 갈망하도록 하는 것으로 오랫동안 믿어져왔다.

❻ By promoting identification across divisions of class, gender, and race, books may promote a fellowship that discourages struggle; but they may also produce a keen sense of injustice that makes progressive struggles possible.

계급, 성별, 그리고 인종의 경계를 넘어 동일시를 촉진함으로써, 책들은 투쟁을 단념시키는 동료 의식을 장려할 수 있을지 모르지만, 이것들은 또한 진보적인 투쟁들을 가능하게 만드는 강한 불의의 감정을 일으킬 수 있다.

❼ Historically, works of literature are credited with producing change: *Uncle Tom's Cabin*, a best-seller in its day, helped create a revulsion against slavery that made possible the American Civil War.

역사적으로, 문학 작품은 변화를 만드는 것으로 믿어져 왔는데 그 시대의 베스트셀러인 '톰 아저씨의 오두막'은 미국 남북전쟁을 가능하게 만든 노예제에 대한 혐오감을 조성하는 것을 도왔다.

# 39 삽입

❶ According to Hobbes, man is not a being who can act morally in spite of his instinct to protect his existence in the state of nature.

홉스에 따르면, 인간은 자연 상태에서 자신의 존재를 보호하려는 그의 본능을 무릅쓰고 도덕적으로 행동할 수 있는 존재가 아니다.

❷ Hence, the only place where morality and moral liberty will begin to find an application begins in a place where a sovereign power, namely the state, emerges.

따라서, 도덕과 도덕적 자유가 적용을 찾기 시작하는 유일한 곳은 군림하는 권력, 즉 국가가 출현하는 곳에서 나타난다.

❸ Hobbes thus describes the state of nature as a circumstance in which man's life is "solitary, poor, nasty, brutish and short".

따라서 홉스는 자연 상태를 인간의 삶이 '고독하고, 가난하며, 불결하고, 잔인하고, 짧은' 상황으로 묘사한다.

❹ It means when people live without a general power to control them all, they are indeed in a state of war.

그것은 사람들이 그들 모두를 통제할 일반적인 권력 없이 살아갈 때, 그들은 실로 전쟁 상태에 놓여 있는 것임을 의미한다.

❺ In other words, Hobbes, who accepted that human beings are not social and political beings in the state of nature, believes that without the power human beings in the state of nature are "antisocial and rational based on their selfishness".

즉 다시 말해, 자연 상태에 있는 인간은 사회적이고 정치적인 존재가 아니라는 것을 인정한 홉스는 그 권력이 없이 자연 상태에 있는 인간은 '이기심에 기초해 반사회적이고 이성적'이라고 믿는다.

❻ Moreover, since society is not a natural phenomenon and there is no natural force bringing people together, what will bring them together as a society is not mutual affection according to Hobbes.

게다가, 사회는 자연적인 현상이 아니며 사람들을 하나로 모으는 자연적인 힘도 없기 때문에, 홉스에 따르면 그들을 사회로 함께 모이게 하는 것은 상호 간의 애정이 아니다.

❼ It is, rather, mutual fear of men's present and future that assembles them, since the cause of fear is a common drive among people in the state of nature.

두려움으로부터의 동기가 자연 상태에 있는 사람들 사이의 공통된 추진력이기 때문에, 오히려, 그들을 모으는 것은 인간의 현재와 미래에 대한 상호 간의 두려움이다.

# 40 요약

❶ There is research that supports the idea that cognitive factors influence the phenomenology of the perceived world. Delk and Fillenbaum asked participants to match the color of figures with the color of their background.

인지적 요인들이 지각된 세계의 현상학에 영향을 미친다는 생각을 뒷받침하는 연구가 있다. Delk와 Fillenbaum은 참가자들에게 형상들의 색상을 배경 색상과 맞추도록 요청했다.

❷ Some of the figures depicted objects associated with a particular color. These included typically red objects such as an apple, lips, and a symbolic heart.

몇몇 형상들은 특정 색상과 연관된 물체들을 묘사했다. 그것들은 사과, 입술, 상징적인 하트 모양과 같이 전형적인 빨간색 물체를 포함했다.

❸ Other objects were presented that are not usually associated with red, such as a mushroom or a bell. However, all the figures were made out of the same red-orange cardboard.

버섯이나 종과 같이 빨간색과 일반적으로 연관이 되지 않는 다른 물체들도 제시되었다. 그러나, 모든 형상들은 동일한 다홍색 판지로 만들어졌다.

❹ Participants then had to match the figure to a background varying from dark to light red. They had to make the background color match the color of the figures.

그리고 나서 참가자들은 그 형상을 진한 빨간색에서 연한 빨간색까지 다양한 배경색과 맞춰야 했다. 그들은 배경색이 형상들의 색과 일치하게 해야 했다.

❺ The researchers found that red-associated objects required more red in the background to be judged a match than did the objects that are not associated with the color red.

연구자들은 빨간색과 연관된 물체들이 빨간색과 연관이 없는 물체가 그러한 것보다 배경과 일치한다고 판단되기 위해서 배경에서 더 빨간색을 요구한다는 것을 발견했다.

❻ This implies that the cognitive association of objects to color influences how we perceive that color.

이것은 색과 물체의 인지적 연관성이 우리가 그 색을 어떻게 지각하는가에 영향을 미친다는 것을 함의한다.

# 41~42 제목, 어휘

❶ In each round of genome copying in our body, there is still about a 70 percent chance that at least one pair of chromosomes will have an error. With each round of genome copying, errors accumulate. This is similar to alterations in medieval books.

우리 몸속 게놈 복제의 각 과정마다, 적어도 한 쌍의 염색체들이 오류를 가질 확률이 여전히 약 70%이다. 게놈 복제의 각 과정마다, 오류들이 쌓인다. 이것은 중세 서적에 있어서의 변화와 유사하다.

❷ Each time a copy was made by hand, some changes were introduced accidentally; as changes stacked up, the copies may have acquired meanings at variance with the original.

하나의 복사본이 사람 손으로 만들어질 때마다, 일부 변화들이 우연히 도입되었고, 변화들이 쌓이면서, 복사본은 원본과 불일치하는 의미를 축적했을 것이다.

❸ Similarly, genomes that have undergone more copying processes will have gathered more mistakes. To make things worse, mutations may damage genes responsible for error checking and repair of genomes, further accelerating the introduction of mutations.

마찬가지로, 더 많은 복제 과정들을 거친 게놈은 더 많은 실수들을 축적하게 될 것이다. 설상가상으로, 변이들은 게놈의 오류 확인과 복구를 책임지는 유전자를 훼손해 변이들의 도입을 더욱 가속할 수도 있다.

❹ Most genome mutations do not have any noticeable effects. It is just like changing the *i* for a *y* in "kingdom" would not distort the word's readability. But sometimes a mutation to a human gene results in, for example, an eye whose iris is of two different colors.

대부분의 게놈 변이들은 어떠한 뚜렷한 영향이 없다. 그것은 마치 'kingdom'에서 'i'를 'y'로 변경하는 것이 그 단어의 가독성을 왜곡하지 않는 것과 같다. 그러나 예를 들어, 때때로 인간 유전자에 대한 변이는 홍채가 두 가지 다른 색을 띠는 눈을 초래하기도 한다.

❺ Similarly, almost everyone has birthmarks, which are due to mutations that occurred as our body's cells multiplied to form skin. If mutations are changes to the genome of one particular cell, how can a patch of cells in an iris or a whole patch of skin, consisting of many individual cells, be affected simultaneously?

마찬가지로, 거의 모두가 모반이 있는데, 이는 우리 몸의 세포가 피부를 형성하기 위하여 증식하면서 발생한 변이들 때문이다. 만약 변이들이 하나의 특정 세포의 게놈에 대한 변화라면, 많은 개별적인 세포들로 구성된 홍채의 세포 집단이나 피부 전체 세포 집단이 어떻게 동시에 영향을 받을 수 있을까?

❻ The answer lies in the cell lineage, the developmental history of a tissue from particular cells through to their fully differentiated state. If the mutation occurred early on in the lineage of the developing iris, then all cells in that patch have inherited that change.

그 대답은 세포 계보, 즉 특정 세포에서 그들의 완전히 차별화된 상태까지의 조직 발달 변천에 있다. 만약 발달 중인 홍채의 계보 초기에 변이가 발생했다면, 그렇다면 그 세포 집단의 모든 세포는 그 변화를 물려받아 왔을 것이다.

## 43~45 순서, 지칭, 세부 내용

❶ Max awoke to the gentle sunlight of an autumn day. Right on schedule, he swung his legs off the bed and took a deep, satisfying breath. He began his morning the same way he usually did, getting dressed and going to school.

Max는 가을날의 부드러운 햇빛에 잠에서 깼다. 시간에 맞추어 그는 다리를 침대 밖으로 휙 내려놓았고 깊고 만족스러운 숨을 내쉬었다. 그는 평소와 똑같은 방식으로 아침을 시작했고 옷을 입고 학교에 갔다.

❷ Today was going to be another perfect day until he ran into Mr. Kapoor, his science teacher. "Just to remind you. Science fair projects are due next Wednesday. Don't forget to submit your final draft on time," Mr. Kapoor said. Max froze.

오늘은 과학 선생님인 Kapoor 선생님을 만나기 전까지는 또 다른 완벽한 날이 될 예정이었다. "그냥 너(Max)에게 알려 주는 거야. 과학 박람회 프로젝트가 다음 주 수요일까지야. 제 시간에 최종안을 제출하는 것을 잊어버리지 마." 라고 Kapoor 선생님이 말했다. Max는 얼어붙었다.

❸ *What? It can't be! It was due next Friday!* After school, he came home worrying that his whole perfectly planned week was going to be ruined. Without his usual greeting, Max headed to his room in haste.

'뭐라고? 그럴 순 없어! 이건 다음 주 금요일까지였다고!' 학교를 마친 후에, 그는 그의 완벽히 계획된 일주일이 망쳐질 것을 걱정하며 집으로 돌아왔다. 그의 일상적인 인사 없이, Max는 급하게 그의 방으로 향했다.

❹ "What's wrong Max?," Jeremy, his dad, followed Max, worrying about him. Max furiously browsed through his planner without answering him, only to find the wrong date written in it.

"무슨 일이니 Max?" 그의 아버지인 Jeremy는 그를 걱정하며 Max를 따라갔다. Max는 그(Jeremy)에게 대답하지 않고 열성적으로 그의 일정표를 뒤적거렸지만, 거기에 잘못 적힌 날짜를 발견할 뿐이었다.

❺ Fighting through tears, Max finally managed to explain the unending pressure to be perfect to his dad. To his surprise, Jeremy laughed. "Max, guess what? Perfect is a great goal, but nobody gets there all the time. What matters is what we do when things get messy." That made him feel a little better.

울음을 참으며, Max는 마침내 가까스로 그의(Max) 아버지에게 완벽해야 한다는 끝나지 않는 압박에 대해 설명했다. 놀랍게도, Jeremy는 웃었다. "Max, 있잖아? 완벽은 훌륭한 목표지만, 누구도 항상 거기에 도달할 수는 없단다. 중요한 건 일이 어질러졌을 때 우리가 무엇을 하는가야." 그것이 그의 기분을 조금 더 나아지게 만들어 주었다.

❻ "You are saying I can fix this?" "Absolutely, try to deal with problems in a logical way," Jeremy said. Max thought for a moment. "I guess.... I can do that by rescheduling tonight's baseball lesson." Jeremy beamed.

"아빠는 제가 (Max) 이것을 해결할 수 있다고 말씀하시는 거예요?" "물론이지. 논리적인 방식으로 문제를 처리해봐." 라고 Jeremy가 말했다. Max는 잠시 동안 생각했다. "아마.... 제가 오늘 밤 야구 레슨 일정을 변경함으로써 그렇게 할 수 있을 것 같아요." Jeremy가 활짝 웃었다.

❼ "See? That's you finding a solution." Max felt a genuine smile spreading. The next Wednesday, he successfully handed in the final draft on time with satisfaction. From then on, he still loved order and routines, but also embraced the messy, unpredictable bits of life too.

"봤지? 네가 해결책을 찾아냈잖니." Max는 진심 어린 미소가 퍼지는 것을 느꼈다. 다음 주 수요일에 그(Max)는 만족하며 성공적으로 최종안을 제시간에 제출했다. 그 이후로 그는 여전히 순서와 정해진 일과를 좋아했지만, 또한 어지럽고 예측 불가능한 삶의 부분들도 기꺼이 맞이했다.

# 2024 고2 11월 모의고사

**❶ 회차 :**    점 / 200점

❶ voca    ❷ text    ❸ [ / ]    ❹ ____    ❺ quiz 1    ❻ quiz 2    ❼ quiz 3    ❽ quiz 4    ❾ quiz 5

## 18

Dear Executive Manager Schulz,
It is a week before the internship program starts. I am writing to bring your [ **attention / pretension** ]¹⁾ to a matter that requires immediate consideration regarding the issue my department has. As the coordinator, it is becoming apparent to me that the budget, previously approved by your department, needs some adjustments in order to meet the emerging modifications. Since my department has [ **fired / hired** ]²⁾ three [ **less / more** ]³⁾ interns than planned initially, the most expensive need is for additional funding to cover their wages, training costs, and materials. I kindly request an additional budget allocation for these expenses. Please refer to the [ **attachment / detachment** ]⁴⁾ for details. Thank you for your [ **pretension / attention** ]⁵⁾.
Best regards, Matt Perry

Schulz 부장님께 인턴십 프로그램을 시작하기 일주일 전입니다. 저희 부서의 사안과 관련하여 즉각적인 고려가 필요한 문제에 대해 당신의 관심을 환기하기 위해 이 글을 씁니다. 업무 담당자로서 최근 생겨난 수정 사항을 충족시키기 위해서, 이전에 당신의 부서로부터 승인받은 예산은 약간의 조정이 필요함이 분명해지고 있습니다. 우리 부서에서 처음에 계획됐던 것보다 세 명의 인턴을 더 고용했기 때문에, 가장 비용이 많이 드는 부족한 부분은 그들의 임금, 훈련 비용, 물품들을 다루기 위한 추가적인 자금입니다. 이 비용들을 위해 추가적인 예산 배당을 정중하게 요청합니다. 자세한 사항은 첨부물을 참고해 주세요. 당신의 관심에 감사드립니다.
Matt Perry 드림

## 19

Katie approached the hotel front desk to check-in but an unexpected event [ **folded / unfolded** ]⁶⁾. The receptionist couldn't find her reservation under the name 'Katie'. "I'm sorry, but I can't seem to locate a reservation under that name," the receptionist said. "No way, I definitely made a reservation on the phone," Katie said, [ **puzzled / puzzling** ]⁷⁾. The receptionist asked, "Can you tell me your phone number?" and Katie told it to him, thinking '[ **What / That** ]⁸⁾ happened? Did I make a mistake?' "Just a moment," the receptionist said, typing deliberately on the keyboard. "I found it! It seems there was a small misspelling. Your reservation is under 'K-A-T-Y'," the receptionist explained. With a sense of ease, Katie watched her reservation [ **appearing / to appear** ]⁹⁾ on the screen. With her heart slowing to a gentle rhythm, she [ **preceded / proceeded** ]¹⁰⁾ with her check-in, thinking that a simple misspelling might have ruined her plans.

Katie는 체크인을 하기 위해 호텔 안내 데스크에 다가갔으나 예상하지 못한 사건이 전개되었다. 접수 담당자는 'Katie'라는 이름으로 된 예약을 찾을 수 없었다. "죄송하지만, 그 이름으로 된 예약을 찾을 수 없는 것 같습니다."라고 접수 담당자가 말했다. "말도 안 돼요, 저는 분명히 전화로 예약했어요."라고 Katie가 어리둥절해하며 말했다. 접수 담당자가 "당신의 전화번호를 말해 주실 수 있을까요?"라고 물어보았고, Katie가 '무슨 일이지? 내가 실수를 저질렀나?'라고 생각하며 전화번호를 그에게 알려 주었다. "잠시만요."라고 접수 담당자가 키보드를 신중하게 치면서 말했다. "알아냈습니다! 작은 오타가 있었던 것 같습니다. 당신의 예약은 'K-A-T-Y'로 되어 있어요."라고 접수 담당자가 설명했다. 편안한 기분으로 Katie는 그녀의 예약이 화면에 나타나는 것을 지켜봤다. 그녀의 심장이 완만한 리듬으로 느려지면서, 그녀는 단순한 오타가 그녀의 계획들을 망쳤을지도 모른다고 생각하며 체크인을 진행했다.

## 20

To be mathematically [ **literate** / literary ]11) means to be able to think critically about societal issues on which mathematics has bearing so as to make informed decisions about how to solve these problems. Dealing with such [ simplified / **complex** ]12) problems through interdisciplinary approaches, mirroring real-world problems [ inquires / **requires** ]13) innovative ways of planning and organizing mathematical teaching methods. Navigating our world means being able to quantify, measure, estimate, classify, compare, find patterns, conjecture, justify, prove, and generalize within critical thinking and when using critical thinking. Therefore, [ **make** / making ]14) decisions, even qualitatively, is not possible without using mathematics and critical thinking. Thus, teaching mathematics should [ **be done** / do ]15) in interaction with [ **critical** / critically ]16) thinking along with a decision-making process. They can be developed into the mathematical context, so that there is no excuse to not [ **explicitly** / implicitly ]17) support students to develop them.

수학적 문해력이 있다는 것은 수학과 관련된 사회적 이슈에 대해 이러한 문제들을 어떻게 해결할지에 대한 정보에 입각한 결정을 하기 위해서 비판적으로 생각할 수 있다는 것을 의미한다. 범교과적인 접근법을 통해 그러한 복잡한 문제들을 다루는 과정에서 실생활 문제들을 반영하는 것은 수학적 교수 방법을 계획하고 조직하는 혁신적인 방법들을 요구한다. 우리의 세계를 탐색한다는 것은 비판적 사고안에서 그리고 비판적 사고를 사용할 때 수량화하고, 측정하고, 추산하고, 분류하고, 비교하고, 패턴을 찾고, 추측하고, 근거를 제시하고, 증명하고, 일반화할 수 있다는 것을 의미한다. 그러므로, 수학과 비판적 사고를 사용하지 않고 의사 결정을 하는 것은 질적인 경우에라도 가능하지 않다. 따라서, 수학을 가르치는 것은 의사 결정 과정과 함께 비판적 사고와의 상호 작용 안에서 이루어져야 한다. 그것들은 수학적인 맥락 안에서 발전될 수 있고, 학생들이 그것들을 발전시킬 수 있도록 명시적으로 도움을 주지 않을 경우 변명의 여지가 없다.

## 21

Imagine that your usually stingy friend delights in buying you a Christmas present after taking a generosity booster. How would you feel? Undoubtedly, there is [ nothing / **something** ]18) praiseworthy about the action. You'd be [ **pleased** / pleasing ]19) to receive the gift. You'd say 'thank you', and mean it. But his change of heart is not [ entire / **entirely** ]20) satisfying. According to Zagzebski, an American philosopher, he is not really generous. When we praise someone's character, we use words for various virtues: 'generous', 'kind', 'courageous', etc. A person who gives one gift isn't generous. Instead, generosity is a stable part of a person's '[ **moral** / mortal ]21) [ identification / **identity** ]22)', an emotional habit that is part of who you are. Thus virtues, as opposed to [ nontypical / **typical** ]23) impulse, are the result of your [ impersonal / **personal** ]24) history. They are part of who you are, as they are part of how your character was formed. Instant virtue is therefore [ **impossible** / possible ]25). Popping a pill cannot make you a better person.

평소에 인색한 여러분의 친구가 관대함 효능촉진제를 먹고 난 이후에 여러분에게 크리스마스 선물을 사 주며 매우 기뻐한다고 상상해 보라. 여러분은 어떻게 느끼겠는가? 의심할 여지 없이, 그 행동에는 칭찬할 만한 점이 있다. 여러분은 선물을 받아서 기뻐할 것이다. 여러분은 '고마워'라고 말하고, 그것은 진심일 것이다. 하지만 그의 마음의 변화는 완전히 만족스럽지는 않다. 미국의 철학자인 Zagzebski에 따르면, 그는 진정으로 관대한 것이 아니다. 우리가 누군가의 인품을 칭찬할 때 '관대한,' '친절한,' '용기있는' 등 다양한 미덕에 대한 단어를 사용한다. 선물을 하나 준 사람이 관대한 것은 아니다. 대신에, 관대함은 누군가의 '도덕적 정체성'의 안정된 일부인데 그것은 여러분의 모습의 일부인 정서적 습관이다. 따라서 미덕은, 비전형적인 충동과는 달리, 여러분 개인 역사의 결과이다. 그것들이 여러분의 인품이 형성되었던 방식의 일부이기 때문에 그것들은 여러분의 모습 중 일부이다. 그러므로 즉각적인 미덕은 있을 수 없다. 약 한 알을 먹는 것이 여러분을 더 나은 사람으로 만들 수는 없다.

## 22

To determine the mass of my bowling ball, I might put it onto a balance and compare it with a known mass, such as a number of metal cubes each weighing 1, 10, or 100 grams. Things get much [ **less / more** ]26) complicated if I want to know the mass of a distant star. How do I measure it? We can roughly say [ **that / what** ]27) measuring the mass of a star involves various theories. If we want to measure the mass of a binary star, we first determine a center of mass between the two stars, then their distance from that center which we can then use, together with a value for the period and a certain instance of Kepler's Third Law, to calculate the mass. In other words, in order to "measure" the star mass, we measure [ **another / other** ]28) quantities and use those values, together with certain equations, to calculate the mass. Measurement is not a simple and unmediated estimation of [ **independent / independently** ]29) existing properties, but a determination of certain magnitudes before the background of a number of [ **rejected / accepted** ]30) theories.

볼링공 질량을 측정하기 위해, 나는 그것을 저울에 올려놓고 각 1g, 10g, 또는 100g이 나가는 여러 개의 금속 큐브 같은 이미 알고 있는 질량과 그것을 비교할 수 있다. 만약 내가 먼 별의 질량을 알고 싶다면 상황은 훨씬 더 복잡해진다. 나는 어떻게 그것을 측정할까? 우리는 별의 질량을 측정하는 것은 다양한 이론을 포함한다고 대략적으로 말할 수 있다. 우리가 쌍성의 질량을 측정하기를 원한다면, 질량을 계산하기 위해 우리는 먼저 두 별들 사이의 질량 중심을, 그 다음에 우리가 그제서야 사용할 수 있는 그 중심으로부터 떨어진 그것들의 거리를 공전 주기의 값과 케플러 제3 법칙의 특정 사례를 가지고 측정한다. 다시 말해서, 별의 질량을 '측정'하기 위해서 우리는 다양한 수치들을 측정하고 그 값들을 특정 방정식들과 함께 사용하여 질량을 계산한다. 측정은 독립적으로 존재하는 값들의 단순하고 중재되지 않은 측정이 아니라, 이미 정립된 여러 이론들을 바탕으로 특정 크기들을 계산하는 것이다.

## 23

Based on discoveries in neuroscience, pain and pleasure [ **are / is** ]31) formed and processed in the [ **different / same** ]32) area of the brain. Our bodies constantly [ **strive / strives** ]33) for homeostasis, [ **which / that** ]34) is defined as the balance of bodily functions. Without the body's [ **effective / affective** ]35) compensatory mechanisms, which may cushion potential highs and lows, we would not be [ **incapable / capable** ]36) of surviving. Pleasure and pain are like two sides of the [ **different / same** ]37) coin; they seem to work together and are heavily reliant on one another and keep balance. If you imagine pleasure and pain as the two [ **opposite / similar** ]38) points on a scale, you can easily understand [ **that / what** ]39) as one of the two points rises, [ **the other / other** ]40) must correspondingly fall. We've all heard the expression, "No pain, no gain." Well, according to psychiatrist Dr. Anna Lembke, there may be some truth to these words. She says [ **that / what** ]41) our attempts to escape being miserable [ **are / is** ]42) in fact making us even [ **less / more** ]43) miserable. This is [ **because of / because** ]44) pain is actually an essential component of our ability to maintain a [ **biased / neutral** ]45) state, and allowing it will in turn [ **reset / resets** ]46) our internal scale back to balance.

뇌 과학의 발견들에 따르면, 고통과 쾌락은 뇌의 같은 영역에서 형성되고 처리된다. 우리 몸은 끊임없이 항상성을 추구하는데, 그것은 몸의 기능들의 균형이라고 정의된다. 잠재적인 변동을 완화시킬 수 있는 몸의 효과적인 보상 기제가 없다면 우리는 생존할 수 없을 것이다. 쾌락과 고통은 동일한 동전의 두 면과 같아서 그들은 함께 작동하는 것 같으며 서로 상당히 의존하고 있고 균형을 유지한다. 만약에 여러분이 쾌락과 고통을 저울 위의 두 반대 지점으로 상상한다면, 여러분은 두 지점 중 한 지점이 올라가면 다른 지점이 상응하여 틀림없이 내려갈 것임을 쉽게 이해할 수 있을 것이다. 우리는 '고통 없이는, 얻는 것도 없다.'라는 표현을 모두 들어본 적이있다. 자, 정신과 의사인 Dr. Anna Lembke에 따르면, 이 말에는 어느 정도의 진실이 있을 수 있다. 그녀는 우리가 비참함에서 벗어나려는 우리의 시도가 사실 우리를 훨씬 더 비참하게 만들고 있다고 말한다. 이는 고통이 실제로 중립적인 상태를 유지하기 위한 우리 능력의 필수적인 구성 요소이기 때문이고, 그 것을 허용하는 것은 결과적으로 우리의 내부 저울을 균형 상태로 다시 맞출 것이다.

## 24

Manufacturers masterfully sow seeds of [ **expect / doubt** ]47) about the adequacy of our current [ **devices / devises** ]48). Suddenly, the phone that was your lifeline a year ago is now a museum piece, unable to keep pace with your digital demands. And thus, the itch to upgrade begins, often before there's a [ **genuine / genuinely** ]49) need. This cycle isn't just [ **confined / defined** ]50) to our digital companions. It spills over into almost every [ **aspect / aspects** ]51) of consumer electronics, from the self-driving car to the smart fridge. Every product [ **seem / seems** ]52) to be on an unstoppable march towards the next version, the next generation that promises to revolutionize your life. [ **That / What** ]53)'s [ **fascinating / fascinated** ]54), or perhaps disturbing, is the utter efficacy of this cycle in shaping our desires. It's not so much that we want the newest device; we're led to believe we need it. The [ **distinction / similarity** ]55) between want and need [ **blur / blurs** ]56), shifting our financial priorities in favor of staying current with trends. For all the logical arguments against this ceaseless upgrading, the temptation remains [ **compelling / unconvincing** ]57).

생산자들은 노련하게 우리의 현재 기기들의 적절성에 대한 의심의 씨앗을 뿌린다. 갑자기, 1년 전의 당신의 목숨줄이었던 휴대폰이 지금은 당신의 디지털 수요를 따라가지 못하는, 시대에 뒤떨어진 것이 되었다. 그래서 종종 진짜 필요가 있기 이전에 업그레이드에 대한 욕구가 시작된다. 이러한 순환은 단지 우리의 디지털 용품에 국한되지 않는다. 이것은 자율 주행 자동차부터 스마트 냉장고에 이르기까지 소비자 전자 기기들의 거의 모든 영역까지 번져나간다. 모든 제품은 다음 버전, 즉, 당신의 삶에 변혁을 일으키겠다는 약속을 하는 다음 세대를 향한 멈출 수 없는 행진을 하는 것으로 보인다. 흥미로운 점, 또는 어쩌면 당황스러운 점은 우리의 욕구를 형성하는 이 순환의 절대적인 효과이다. 우리가 가장 최신 기기를 원하는 것이 아니라, 우리가 그것을 원한다고 믿도록 유도된 것이다. 최신 트렌드를 유지하는 것을 선호하는 쪽으로 우리의 재정적인 우선순위를 바꾸면서, 원하는 것과 필요한 것 사이의 구분이 흐릿해진다. 이런 끊임없는 업그레이드를 하는 것에 대한 논리적인 논쟁에도 불구하고, 매력은 여전히 강력하다.

## 29

Conditioned Place [ **Inference / Preference** ]58) is a way of finding out [ **what / that** ]59) animals want. Researchers train them to [ **associate / detach** ]60) one place with an experience such as food or a loud noise and [ **another / the other** ]61) place with something completely [ **different / uniform** ]62), usually where nothing happens. The two places are made obviously [ **uniform / different** ]63) to make it as easy as possible for the animal to [ **detach / associate** ]64) each place with [ **that / what** ]65) happened to it there. The animal's [ **inference / preference** ]66) for being in one place or another is measured both before and after its experiences in the two places. If there is a shift in where the animal chooses to spend its time for the [ **award / reward** ]67), this suggests that it liked the experience and is trying [ **repeating / to repeat** ]68) it. Conversely, if it now avoids the place the stimulus appeared and [ **start / starts** ]69) to prefer the place it did not experience it, then this suggests that it found the stimulus [ **unpleasant / unpleasantly** ]70). For example, mice with cancer show a [ **preference / inference** ]71) for the place where they have been given morphine, a drug used to relieve pain, rather than where they have received saline whereas healthy mice developed no such [ **inference / preference** ]72). This suggests that the mice with cancer wanted the morphine.

조건부 장소 선호도는 동물들이 무엇을 원하는지 알아내는 하나의 방법이다. 연구자들은 그것들이 한 장소를 음식이나 시끄러운 소리와 같은 경험과 연관시키고 또 다른 장소를 완벽히 다른 어떤 것과 연관시키도록 훈련시키는데 대개 그곳에서는 아무것도 일어나지 않는다. 그 두 장소는 그 동물이 각 장소를 거기에서 그것에게 일어난 일과 연관시키는 것을 가능하게 쉽게 만들기 위해 명백히 다르게 만들어진다. 한 장소나 다른 장소에 있는 것에 대한 그 동물의 선호도는 두 장소에서 경험하기 전과 후에 모두 측정된다. 만약 동물이 보상을 위해 어디에서 시간을 보내기로 선택하는지에 변화가 있다면, 이것은 그것이 그 경험을 좋아했고 그것을 반복하려고 노력하는 중이라는 것을 시사한다. 반대로, 만약 그것이 이제 자극이 나타났던 장소를 피하고 그것이 그것을 경험하지 않았던 장소를 선호하기 시작한다면, 그러면 이것은 그것이 그 자극을 불쾌하게 느꼈다는 것을 시사한다. 예를 들어, 암에 걸린 쥐가 식염수를 받아 왔었던 곳보다 통증을 완화시키는 데 사용되는 약인 모르핀이 주어졌었던 장소에 대한 선호를 보여 준 반면, 건강한 쥐는 그러한 선호가 생기지 않았다. 이것은 암에 걸린 쥐가 그 모르핀을 원했음을 시사한다.

## 30

Near the equator, many species of bird **[ breed / breeds ]**73) all year round. But in temperate and polar regions, the breeding seasons of birds are often sharply defined. They are triggered mainly by changes in day length. If all goes well, the **[ income / outcome ]**74) is that birds **[ shrink / raise ]**75) their young when the food supply is at its peak. Most birds are not simply reluctant to breed at **[ other / the other ]**76) times but they are also physically incapable of doing so. This is **[ because / because of ]**77) their reproductive system shrinks, which helps flying birds save weight. The main **[ exception / expectation ]**78) to this rule are nomadic desert species. These can initiate their breeding cycle within days of rain. It's for making the most of the sudden breeding opportunity. Also, **[ different / uniform ]**79) species divide the breeding season up in different ways. Most seabirds **[ decline / raise ]**80) a single brood. In **[ warm / cool ]**81) regions, however, songbirds may **[ shrink / raise ]**82) several families in a few months. In an exceptionally good year, a pair of House Sparrows, a kind of songbird, can **[ raise / decline ]**83) **[ successive / successful ]**84) broods through a marathon reproductive effort.

적도 근처에서, 새의 많은 종들은 일 년 내내번식한다. 하지만 온대와 극지방에서는 새들의 번식기들이 대개 뚜렷하게 정해진다. 그것들은 주로 낮의 길이의 변화에 의해 촉발된다. 만약에 모든 것이 잘 진행된다면, 결과는 새들이 먹이 공급이 최고조에 이를 때 새끼들을 기르는 것이다. 대부분의 새들은 다른 때에 번식하기를 단지 꺼리는 것뿐만 아니라 또한 신체적으로 그렇게 할 수 없는 것이다. 이것은 왜냐하면 그들의 번식 기관이 줄어들기 때문이고, 이 사실은 나는 새들이 몸무게를 줄일 수 있도록 도와준다. 유목성 사막 종은 이 규칙의 주요 예외이다. 이들은 비가 오는 날들에 번식 주기를 시작할 수 있다. 그것은 갑작스러운 번식 기회를 최대한으로 활용하기 위한 것이다. 또한, 다른 종들은 번식기간을 다른 방식으로 나눈다. 대부분의 바닷새들은 한 무리의 함께 태어난 새끼를 기른다. 그러나, 따뜻한 지역에서는, 명금(鳴禽)들이 몇 달 안에 여러 자녀들을 기를 수도 있다. 유난히 좋은 해에는 명금(鳴禽)의 한 종류인 참새 한 쌍은 마라톤과 같은 번식 노력을 통해 잇따라 태어난 여러 무리의 함께 태어난 새끼들을 기를 수 있다.

## 31

One factor that may **[ hinder / foster ]**85) creativity is unawareness of the resources required in each activity in students' learning. Often students are unable to identify the resources they need to perform the task required of them. **[ Uniform / Different ]**86) resources may be compulsory for **[ specific / vague ]**87) learning tasks, and recognizing them may simplify the activity's performance. For example, it may be that students desire to conduct some experiments in their projects. There must be a prior investigation of whether the students will have **[ access / assess ]**88) to the laboratory, equipment, and chemicals required for the experiment. It means preparation is **[ optional / vital ]**89) for the students to succeed, and it may be about human and financial resources such as laboratory technicians, money to purchase chemicals, and equipment for their learning where applicable. Even if some of the resources required for a task may not be **[ unavailable / available ]**90), identifying them in advance may help students' creativity. It may even lead to changing the topic, finding **[ alternate / alternative ]**91) resources, and other means.

창의성을 방해할 수도 있는 한 가지 요소는 학생들의 학습에서 각 활동에 요구되는 자원에 대한 인식이 없다는 것이다. 종종 학생들은 그들에게 요구되는 과제를 수행하는 데 필요한 자원들을 식별할 수 없다. 여러 가지의 자원들이 특정 학습 과제들에 대해 필수적일 수 있어서 그것들을 인식하는 것은 활동의 수행을 평이하게 해 줄 수도 있다. 예를 들어, 학생들이 프로젝트에서 어떤 실험을 수행하기를 원할 수도 있다. 학생들이 실험에 요구되는 실험실, 장비, 그리고 화학 물질에 접근할 수 있을지 여부에대한 사전 조사가 있어야 한다. 그것은 학생들이 성공하기 위해 준비가 필수적이라는 것을 의미하며, 그들의 학습을 위해 적용할 수 있는 경우에 그것은 실험실 기술자, 화학 물질 구입 자금, 그리고 장비와 같은 인적 그리고 재정적 자원에 대한 것일 수도 있다. 과제에 요구되는 자원들 중 일부가 이용 가능하지 않을 수도 있지만, 사전에 그것들을 식별하는 것은 학생들의 창의성에 도움이 될 수도 있다. 그것은 심지어 주제 변경, 대체 자원들 찾기, 그리고 다른 방법으로 이어질 수도 있다.

## 32

All translators feel some pressure from the community of readers for whom they are doing their work. And all translators [ **arrive / depart** ]92) at their interpretations in dialogue with [ **other / the other** ]93) people. The English poet Alexander Pope had pretty good Greek, but when he set about translating Homer's *Iliad* in the early 18th century he was not on his own. He had Greek commentaries to refer to, and translations that had already been done in English, Latin, and French — and of course he had dictionaries. Translators always draw on [ **more / less** ]94) than one source text. Even when the scene of translation [ **consist / consists** ]95) of just one person with a pen, paper, and the book that is being translated, or even when it is just one person translating orally for another, that person's linguistic knowledge arises from lots of other texts and other conversations. And then his or her idea of the translation's purpose will be influenced by the expectations of the person or people it is for. In both these senses every [ **translation / translations** ]96) is a crowd translation.

모든 번역가들은 그들이 대상으로 작업하고 있는 독자들의 공동체로부터 약간의 압박을 느낀다. 그리고 모든 번역가들은 다른 사람들과의 대화에서 그들의 해석에 도달한다. 영국의 시인 알렉산더 포프는 그리스어를 꽤 잘했지만, 18세기 초에 호머의 'Iliad'를 번역하는 것에 대해 착수했을 때 그는 혼자한 것이 아니었다. 그는 참고할 그리스어 해설과 이미 영어, 라틴어, 프랑스어로 된 번역본을 가지고 있었고, 물론 사전도 가지고 있었다. 번역가들은 항상 한 가지 이상의 원문을 활용한다. 심지어 번역 현장이 하나의 펜, 종이, 그리고 번역 중인 책을 가진 단 한 사람으로 구성되어 있거나, 한 사람이 다른 사람을 위해 구두로 번역 중일 때에도, 그 사람의 언어적 지식은 많은 다른 텍스트와 다른 대화에서 발생한다. 그러고 나서 번역의 목적에 대한 그 또는 그녀의 생각은 이것의 대상이 되는 사람 또는 사람들의 기대에 의해 영향을 받는다. 이 두 가지 의미에서 모든 번역은 군중 번역이다.

## 33

Some people argue that there is a single, logically [ **consistent / consistently** ]97) concept known as reading that can be neatly set apart from everything else people do with books. Is reading really that simple? The most productive way to think about reading is as a loosely related set of behaviors that belong together owing to family resemblances, as Ludwig Wittgenstein used the phrase, without having in [ **common / abnormal** ]98) a single defining trait. Consequently, efforts to distinguish reading from nonreading [ **are / is** ]99) destined to fail [ **because of / because** ]100) there is no agreement on [ **what / that** ]101) qualifies as reading in the first place. The more one tries to figure out [ **where / which** ]102) the border lies between reading and not-reading, the [ **more / less** ]103) edge cases will be found to stretch the term's flexible boundaries. Thus, it is worth attempting to collect together these exceptional forms of reading into a single forum, one highlighting the challenges [ **faced / facing** ]104) by anyone wishing to establish the boundaries where reading begins and ends. The [ **attempt / contempt** ]105) moves toward an understanding of reading as a spectrum that is [ **expansive / expensive** ]106) enough to accommodate the [ **distinct / vague** ]107) reading activities.

몇몇 사람들은 사람들이 책을 가지고 하는 모든 다른 행동들로부터 깔끔하게 분리될 수 있는, 읽기로 알려진 유일하고 논리적으로 일관성 있는 개념이 있다고 주장한다. 읽기는 정말로 그렇게 단순할까? 읽기에 대해 생각하는 가장 생산적인 방식은 하나의 명백한 특성을 공통적으로 가지지 않은 채 Ludwig Wittgenstein이 그 어구를 사용한 것처럼 가족 유사성 때문에 함께 속하게 되는 헐겁게 연결된 행동의 묶음으로서이다. 결론적으로, 읽기와 읽기가 아닌 것을 구분하려는 노력은 실패로 돌아가는데, 왜냐하면 애초에 무엇이 읽기로서의 자격을 주는가에 대한 동의가 없기 때문이다. 읽기와 읽기가 아닌 것 사이의 경계가 어디에 있는가를 알려고 하면 할수록, 더욱 많은 특이 사례들이 그 용어의 유연한 경계를 확장하고 있다는 것이 밝혀질 것이다. 그러므로, 이러한 예외적인 읽기의 형태들을 모두 함께 하나의 토론의 장으로 모으려는 시도는 해 볼 가치가 있으며, 그 토론의 장은 어디서 읽기가 시작되고 끝나는가에 대한 경계를 정하기를 원하는 누구나에 의해 마주하게 될 어려움들을 돋보이게 한다. 그러한 시도는 별개의 읽기 활동들을 다 수용할 만큼 충분히 광 범위한 스펙트럼으로서 읽기를 이해하는 것으로 발전한다.

## 34

Weber's law concerns the perception of difference between two stimuli. It suggests [ **that / what** ]108) we might not be able to detect a 1-mm difference when we are looking at lines 466 mm and 467 mm in length, but we may be able to detect a 1-mm difference when we are comparing a line 2 mm long with one 3 mm long. [ **Another / Other** ]109) example of this [ **principal / principle** ]110) is that we can detect 1 candle when it is lit in an otherwise [ **dark / bright** ]111) room. But when 1 candle is lit in a room in which 100 candles are already burning, we may not notice the light from this candle. Therefore, the Just-noticeable difference (JND) varies as a function of the strength of the signals. For example, the JND is greater for very loud noises than it is for much [ **more / less** ]112) quiet sounds. When a sound is very weak, we can tell that another sound is louder, even if it is [ **bare / barely** ]113) louder. When a sound is very loud, to tell that another sound is even louder, it has to be much louder. Thus, Weber's law means that it is harder to [ **distinguish / link** ]114) between two samples when those samples are larger or stronger levels of the stimuli.

베버의 법칙은 두 자극 사이의 차이에 대한 감지에 관한 것이다. 이것은 우리가 466mm와 467mm 길이인 선들을 볼 때 1mm의 차이를 감지할 수 없지만, 우리가 2mm 길이와 3mm 길이인 선을 비교할 때는 1mm의 차이를 감지할 수 있을지도 모른다는 것을 암시한다. 이 원리의 또 다른 예는 촛불이 켜지지 않았으면 어두웠을 방안에 하나의 촛불이 켜졌을 때 이것을 감지할 수 있다는 것이다. 그러나 100개의 촛불이 이미 타고 있는 방에 하나의 촛불이 켜졌을 때, 우리는 이 촛불의 빛을 알아차리지 못할지도 모른다. 그러므로, 겨우 알아차릴 수 있는 차이 (JND)는 신호의 세기에 대한 함수에 의해 달라진다. 예를 들어, JND는 훨씬 더 작은 소리에 대한 것보다 매우 큰 소음에 대해 더 크다. 한 소리가 매우 약할 때, 우리는 그것이 간신히 더 클지라도, 또 다른 소리가 더 크다는 것을 구분할 수 있다. 어떤 소리가 매우 클 때, 다른 소리가 훨씬 더 크다는 것을 구분하기 위해서는, 그 소리는 훨씬 더 커야 한다. 그러므로, 베버의 법칙은 그 표본들이 자극의 수준이 더 크거나 강할 때 두 표본을 구별하기가 더 어렵다는 것을 의미한다.

## 35

Any new resource (e.g., a new airport, a new mall) always opens with people benefiting individually by sharing a [ **common / peculiar** ]115) resource (e.g., the city or state budget). Soon, at some point, the amount of traffic grows too large for the "commons" to support. Traffic jams, overcrowding, and overuse lessen the benefits of the [ **common / irregular** ]116) resource for everyone — the tragedy of the commons! If the new resource cannot be [ **diminished / expanded** ]117) or provided with additional space, it becomes a problem, and you cannot solve the problem on your own, in isolation from your fellow drivers or walkers or competing users. The total activity on this new resource keeps [ **increase / increasing** ]118), and so [ **do / does** ]119) individual activity; but if the dynamic of [ **common / unconventional** ]120) use and overuse continues too long, both begin to fall after a peak, leading to a crash. [ **That / What** ]121) makes the "tragedy of commons" tragic is the crash dynamic — the destruction or degeneration of the [ **unique / common** ]122) resource's ability to regenerate [ **it / itself** ]123).

어떤 새로운 자원(예를 들어, 새로운 공항, 새로운 쇼핑센터)은 항상 공동의 자원(예를 들어, 시 또는 주 예산)을 공유함으로써 사람들이 개별적으로 이익을 얻으면서 시작된다. 곧, 어느 시점에서, 교통량은 '공유지'가 견디기에 너무 커진다. 교통 체증, 과밀, 그리고 과도한 사용은 모두를 위한 공유 자원의 혜택을 줄이는데, 이것은 즉 공유지의 비극이다! 만약 새로운 자원이 확장될 수 없거나 추가적인 공간이 제공될 수 없다면, 이것은 문제가 되고, 여러분은 여러분의 동료 운전자나 보행자 또는 경쟁 사용자들로부터 고립된 상태로 혼자서 문제를 해결할 수 없다. 이 새로운 자원에 대한 총활동은 계속 증가하고, 개인 활동도 증가한다. 그러나 만약 공동 사용과 과도한 사용의 역학이 너무 오래 지속되면, 둘 다 정점 이후에 떨어지기 시작하고, 몰락으로 이어진다. (마찬가지로, 지식 그리고 정보와 같은 공동의 자원은 사용자의 수가 증가할 때 상대적 가치가 떨어지는 무한한 것이지만, 과도하게 사용된다고 할지라도 완전히 소모되지는 않을 것이다.) '공유지의 비극'을 더 비극적이게 만드는 것은 몰락 역학, 즉 그 스스로를 재생산할 수 있는 공동 자원의 능력의 파괴 또는 퇴보이다.

## 36

Theoretically, our brain would have the capacity to store all experiences throughout life, [ **reached / reaching** ]124) the quality of a DVD. However, this theoretical capacity is offset by the energy demand associated with the process of [ **store / storing** ]125) and [ **retrieve / retrieving** ]126) information in memory. As a result, the brain develops efficient strategies, becoming [ **dependent / independent** ]127) on shortcuts. When we observe a face, the visual image captured by the eyes is [ **highly / high** ]128) variable, depending on the point of view, lighting conditions and other contextual factors. Nevertheless, we are able to recognize the face as the [ **different / same** ]129), maintaining the underlying [ **identification / identity** ]130). The brain, rather than focusing on the details of visualization, creates and stores general patterns that allow for consistent recognition across diverse circumstances. This ability to match [ **that / what** ]131) we see with general visual memory patterns serves as an [ **effective / affective** ]132) mechanism for optimizing brain performance and [ **save / saving** ]133) energy. The brain, being naturally against unnecessary effort, constantly [ **seek / seeks** ]134) to simplify and generalize information to [ **facilitate / impede** ]135) the cognitive process.

이론적으로는 우리의 뇌는 DVD의 품질에 도달할 정도로, 삶의 모든 경험들을 저장할 수 있는 수용력을 가지고 있을 것이다. 그러나, 이 이론상의 수용력은 기억에 정보를 저장하고 상기하는 과정과 관련된 에너지 수요로 인해 상쇄된다. 그 결과, 뇌는 효율적인 전략들을 수립하고, 지름길에 의존하게 된다. 우리가 얼굴을 관찰할 때, 눈에 의해 포착되는 시각적 이미지는 시점, 조명 조건 및 기타 상황적 요인들에 따라 매우 다양하다. 그럼에도 불구하고, 우리는 근본적인 정체성을 유지하면서 얼굴을 같은 것으로 인식할 수 있다. 뇌는 시각화의 세부 사항에 집중하기보다 다양한 상황들에서 일관된 인식을 가능하게 하는 일반적인 패턴을 생성하고 저장한다. 우리가 보는 것과 일반적인 시각 기억 패턴을 일치시키는 이 능력은 뇌의 수행을 최적화하고 에너지를 절약하는 효과적인 기제로 작용한다. 불필요한 노력에 자연스럽게 대항하는 뇌는 인지 과정을 돕기 위해서 끊임없이 정보를 단순화하고 일반화하는 것을 추구한다.

## 37

Where scientific research is concerned, explanatory tales are expected to adhere closely to experimental data and to illuminate the regular and predictable features of experience. However, this paradigm sometimes [ **conceals / reveals** ]136) the fact that theories are deeply loaded with creative elements that shape the [ **destruction / construction** ]137) of research projects and the interpretations of evidence. Scientific explanations do not just relate a chronology of facts. They construct frameworks for systematically chosen data in order to [ **provide / providing** ]138) a consistent and meaningful explanation of [ **that / what** ]139) is observed. Such constructions lead us to imagine [ **specific / vague** ]140) kinds of subject matter in particular sorts of relations, and the storylines they inspire will prove more [ **affective / effective** ]141) for analyzing some features of experience over others. When we neglect the creative contributions of such scientific imagination and treat models and interpretive explanations as straightforward facts — even worse, as facts including all of reality — we can [ **informed / blind** ]142) ourselves to the limitations of a given model and fail to note its potential for misunderstanding a situation to which it ill applies.

과학 연구에 관해서는, 설명하는 이야기들이 실험의 데이터에 엄밀히 충실할 것으로 기대되고 경험의 규칙적이고 예측 가능한 특징들을 밝힐 것으로 기대된다. 그러나, 이러한 패러다임은 때때로 이론들이 연구 프로젝트의 구성과 증거의 해석을 형성하는 창의적인 요소들로 철저히 채워져 있다는 사실을 감춘다. 과학적 설명들은 단순히 사실들의 연대기를 말하는 것은 아니다. 그것들은 관찰된 것에 대한 일관적이고 의미 있는 설명을 제공하기 위해 체계적으로 선택된 데이터에 대한 틀을 구축한다. 그러한 구성들은 우리가 특정한 유형의 관계에서 구체적인 종류의 주제를 상상하도록 하며, 그것들이 고취하는 줄거리는 다른 것들보다 경험의 일부 특징을 분석하는 데 더 효과적일 것으로 판명될 것이다. 우리가 그러한 과학적 상상의 창의적 기여를 무시하고 모델과 해석적 설명을 단순한 사실, 훨씬 더 심하게는 현실을 전부 포괄하는 사실로 간주할 때, 우리는 주어진 모델의 한계에 대해 우리 스스로를 눈멀게 하며 그것이 잘못 적용되는 상황에 대해 오해할 가능성을 알아차리지 못할 수 있다.

## 38

We encounter contrary claims about the relation of literature to action. Theorists have maintained that literature [ **encourages / inhibits** ]143) solitary reading and reflection as the way to engage with the world and thus counters the [ **social / sociable** ]144) and political activities that might produce [ **social / sociable** ]145) change. At best it [ **encourages / inhibits** ]146) detachment or appreciation of [ **complexity / simplicity** ]147), and at worst passivity and acceptance of [ **that / what** ]148) is. But on the other hand, literature has historically been seen as dangerous: it promotes the questioning of authority and [ **sociable / social** ]149) arrangements. Plato banned poets from his [ **idle / ideal** ]150) republic [ **because / because of** ]151) they could only do harm, and novels have long been credited with making people [ **dissatisfied / satisfied** ]152) with their lives and eager for something new. By promoting identification across divisions of class, gender, and race, books may promote a fellowship that discourages struggle; but they
may also produce a keen sense of injustice that makes [ **conservative / progressive** ]153) struggles [ **impossible / possible** ]154). Historically, works of literature are credited with producing change: *Uncle Tom's Cabin*, a best-seller in its day, helped create a revulsion against slavery that made possible the American Civil War.

우리는 문학과 행동의 관계에 대한 상반된 주장들과 마주한다. 이론가들은 문학이 세상과 관계를 맺는 방법으로써 고독한 독서와 성찰을 장려하고 따라서 사회 변화를 일으킬 수 있을지도 모르는 사회적이고 정치적인 활동들에 거스른다고 주장해 왔다. 기껏해야 이것은 단절 또는 복잡성에 대한 인정을, 최악의 경우 수동성과 있는 그대로에 대한 수용을 조장한다. 그러나 다른 한편으로, 문학은 역사적으로 권위와 사회적 합의에 대한 의문을 제기하는 것을 조장하므로 위험하다고 여겨져 왔다. 플라톤은 그들이 해를 끼치는 것만 할 수 있기 때문에 그의 이상적인 공화국으로부터 시인들을 추방했고, 소설은 사람들이 그들의 삶에 불만을 품게 만들고 새로운 무언가를 갈망하도록 하는 것으로 오랫동안 믿어져 왔다. 계급, 성별, 그리고 인종의 경계를 넘어 동일시를 촉진함으로써, 책들은 투쟁을 단념시키는 동료 의식을 장려할 수 있을지 모르지만, 이것들은 또한 진보적인 투쟁들을 가능하게 만드는 강한 불의의 감정을 일으킬 수 있다. 역사적으로, 문학 작품은 변화를 만드는 것으로 믿어져 왔는데 그 시대의 베스트셀러인 '톰 아저씨의 오두막'은 미국 남북 전쟁을 가능하게 만든 노예제에 대한 혐오감을 조성하는 것을 도왔다.

## 39

According to Hobbes, man is not a being who can act morally in spite of his instinct to protect his existence in the state of nature. Hence, the only place where morality and [ **mortal / moral** ]155) liberty will begin to find an [ **appliance / application** ]156) begins in a place where a sovereign power, namely the state, [ **emerges / disappears** ]157). Hobbes thus describes the state of nature as a circumstance in which man's life is "solitary, poor, nasty, brutish and short". It means when people live without a general power to control them all, they are indeed in a state of war. In other words, Hobbes, who [ **accepted / rejected** ]158) that human beings are not [ **sociable / social** ]159) and political beings in the state of nature, believes that without the power human beings in the state of nature are "antisocial and rational based on their selfishness". Moreover, since society is not a [ **artificial / natural** ]160) phenomenon and there is no [ **natural / artificial** ]161) force bringing people together, [ **that / what** ]162) will bring them together as a society is not mutual affection according to Hobbes. It is, rather, mutual [ **bravery / fear** ]163) of men's present and future that assembles them, since the cause of [ **bravery / fear** ]164) is a [ **unconventional / common** ]165) drive among people in the state of nature.

홉스에 따르면, 인간은 자연 상태에서 자신의 존재를 보호하려는 그의 본능을 무릅쓰고 도덕적으로행동할 수 있는 존재가 아니다. 따라서, 도덕과 도덕적 자유가 적용을 찾기 시작하는 유일한 곳은 군림하는 권력, 즉 국가가 출현하는 곳에서 나타난다. 따라서 홉스는 자연 상태를 인간의 삶이 '고독하고, 가난하며, 불결하고, 잔인하고, 짧은' 상황으로 묘사한다. 그것은 사람들이 그들 모두를 통제할 일반적인 권력 없이 살아갈 때, 그들은 실로 전쟁 상태에 놓여 있는 것임을 의미한다. 즉 다시 말해, 자연 상태에 있는 인간은 사회적이고 정치적인 존재가 아니라는 것을 인정한 홉스는 그 권력이 없이 자연 상태에 있는 인간은 '이기심에 기초해 반사회적이고 이성적'이라고 믿는다. 게다가, 사회는 자연적인 현상이 아니며 사람들을 하나로 모으는 자연적인 힘도 없기 때문에, 홉스에 따르면 그들을 사회로 함께 모이게 하는 것은 상호 간의 애정이 아니다. 두려움으로부터의 동기가 자연 상태에 있는 사람들 사이의 공통된 추진력이기 때문에, 오히려, 그들을 모으는 것은 인간의 현재와 미래에 대한 상호 간의 두려움이다.

# 40

There is research that supports the idea that cognitive factors influence the phenomenology of the [ **perceived / perceiving** ]166) world. Delk and Fillenbaum asked participants to match the color of figures with the color of their background. Some of the figures depicted objects associated with a [ **particular / general** ]167) color. These included typically red objects such as an apple, lips, and a symbolic heart. Other objects [ **presented / were presented** ]168) that are not usually associated with red, such as a mushroom or a bell. However, all the figures were made out of the [ **same / different** ]169) red-orange cardboard. Participants then had to match the figure to a background varying from [ **bright / dark** ]170) to light red. They had to make the background color match the color of the figures. The researchers found that red-associated objects required [ **less / more** ]171) red in the background to be judged a match than did the objects that are not associated with the color red. This implies that the cognitive association of objects to color influences how we [ **ignore / perceive** ]172) that color.

인지적 요인들이 지각된 세계의 현상학에 영향을 미친다는 생각을 뒷받침하는 연구가 있다. Delk와 Fillenbaum은 참가자들에게 형상들의 색상을 배경 색상과 맞추도록 요청했다. 몇몇 형상들은 특정 색상과 연관된 물체들을 묘사했다. 그것들은 사과, 입술, 상징적인 하트 모양과 같이 전형적인 빨간색 물체를 포함했다. 버섯이나 종과 같이 빨간색과 일반적으로 연관이 되지 않는 다른 물체들도 제시되었다. 그러나, 모든 형상들은 동일한 다홍색 판지로 만들어졌다. 그리고 나서 참가자들은 그 형상을 진한 빨간색에서 연한 빨간색까지 다양한 배경색과 맞춰야 했다. 그들은 배경색이 형상들의 색과 일치하게 해야 했다. 연구자들은 빨간색과 연관된 물체들이 빨간색과 연관이 없는 물체가 그러한 것보다 배경과 일치한다고 판단되기 위해서 배경에서 더 빨간색을 요구한다는 것을 발견했다. 이것은 색과 물체의 인지적 연관성이 우리가 그 색을 어떻게 지각하는가에 영향을 미친다는 것을 함의한다. 한 연구에서, 참가자들은 일반적으로 빨간색인 물체의 색상과 같은 색상의 배경을 일치시키도록 요청받았을 때, 더 진한 빨강을 선택했는데, 이는 물체들의 색상에 대한 그들의 지식이 그들의 지각적 판단에 영향을 미쳤다는 것을 보여준다.

# 41, 42

In each round of genome copying in our body, there is still about a 70 percent chance that at [ **least / most** ]173) one pair of chromosomes will have an error. With each round of genome copying, errors accumulate. This is similar to alterations in medieval books. Each time a copy was made by hand, some changes were introduced accidentally; as changes stacked up, the copies may have acquired meanings at variance with the [ **stereotype / original** ]174). Similarly, genomes that have undergone [ **less / more** ]175) copying processes will have gathered [ **more / less** ]176) mistakes. To make things worse, mutations may damage genes responsible for error checking and repair of genomes, further accelerating the introduction of mutations.

Most genome mutations do not have any noticeable [ **effects / affects** ]177). It is just like changing the *i* for a *y* in "kingdom" would not [ **distort / clarify** ]178) the word's readability. But sometimes a mutation to a human gene results in, for example, an eye whose iris is of two [ **different / uniform** ]179) colors. Similarly, almost everyone has birthmarks, which are due to mutations that occurred as our body's cells multiplied to form skin. If mutations are changes to the genome of one [ **general / particular** ]180) cell, how can a patch of cells in an iris or a whole patch of skin, consisting of many individual cells, be affected [ **spontaneously / simultaneously** ]181)? The answer lies in the cell lineage, the developmental history of a tissue from [ **particular / general** ]182) cells through to their fully differentiated state. If the mutation occurred early on in the lineage of the developing iris, then all cells in that patch have inherited that change.

우리 몸속 게놈 복제의 각 과정마다, 적어도 한 쌍의 염색체들이 오류를 가질 확률이 여전히 약 70%이다. 게놈 복제의 각 과정마다, 오류들이 쌓인다. 이것은 중세 서적에 있어서의 변화와 유사하다. 하나의 복사본이 사람 손으로 만들어질 때마다, 일부 변화들이 우연히 도입되었고, 변화들이 쌓이면서, 복사본은 원본과 불일치하는 의미를 축적했을 것이다. 마찬가지로, 더 많은 복제 과정들을 거친 게놈은 더 많은 실수들을 축적하게 될 것이다. 설상가상으로, 변이들은 게놈의 오류 확인과 복구를 책임지는 유전자를 훼손해 변이들의 도입을 더욱 가속할 수도 있다.

대부분의 게놈 변이들은 어떠한 뚜렷한 영향이 없다. 그것은 마치 'kingdom'에서 'i'를 'y'로 변경하는 것이 그 단어의 가독성을 보장하지(→왜곡하지) 않는 것과 같다. 그러나 예를 들어, 때때로 인간 유전자에 대한 변이는 홍채가 두 가지 다른 색을 띠는 눈을 초래하기도 한다. 마찬가지로, 거의 모두가 모반이 있는데, 이는 우리 몸의 세포가 피부를 형성하기 위하여 증식하면서 발생한 변이들 때문이다. 만약 변이들이 하나의 특정 세포의 게놈에 대한 변화라면, 많은 개별적인 세포들로 구성된 홍채의 세포 집단이나 피부 전체 세포 집단이 어떻게 동시에 영향을 받을 수 있을까? 그 대답은 세포 계보, 즉 특정 세포에서 그들의 완전히 차별화된 상태까지의 조직 발달 변천에 있다. 만약 발달 중인 홍채의 계보 초기에 변이가 발생했다면, 그렇다면 그 세포 집단의 모든 세포는 그 변화를 물려받아 왔을 것이다.

# 43 ~ 45

Max awoke to the gentle sunlight of an autumn day. Right on schedule, he swung his legs off the bed and took a deep, [ **satisfied / satisfying** ]183) breath. He began his morning the [ **different / same** ]184) way he usually did, getting dressed and going to school. Today was going to be another [ **flawed / perfect** ]185) day until he ran into Mr. Kapoor, his science teacher. "Just to remind you. Science [ **fair / unfair** ]186) projects are due next Wednesday. Don't forget to submit your final draft on time," Mr. Kapoor said. Max froze. [ **What / That** ]187)? *It can't be! It was due next Friday!* After school, he came home worrying that his whole perfectly planned week was going to [ **be ruined / ruin** ]188) . Without his usual greeting, Max headed to his room in haste. "[ **That / What** ]189)'s [ **appropriate / wrong** ]190) Max?," Jeremy, his dad, followed Max, worrying about him. Max furiously browsed through his planner without answering him, only to find the [ **wrong / appropriate** ]191) date written in it. Fighting through tears, Max finally managed to [ **explain / explaining** ]192) the unending pressure to be [ **flawed / perfect** ]193) to his dad. To his surprise, Jeremy laughed. "Max, guess what? [ **Flawed / Perfect** ]194) is a great goal, but nobody gets there all the time. [ **What / That** ]195) matters is [ **what / that** ]196) we do when things get messy." That made him [ **feel / to feel** ]197) a little better. "You are saying I can fix this?" "Absolutely, try to deal with problems in a logical way," Jeremy said. Max thought for a moment. "I guess.... I can do that by rescheduling tonight's baseball lesson." Jeremy beamed. "See? That's you finding a solution." Max felt a genuine smile [ **spreading / to spread** ]198). The next Wednesday, he successfully handed in the final draft on time with satisfaction. From then on, he still loved order and routines, but also [ **embraced / embracing** ]199) the messy, [ **predictable / unpredictable** ]200) bits of life too.

Max는 가을날의 부드러운 햇빛에 잠에서 깼다. 시간에 맞추어 그는 다리를 침대 밖으로 휙 내려놓았고 깊고 만족스러운 숨을 내쉬었다. 그는 평소와 똑같은 방식으로 아침을 시작했고 옷을 입고 학교에 갔다. 오늘은 과학 선생님인 Kapoor 선생님을 만나기 전까지는 또 다른 완벽한 날이 될 예정이었다. "그냥 너에게 알려 주는 거야. 과학 박람회 프로젝트가 다음 주 수요일까지야. 제 시간에 최종안을 제출하는 것을 잊어버리지 마."라고 Kapoor 선생님이 말했다. Max는 얼어붙었다. '뭐라고? 그럴 순 없어! 이건 다음 주 금요일까지였다고!' 학교를 마친 후에, 그는 그의 완벽히 계획된 일주일이 망쳐질 것을 걱정하며 집으로 돌아왔다. 그의 일상적인 인사 없이, Max는 급하게 그의 방으로 향했다. "무슨 일이니 Max?" 그의 아버지인 Jeremy는 그를 걱정하며 Max를 따라갔다. Max는 그에게 대답하지 않고 열성적으로 그의 일정표를 뒤적거렸지만, 거기에 잘못 적힌 날짜를 발견할 뿐이었다. 울음을 참으며, Max는 마침내 가까스로 그의 아버지에게 완벽해야 한다는 끝나지 않는 압박에 대해 설명했다. 놀랍게도, Jeremy는 웃었다. "Max, 있잖아? 완벽은 훌륭한 목표지만, 누구도 항상 거기에 도달할 수는 없단다. 중요한 건 일이 어질러졌을 때 우리가 무엇을 하는가야." 그것이 그의 기분을 조금 더 나아지게 만들어 주었다. "아빠는 제가 이것을 해결할 수 있다고 말씀하시는 거예요?" "물론이지. 논리적인 방식으로 문제를 처리해봐."라고 Jeremy가 말했다. Max는 잠시동안 생각했다. "아마.... 제가 오늘 밤 야구 레슨 일정을 변경함으로써 그렇게 할 수 있을 것 같아요." Jeremy가 활짝 웃었다. "봤지? 네가 해결책을 찾아냈잖니." Max는 진심 어린 미소가 퍼지는 것을 느꼈다. 다음 주 수요일에 그는 만족하며 성공적으로 최종안을 제시간에 제출했다. 그 이후로 그는 여전히 순서와 정해진 일과를 좋아했지만, 또한 어지럽고 예측 불가능한 삶의 부분들도 기꺼이 맞이했다.

## 18

Dear Executive Manager Schulz,
It is a week before the internship program starts. I am writing to bring your [ **attention / pretension** ]¹⁾ to a matter that requires immediate consideration regarding the issue my department has. As the coordinator, it is becoming apparent to me that the budget, previously approved by your department, needs some adjustments in order to meet the emerging modifications. Since my department has [ **fired / hired** ]²⁾ three [ **less / more** ]³⁾ interns than planned initially, the most expensive need is for additional funding to cover their wages, training costs, and materials. I kindly request an additional budget allocation for these expenses. Please refer to the [ **attachment / detachment** ]⁴⁾ for details. Thank you for your [ **pretension / attention** ]⁵⁾.
Best regards, Matt Perry

## 19

Katie approached the hotel front desk to check-in but an unexpected event [ **folded / unfolded** ]⁶⁾. The receptionist couldn't find her reservation under the name 'Katie'. "I'm sorry, but I can't seem to locate a reservation under that name," the receptionist said. "No way, I definitely made a reservation on the phone," Katie said, [ **puzzled / puzzling** ]⁷⁾. The receptionist asked, "Can you tell me your phone number?" and Katie told it to him, thinking '[ **What / That** ]⁸⁾ happened? Did I make a mistake?' "Just a moment," the receptionist said, typing deliberately on the keyboard. "I found it! It seems there was a small misspelling. Your reservation is under 'K-A-T-Y'," the receptionist explained. With a sense of ease, Katie watched her reservation [ **appearing / to appear** ]⁹⁾ on the screen. With her heart slowing to a gentle rhythm, she [ **preceded / proceeded** ]¹⁰⁾ with her check-in, thinking that a simple misspelling might have ruined her plans.

## 20

To be mathematically [ **literate / literary** ]¹¹⁾ means to be able to think critically about societal issues on which mathematics has bearing so as to make informed decisions about how to solve these problems. Dealing with such [ **simplified / complex** ]¹²⁾ problems through interdisciplinary approaches, mirroring real-world problems [ **inquires / requires** ]¹³⁾ innovative ways of planning and organizing mathematical teaching methods. Navigating our world means being able to quantify, measure, estimate, classify, compare, find patterns, conjecture, justify, prove, and generalize within critical thinking and when using critical thinking. Therefore, [ **make / making** ]¹⁴⁾ decisions, even qualitatively, is not possible without using mathematics and critical thinking. Thus, teaching mathematics should [ **be done / do** ]¹⁵⁾ in interaction with [ **critical / critically** ]¹⁶⁾ thinking along with a decision-making process. They can be developed into the mathematical context, so that there is no excuse to not [ **explicitly / implicitly** ]¹⁷⁾ support students to develop them.

## 21

Imagine that your usually stingy friend delights in buying you a Christmas present after taking a generosity booster. How would you feel? Undoubtedly, there is [ **nothing / something** ]18) praiseworthy about the action. You'd be [ **pleased / pleasing** ]19) to receive the gift. You'd say 'thank you', and mean it. But his change of heart is not [ **entire / entirely** ]20) satisfying. According to Zagzebski, an American philosopher, he is not really generous. When we praise someone's character, we use words for various virtues: 'generous', 'kind', 'courageous', etc. A person who gives one gift isn't generous. Instead, generosity is a stable part of a person's '[ **moral / mortal** ]21) [ **identification / identity** ]22)', an emotional habit that is part of who you are. Thus virtues, as opposed to [ **nontypical / typical** ]23) impulse, are the result of your [ **impersonal / personal** ]24) history. They are part of who you are, as they are part of how your character was formed. Instant virtue is therefore [ **impossible / possible** ]25). Popping a pill cannot make you a better person.

## 22

To determine the mass of my bowling ball, I might put it onto a balance and compare it with a known mass, such as a number of metal cubes each weighing 1, 10, or 100 grams. Things get much [ **less / more** ]26) complicated if I want to know the mass of a distant star. How do I measure it? We can roughly say [ **that / what** ]27) measuring the mass of a star involves various theories. If we want to measure the mass of a binary star, we first determine a center of mass between the two stars, then their distance from that center which we can then use, together with a value for the period and a certain instance of Kepler's Third Law, to calculate the mass. In other words, in order to "measure" the star mass, we measure [ **another / other** ]28) quantities and use those values, together with certain equations, to calculate the mass. Measurement is not a simple and unmediated estimation of [ **independent / independently** ]29) existing properties, but a determination of certain magnitudes before the background of a number of [ **rejected / accepted** ]30) theories.

## 23

Based on discoveries in neuroscience, pain and pleasure [ **are / is** ]31) formed and processed in the [ **different / same** ]32) area of the brain. Our bodies constantly [ **strive / strives** ]33) for homeostasis, [ **which / that** ]34) is defined as the balance of bodily functions. Without the body's [ **effective / affective** ]35) compensatory mechanisms, which may cushion potential highs and lows, we would not be [ **incapable / capable** ]36) of surviving. Pleasure and pain are like two sides of the [ **different / same** ]37) coin; they seem to work together and are heavily reliant on one another and keep balance. If you imagine pleasure and pain as the two [ **opposite / similar** ]38) points on a scale, you can easily understand [ **that / what** ]39) as one of the two points rises, [ **the other / other** ]40) must correspondingly fall. We've all heard the expression, "No pain, no gain." Well, according to psychiatrist Dr. Anna Lembke, there may be some truth to these words. She says [ **that / what** ]41) our attempts to escape being miserable [ **are / is** ]42) in fact making us even [ **less / more** ]43) miserable. This is [ **because of / because** ]44) pain is actually an essential component of our ability to maintain a [ **biased / neutral** ]45) state, and allowing it will in turn [ **reset / resets** ]46) our internal scale back to balance.

## 24

Manufacturers masterfully sow seeds of [ **expect / doubt** ]47) about the adequacy of our current [ **devices / devises** ]48). Suddenly, the phone that was your lifeline a year ago is now a museum piece, unable to keep pace with your digital demands. And thus, the itch to upgrade begins, often before there's a [ **genuine / genuinely** ]49) need. This cycle isn't just [ **confined / defined** ]50) to our digital companions. It spills over into almost every [ **aspect / aspects** ]51) of consumer electronics, from the self-driving car to the smart fridge. Every product [ **seem / seems** ]52) to be on an unstoppable march towards the next version, the next generation that promises to revolutionize your life. [ **That / What** ]53)'s [ **fascinating / fascinated** ]54), or perhaps disturbing, is the utter efficacy of this cycle in shaping our desires. It's not so much that we want the newest device; we're led to believe we need it. The [ **distinction / similarity** ]55) between want and need [ **blur / blurs** ]56), shifting our financial priorities in favor of staying current with trends. For all the logical arguments against this ceaseless upgrading, the temptation remains [ **compelling / unconvincing** ]57).

## 29

Conditioned Place [ **Inference / Preference** ]58) is a way of finding out [ **what / that** ]59) animals want. Researchers train them to [ **associate / detach** ]60) one place with an experience such as food or a loud noise and [ **another / the other** ]61) place with something completely [ **different / uniform** ]62), usually where nothing happens. The two places are made obviously [ **uniform / different** ]63) to make it as easy as possible for the animal to [ **detach / associate** ]64) each place with [ **that / what** ]65) happened to it there. The animal's [ **inference / preference** ]66) for being in one place or another is measured both before and after its experiences in the two places. If there is a shift in where the animal chooses to spend its time for the [ **award / reward** ]67), this suggests that it liked the experience and is trying [ **repeating / to repeat** ]68) it. Conversely, if it now avoids the place the stimulus appeared and [ **start / starts** ]69) to prefer the place it did not experience it, then this suggests that it found the stimulus [ **unpleasant / unpleasantly** ]70). For example, mice with cancer show a [ **preference / inference** ]71) for the place where they have been given morphine, a drug used to relieve pain, rather than where they have received saline whereas healthy mice developed no such [ **inference / preference** ]72). This suggests that the mice with cancer wanted the morphine.

## 30

Near the equator, many species of bird [ **breed / breeds** ]73) all year round. But in temperate and polar regions, the breeding seasons of birds are often sharply defined. They are triggered mainly by changes in day length. If all goes well, the [ **income / outcome** ]74) is that birds [ **shrink / raise** ]75) their young when the food supply is at its peak. Most birds are not simply reluctant to breed at [ **other / the other** ]76) times but they are also physically incapable of doing so. This is [ **because / because of** ]77) their reproductive system shrinks, which helps flying birds save weight. The main [ **exception / expectation** ]78) to this rule are nomadic desert species. These can initiate their breeding cycle within days of rain. It's for making the most of the sudden breeding opportunity. Also, [ **different / uniform** ]79) species divide the breeding season up in different ways. Most seabirds [ **decline / raise** ]80) a single brood. In [ **warm / cool** ]81) regions, however, songbirds may [ **shrink / raise** ]82) several families in a few months. In an exceptionally good year, a pair of House Sparrows, a kind of songbird, can [ **raise / decline** ]83) [ **successive / successful** ]84) broods through a marathon reproductive effort.

# 31

One factor that may [ **hinder / foster** ]85) creativity is unawareness of the resources required in each activity in students' learning. Often students are unable to identify the resources they need to perform the task required of them. [ **Uniform / Different** ]86) resources may be compulsory for [ **specific / vague** ]87) learning tasks, and recognizing them may simplify the activity's performance. For example, it may be that students desire to conduct some experiments in their projects. There must be a prior investigation of whether the students will have [ **access / assess** ]88) to the laboratory, equipment, and chemicals required for the experiment. It means preparation is [ **optional / vital** ]89) for the students to succeed, and it may be about human and financial resources such as laboratory technicians, money to purchase chemicals, and equipment for their learning where applicable. Even if some of the resources required for a task may not be [ **unavailable / available** ]90), identifying them in advance may help students' creativity. It may even lead to changing the topic, finding [ **alternate / alternative** ]91) resources, and other means.

# 32

All translators feel some pressure from the community of readers for whom they are doing their work. And all translators [ **arrive / depart** ]92) at their interpretations in dialogue with [ **other / the other** ]93) people. The English poet Alexander Pope had pretty good Greek, but when he set about translating Homer's *Iliad* in the early 18th century he was not on his own. He had Greek commentaries to refer to, and translations that had already been done in English, Latin, and French — and of course he had dictionaries. Translators always draw on [ **more / less** ]94) than one source text. Even when the scene of translation [ **consist / consists** ]95) of just one person with a pen, paper, and the book that is being translated, or even when it is just one person translating orally for another, that person's linguistic knowledge arises from lots of other texts and other conversations. And then his or her idea of the translation's purpose will be influenced by the expectations of the person or people it is for. In both these senses every [ **translation / translations** ]96) is a crowd translation.

# 33

Some people argue that there is a single, logically [ **consistent / consistently** ]97) concept known as reading that can be neatly set apart from everything else people do with books. Is reading really that simple? The most productive way to think about reading is as a loosely related set of behaviors that belong together owing to family resemblances, as Ludwig Wittgenstein used the phrase, without having in [ **common / abnormal** ]98) a single defining trait. Consequently, efforts to distinguish reading from nonreading [ **are / is** ]99) destined to fail [ **because of / because** ]100) there is no agreement on [ **what / that** ]101) qualifies as reading in the first place. The more one tries to figure out [ **where / which** ]102) the border lies between reading and not-reading, the [ **more / less** ]103) edge cases will be found to stretch the term's flexible boundaries. Thus, it is worth attempting to collect together these exceptional forms of reading into a single forum, one highlighting the challenges [ **faced / facing** ]104) by anyone wishing to establish the boundaries where reading begins and ends. The [ **attempt / contempt** ]105) moves toward an understanding of reading as a spectrum that is [ **expansive / expensive** ]106) enough to accommodate the [ **distinct / vague** ]107) reading activities.

## 34

Weber's law concerns the perception of difference between two stimuli. It suggests [ **that / what** ]108) we might not be able to detect a 1-mm difference when we are looking at lines 466 mm and 467 mm in length, but we may be able to detect a 1-mm difference when we are comparing a line 2 mm long with one 3 mm long. [ **Another / Other** ]109) example of this [ **principal / principle** ]110) is that we can detect 1 candle when it is lit in an otherwise [ **dark / bright** ]111) room. But when 1 candle is lit in a room in which 100 candles are already burning, we may not notice the light from this candle. Therefore, the Just-noticeable difference (JND) varies as a function of the strength of the signals. For example, the JND is greater for very loud noises than it is for much [ **more / less** ]112) quiet sounds. When a sound is very weak, we can tell that another sound is louder, even if it is [ **bare / barely** ]113) louder. When a sound is very loud, to tell that another sound is even louder, it has to be much louder. Thus, Weber's law means that it is harder to [ **distinguish / link** ]114) between two samples when those samples are larger or stronger levels of the stimuli.

## 35

Any new resource (e.g., a new airport, a new mall) always opens with people benefiting individually by sharing a [ **common / peculiar** ]115) resource (e.g., the city or state budget). Soon, at some point, the amount of traffic grows too large for the "commons" to support. Traffic jams, overcrowding, and overuse lessen the benefits of the [ **common / irregular** ]116) resource for everyone — the tragedy of the commons! If the new resource cannot be [ **diminished / expanded** ]117) or provided with additional space, it becomes a problem, and you cannot solve the problem on your own, in isolation from your fellow drivers or walkers or competing users. The total activity on this new resource keeps [ **increase / increasing** ]118), and so [ **do / does** ]119) individual activity; but if the dynamic of [ **common / unconventional** ]120) use and overuse continues too long, both begin to fall after a peak, leading to a crash. [ **That / What** ]121) makes the "tragedy of commons" tragic is the crash dynamic — the destruction or degeneration of the [ **unique / common** ]122) resource's ability to regenerate [ **it / itself** ]123).

## 36

Theoretically, our brain would have the capacity to store all experiences throughout life, [ **reached / reaching** ]124) the quality of a DVD. However, this theoretical capacity is offset by the energy demand associated with the process of [ **store / storing** ]125) and [ **retrieve / retrieving** ]126) information in memory. As a result, the brain develops efficient strategies, becoming [ **dependent / independent** ]127) on shortcuts. When we observe a face, the visual image captured by the eyes is [ **highly / high** ]128) variable, depending on the point of view, lighting conditions and other contextual factors. Nevertheless, we are able to recognize the face as the [ **different / same** ]129), maintaining the underlying [ **identification / identity** ]130). The brain, rather than focusing on the details of visualization, creates and stores general patterns that allow for consistent recognition across diverse circumstances. This ability to match [ **that / what** ]131) we see with general visual memory patterns serves as an [ **effective / affective** ]132) mechanism for optimizing brain performance and [ **save / saving** ]133) energy. The brain, being naturally against unnecessary effort, constantly [ **seek / seeks** ]134) to simplify and generalize information to [ **facilitate / impede** ]135) the cognitive process.

## 37

Where scientific research is concerned, explanatory tales are expected to adhere closely to experimental data and to illuminate the regular and predictable features of experience. However, this paradigm sometimes [ **conceals / reveals** ]136) the fact that theories are deeply loaded with creative elements that shape the [ **destruction / construction** ]137) of research projects and the interpretations of evidence. Scientific explanations do not just relate a chronology of facts. They construct frameworks for systematically chosen data in order to [ **provide / providing** ]138) a consistent and meaningful explanation of [ **that / what** ]139) is observed. Such constructions lead us to imagine [ **specific / vague** ]140) kinds of subject matter in particular sorts of relations, and the storylines they inspire will prove more [ **affective / effective** ]141) for analyzing some features of experience over others. When we neglect the creative contributions of such scientific imagination and treat models and interpretive explanations as straightforward facts — even worse, as facts including all of reality — we can [ **informed / blind** ]142) ourselves to the limitations of a given model and fail to note its potential for misunderstanding a situation to which it ill applies.

## 38

We encounter contrary claims about the relation of literature to action. Theorists have maintained that literature [ **encourages / inhibits** ]143) solitary reading and reflection as the way to engage with the world and thus counters the [ **social / sociable** ]144) and political activities that might produce [ **social / sociable** ]145) change. At best it [ **encourages / inhibits** ]146) detachment or appreciation of [ **complexity / simplicity** ]147), and at worst passivity and acceptance of [ **that / what** ]148) is. But on the other hand, literature has historically been seen as dangerous: it promotes the questioning of authority and [ **sociable / social** ]149) arrangements. Plato banned poets from his [ **idle / ideal** ]150) republic [ **because / because of** ]151) they could only do harm, and novels have long been credited with making people [ **dissatisfied / satisfied** ]152) with their lives and eager for something new. By promoting identification across divisions of class, gender, and race, books may promote a fellowship that discourages struggle; but they may also produce a keen sense of injustice that makes [ **conservative / progressive** ]153) struggles [ **impossible / possible** ]154). Historically, works of literature are credited with producing change: *Uncle Tom's Cabin*, a best-seller in its day, helped create a revulsion against slavery that made possible the American Civil War.

## 39

According to Hobbes, man is not a being who can act morally in spite of his instinct to protect his existence in the state of nature. Hence, the only place where morality and [ **mortal / moral** ]155) liberty will begin to find an [ **appliance / application** ]156) begins in a place where a sovereign power, namely the state, [ **emerges / disappears** ]157). Hobbes thus describes the state of nature as a circumstance in which man's life is "solitary, poor, nasty, brutish and short". It means when people live without a general power to control them all, they are indeed in a state of war. In other words, Hobbes, who [ **accepted / rejected** ]158) that human beings are not [ **sociable / social** ]159) and political beings in the state of nature, believes that without the power human beings in the state of nature are "antisocial and rational based on their selfishness". Moreover, since society is not a [ **artificial / natural** ]160) phenomenon and there is no [ **natural / artificial** ]161) force bringing people together, [ **that / what** ]162) will bring them together as a society is not mutual affection according to Hobbes. It is, rather, mutual [ **bravery / fear** ]163) of men's present and future that assembles them, since the cause of [ **bravery / fear** ]164) is a [ **unconventional / common** ]165) drive among people in the state of nature.

## 40

There is research that supports the idea that cognitive factors influence the phenomenology of the [ **perceived / perceiving** ]166) world. Delk and Fillenbaum asked participants to match the color of figures with the color of their background. Some of the figures depicted objects associated with a [ **particular / general** ]167) color. These included typically red objects such as an apple, lips, and a symbolic heart. Other objects [ **presented / were presented** ]168) that are not usually associated with red, such as a mushroom or a bell. However, all the figures were made out of the [ **same / different** ]169) red-orange cardboard. Participants then had to match the figure to a background varying from [ **bright / dark** ]170) to light red. They had to make the background color match the color of the figures. The researchers found that red-associated objects required [ **less / more** ]171) red in the background to be judged a match than did the objects that are not associated with the color red. This implies that the cognitive association of objects to color influences how we [ **ignore / perceive** ]172) that color.

## 41, 42

In each round of genome copying in our body, there is still about a 70 percent chance that at [ **least / most** ]173) one pair of chromosomes will have an error. With each round of genome copying, errors accumulate. This is similar to alterations in medieval books. Each time a copy was made by hand, some changes were introduced accidentally; as changes stacked up, the copies may have acquired meanings at variance with the [ **stereotype / original** ]174). Similarly, genomes that have undergone [ **less / more** ]175) copying processes will have gathered [ **more / less** ]176) mistakes. To make things worse, mutations may damage genes responsible for error checking and repair of genomes, further accelerating the introduction of mutations.

Most genome mutations do not have any noticeable [ **effects / affects** ]177). It is just like changing the *i* for a *y* in "kingdom" would not [ **distort / clarify** ]178) the word's readability. But sometimes a mutation to a human gene results in, for example, an eye whose iris is of two [ **different / uniform** ]179) colors. Similarly, almost everyone has birthmarks, which are due to mutations that occurred as our body's cells multiplied to form skin. If mutations are changes to the genome of one [ **general / particular** ]180) cell, how can a patch of cells in an iris or a whole patch of skin, consisting of many individual cells, be affected [ **spontaneously / simultaneously** ]181)? The answer lies in the cell lineage, the developmental history of a tissue from [ **particular / general** ]182) cells through to their fully differentiated state. If the mutation occurred early on in the lineage of the developing iris, then all cells in that patch have inherited that change.

# 43 ~ 45

Max awoke to the gentle sunlight of an autumn day. Right on schedule, he swung his legs off the bed and took a deep, **[ satisfied / satisfying ]**183) breath. He began his morning the **[ different / same ]**184) way he usually did, getting dressed and going to school. Today was going to be another **[ flawed / perfect ]**185) day until he ran into Mr. Kapoor, his science teacher. "Just to remind you. Science **[ fair / unfair ]**186) projects are due next Wednesday. Don't forget to submit your final draft on time," Mr. Kapoor said. Max froze. **[ What / That ]**187)? *It can't be! It was due next Friday!* After school, he came home worrying that his whole perfectly planned week was going to **[ be ruined / ruin ]**188) . Without his usual greeting, Max headed to his room in haste. "**[ That / What ]**189)'s **[ appropriate / wrong ]**190) Max?," Jeremy, his dad, followed Max, worrying about him. Max furiously browsed through his planner without answering him, only to find the **[ wrong / appropriate ]**191) date written in it. Fighting through tears, Max finally managed to **[ explain / explaining ]**192) the unending pressure to be **[ flawed / perfect ]**193) to his dad. To his surprise, Jeremy laughed. "Max, guess what? **[ Flawed / Perfect ]**194) is a great goal, but nobody gets there all the time. **[ What / That ]**195) matters is **[ what / that ]**196) we do when things get messy." That made him **[ feel / to feel ]**197) a little better. "You are saying I can fix this?" "Absolutely, try to deal with problems in a logical way," Jeremy said. Max thought for a moment. "I guess.... I can do that by rescheduling tonight's baseball lesson." Jeremy beamed. "See? That's you finding a solution." Max felt a genuine smile **[ spreading / to spread ]**198). The next Wednesday, he successfully handed in the final draft on time with satisfaction. From then on, he still loved order and routines, but also **[ embraced / embracing ]**199) the messy, **[ predictable / unpredictable ]**200) bits of life too.

# 2024 고2 11월 모의고사 ❶ 회차 : 점 / 320점

❶ voca　　❷ text　　❸ [ / ]　　④ _____　　❺ quiz 1　　❻ quiz 2　　❼ quiz 3　　❽ quiz 4　　❾ quiz 5

2024_H2_11_18

Dear Executive Manager Schulz,
It is a week before the **i**_____<sup>1)</sup> program starts. I am writing to bring your **a**_____<sup>2)</sup> to a matter that requires immediate **c**_____<sup>3)</sup> regarding the issue my department has. As the **c**_____<sup>4)</sup> , it is becoming **a**_____<sup>5)</sup> to me that the **b**_____<sup>6)</sup> , previously **a**_____<sup>7)</sup> by your department, needs some **a**_____<sup>8)</sup> in order to meet the emerging **m**_____<sup>9)</sup> . Since my department has **h**_____<sup>10)</sup> three more interns than planned initially, the most expensive need is for additional **f**_____<sup>11)</sup> to cover their **w**_____<sup>12)</sup> , training costs, and materials. I kindly request an additional budget **a**_____<sup>13)</sup> for these **e**_____<sup>14)</sup> . Please refer to the attachment for details. Thank you for your attention.
Best regards, Matt Perry

Schulz 부장님께 인턴십 프로그램을 시작하기 일주일 전입니다. 저희 부서의 사안과 관련하여 즉각적인 고려가 필요한 문제에 대해 당신의 관심을 환기하기 위해 이 글을 씁니다. 업무 담당자로서 최근 생겨난 수정 사항을 충족시키기 위해서, 이전에 당신의 부서로부터 승인받은 예산은 약간의 조정이 필요함이 분명해지고 있습니다. 우리 부서에서 처음에 계획됐던 것보다 세 명의 인턴을 더 고용했기 때문에, 가장 비용이 많이 드는 부족한 부분은 그들의 임금, 훈련 비용, 물품들을 다루기 위한 추가적인 자금입니다. 이 비용들을 위해 추가적인 예산 배당을 정중하게 요청합니다. 자세한 사항은 첨부물을 참고해 주세요. 당신의 관심에 감사드립니다.
Matt Perry 드림

2024_H2_11_19

Katie **a**_____<sup>15)</sup> the hotel front desk to check-in but an unexpected event **u**_____<sup>16)</sup> . The **r**_____<sup>17)</sup> couldn't find her **r**_____<sup>18)</sup> under the name 'Katie'. "I'm sorry, but I can't seem to locate a reservation under that name," the receptionist said. "No way, I definitely made a reservation on the phone," Katie said, **p**_____<sup>19)</sup> . The receptionist asked, "Can you tell me your phone number?" and Katie told it to him, thinking 'What happened? Did I make a mistake?' "Just a moment," the receptionist said, typing **d**_____<sup>20)</sup> on the keyboard. "I found it! It seems there was a small misspelling. Your reservation is under 'K-A-T-Y'," the receptionist explained. With a sense of ease, Katie watched her reservation appearing on the screen. With her heart slowing to a gentle rhythm, she **p**_____<sup>21)</sup> with her check-in, thinking that a simple misspelling might have **r**_____<sup>22)</sup> her plans.

Katie는 체크인을 하기 위해 호텔 안내 데스크에 다가갔으나 예상하지 못한 사건이 전개되었다. 접수 담당자는 'Katie'라는 이름으로 된 예약을 찾을 수 없었다. "죄송하지만, 그 이름으로 된 예약을 찾을 수 없는 것 같습니다."라고 접수 담당자가 말했다. "말도 안 돼요, 저는 분명히 전화로 예약했어요."라고 Katie가 어리둥절해하며 말했다. 접수 담당자가 "당신의 전화 번호를 말해 주실 수 있을까요?"라고 물어보았고, Katie가 '무슨 일이지? 내가 실수를 저질렀나?'라고 생각하며 전화번호를 그에게 알려 주었다. "잠시만요."라고 접수 담당자가 키보드를 신중하게 치면서 말했다. "알아냈습니다! 작은 오타가 있었던 것 같습니다. 당신의 예약은 'K-A-T-Y'로 되어 있어요."라고 접수 담당자가 설명했다. 편안한 기분으로 Katie는 그녀의 예약이 화면에 나타나는 것을 지켜봤다. 그녀의 심장이 완만한 리듬으로 느려지면서, 그녀는 단순한 오타가 그녀의 계획들을 망쳤을지도 모른다고 생각하며 체크인을 진행했다.

2024_H2_11_20

To be mathematically l_____ 23) means to be able to think c_____ 24) about s_____ 25) issues on which mathematics has b_____ 26) so as to make i_____ 27) decisions about how to solve these problems. Dealing with such c_____ 28) problems through i_____ 29) approaches, m_____ 30) real-world problems requires i_____ 31) ways of planning and organizing mathematical teaching methods. N_____ 32) our world means being able to q_____ 33) , measure, estimate, classify, compare, find patterns, c_____ 34) , justify, prove, and generalize within critical thinking and when using critical thinking. Therefore, making decisions, even q_____ 35) is not possible without using mathematics and critical thinking. Thus, teaching mathematics should be done in i_____ 36) with critical thinking along with a decision-making process. They can be d_____ 37) into the mathematical c_____ 38) , so that there is no excuse to not e_____ 39) support students to develop them.

수학적 문해력이 있다는 것은 수학과 관련된 사회적 이슈에 대해 이러한 문제들을 어떻게 해결할지에 대한 정보에 입각한 결정을 하기 위해서 비판적으로 생각할 수 있다는 것을 의미한다. 범교과적인 접근법을 통해 그러한 복잡한 문제들을 다루는 과정에서 실생활 문제들을 반영하는 것은 수학적 교수 방법을 계획하고 조직하는 혁신적인 방법들을 요구한다. 우리의 세계를 탐색한다는 것은 비판적 사고안에서 그리고 비판적 사고를 사용할 때 수량화하고, 측정하고, 추산하고, 분류하고, 비교하고, 패턴을 찾고, 추측하고, 근거를 제시하고, 증명하고, 일반화할 수 있다는 것을 의미한다. 그러므로, 수학과 비판적 사고를 사용하지 않고 의사 결정을 하는 것은 질적인 경우에라도 가능하지 않다. 따라서, 수학을 가르치는 것은 의사 결정 과정과 함께 비판적 사고와의 상호 작용 안에서 이루어져야 한다. 그것들은 수학적인 맥락 안에서 발전될 수 있고, 학생들이 그것들을 발전시킬 수 있도록 명시적으로 도움을 주지 않을 경우 변명의 여지가 없다.

2024_H2_11_21

Imagine that your usually s_____ 40) friend d_____ 41) in buying you a Christmas present after taking a g_____ 42) booster. How would you feel? U_____ 43) there is something p_____ 44) about the action. You'd be p_____ 45) to receive the gift. You'd say 'thank you', and mean it. But his change of heart is not entirely satisfying. According to Zagzebski, an American philosopher, he is not really g_____ 46) . When we praise someone's character, we use words for v_____ 47) v_____ 48) : 'generous', 'kind', ' c_____ 49) ', etc. A person who gives one gift isn't generous. Instead, generosity is a stable part of a person's 'moral i_____ 50) ', an emotional habit that is part of who you are. Thus virtues, as opposed to n_____ 51) i_____ 52) , are the result of your personal history. They are part of who you are, as they are part of how your character was formed. I_____ 53) virtue is therefore impossible. P_____ 54) a p_____ 55) cannot make you a better person.

평소에 인색한 여러분의 친구가 관대함 효능촉진제를 먹고 난 이후에 여러분에게 크리스마스 선물을 사 주며 매우 기뻐한다고 상상해 보라. 여러분은 어떻게 느끼겠는가? 의심할 여지 없이, 그 행동에는 칭찬할 만한 점이 있다. 여러분은 선물을 받아서 기뻐할 것이다. 여러분은 '고마워'라고 말하고, 그것은 진심일 것이다. 하지만 그의 마음의 변화는 완전히 만족스럽지는 않다. 미국의 철학자인 Zagzebski에 따르면, 그는 진정으로 관대한 것이 아니다. 우리가 누군가의 인품을 칭찬할 때 '관대한,' '친절한,' '용기있는' 등 다양한 미덕에 대한 단어를 사용한다. 선물을 하나 준 사람이 관대한 것은 아니다. 대신에, 관대함은 누군가의 '도덕적 정체성'의 안정된 일부인데 그것은 여러분의 모습의 일부인 정서적 습관이다. 따라서 미덕은, 비전형적인 충동과는 달리, 여러분 개인 역사의 결과이다. 그것들이 여러분의 인품이 형성되었던 방식의 일부이기 때문에 그것들은 여러분의 모습 중 일부이다. 그러므로 즉각적인 미덕은 있을 수 없다. 약 한 알을 먹는 것이 여러분을 더 나은 사람으로 만들 수는 없다.

2024_H2_11_22

To **d**_____ 56) the mass of my bowling ball, I might put it onto a balance and compare it with a known **m**_____ 57) , such as a number of metal cubes each weighing 1, 10, or 100 grams. Things get much more **c**_____ 58) if I want to know the **m**_____ 59) of a **d**_____ 60) star. How do I measure it? We can **r**_____ 61) say that measuring the mass of a star **i**_____ 62) various theories. If we want to measure the mass of a **b**_____ 63) star, we first determine a center of mass between the two stars, then their **d**_____ 64) from that center which we can then use, together with a value for the period and a certain instance of Kepler's Third Law, to calculate the mass. In other words, in order to "measure" the star mass, we measure other **q**_____ 65) and use those values, together with certain **e**_____ 66) , to calculate the mass. Measurement is not a simple and **u**_____ 67) estimation of independently existing **p**_____ 68) , but a determination of certain **m**_____ 69) before the background of a number of accepted **t**_____ 70) .

볼링공 질량을 측정하기 위해, 나는 그것을 저울에 올려놓고 각 1g, 10g, 또는 100g이 나가는 여러 개의 금속 큐브 같은 이미 알고 있는 질량과 그것을 비교할 수 있다. 만약 내가 먼 별의 질량을 알고 싶다면 상황은 훨씬 더 복잡해진다. 나는 어떻게 그것을 측정할까? 우리는 별의 질량을 측정하는 것은 다양한 이론을 포함한다고 대략적으로 말할 수 있다. 우리가 쌍성의 질량을 측정하기를 원한다면, 질량을 계산하기 위해 우리는 먼저 두 별들 사이의 질량 중심을, 그 다음에 우리가 그제서야 사용할 수 있는 그 중심으로부터 떨어진 그것들의 거리를 공전 주기의 값과 케플러 제3 법칙의 특정한 사례를 가지고 측정한다. 다시 말해서, 별의 질량을 '측정'하기 위해서 우리는 다양한 수치들을 측정하고 그 값들을 특정 방정식들과 함께 사용하여 질량을 계산한다. 측정은 독립적으로 존재하는 값들의 단순하고 중재되지 않은 측정이 아니라, 이미 정립된 여러 이론들을 바탕으로 특정 크기들을 계산하는 것이다.

2024_H2_11_23

Based on discoveries in **n**_____ 71) , pain and pleasure are formed and processed in the same **a**_____ 72) of the brain. Our bodies constantly **s**_____ 73) for **h**_____ 74) , which is **d**_____ 75) as the balance of **b**_____ 76) functions. Without the body's effective **c**_____ 77) mechanisms, which may cushion potential highs and lows, we would not be **c**_____ 78) of surviving. **P**_____ 79) and pain are like two sides of the same coin; they seem to work together and are heavily **r**_____ 80) on one another and keep **b**_____ 81) . If you imagine pleasure and pain as the two opposite points on a scale, you can easily understand that as one of the two points rises, the other must **c**_____ 82) fall. We've all heard the **e**_____ 83) , "No pain, no gain." Well, according to **p**_____ 84) Dr. Anna Lembke, there may be some truth to these words. She says that our attempts to escape being **m**_____ 85) are in fact making us even more **m**_____ 86) . This is because pain is actually an **e**_____ 87) **c**_____ 88) of our ability to maintain a **n**_____ 89) state, and allowing it will in turn reset our **i**_____ 90) scale back to balance.

뇌 과학의 발견들에 따르면, 고통과 쾌락은 뇌의 같은 영역에서 형성되고 처리된다. 우리 몸은 끊임없이 항상성을 추구하는데, 그것은 몸의 기능들의 균형이라고 정의된다. 잠재적인 변동을 완화시킬 수 있는 몸의 효과적인 보상 기제가 없다면 우리는 생존할 수 없을 것이다. 쾌락과 고통은 동일한 동전의 두 면과 같아서 그들은 함께 작동하는 것 같으며 서로 상당히 의존하고 있고 균형을 유지한다. 만약에 여러분이 쾌락과 고통을 저울 위의 두 반대 지점으로 상상한다면, 여러분은 두 지점 중 한 지점이 올라가면 다른 한 지점이 상응하여 틀림없이 내려갈 것임을 쉽게 이해할 수 있을 것이다. 우리는 '고통 없이는, 얻는 것도 없다.'라는 표현을 모두 들어본 적이있다. 자, 정신과 의사인 Dr. Anna Lembke에 따르면, 이 말에는 어느 정도의 진실이 있을 수 있다. 그녀는 우리가 비참함에서 벗어나려는 우리의 시도가 사실 우리를 훨씬 더 비참하게 만들고 있다고 말한다. 이는 고통이 실제로 중립적인 상태를 유지하기 위한 우리 능력의 필수적인 구성 요소이기 때문이고, 그것을 허용하는 것은 결과적으로 우리의 내부 저울을 균형 상태로 다시 맞출 것이다.

## 2024_H2_11_24

M_____91) m_____92) sow seeds of doubt about the a_____93) of our current devices. Suddenly, the phone that was your lifeline a year ago is now a museum piece, unable to keep pace with your digital demands. And thus, the i_____94) to u_____95) begins, often before there's a g_____96) need. This cycle isn't just c_____97) to our digital c_____98) . It s_____99) over into almost every a_____100) of consumer electronics, from the self-driving car to the smart fridge. Every product seems to be on an u_____101) march towards the next version, the next g_____102) that promises to r_____103) your life. What's fascinating, or perhaps disturbing, is the utter e_____104) of this c_____105) in shaping our desires. It's not so much that we want the newest device; we're led to believe we need it. The d_____106) between want and need b_____107) , shifting our f_____108) p_____109) in favor of staying c_____110) with trends. For all the l_____111) arguments against this c_____112) upgrading, the t_____113) remains c_____114) .

생산자들은 노련하게 우리의 현재 기기들의 적절성에 대한 의심의 씨앗을 뿌린다. 갑자기, 1년 전의 당신의 목숨줄이었던 휴대폰이 지금은 당신의 디지털 수요를 따라가지 못하는, 시대에 뒤떨어진 것이 되었다. 그래서 종종 진짜 필요가 있기 이전에 업그레이드에 대한 욕구가 시작된다. 이러한 순환은 단지 우리의 디지털 용품에 국한되지 않는다. 이것은 자율 주행 자동차부터 스마트 냉장고에 이르기까지 소비자 전자 기기들의 거의 모든 영역까지 번져나간다. 모든 제품은 다음 버전, 즉, 당신의 삶에 변혁을 일으키겠다는 약속을 하는 다음 세대를 향한 멈출 수 없는 행진을 하는 것으로 보인다. 흥미로운 점, 또는 어쩌면 당황스러운 점은 우리의 욕구를 형성하는 이 순환의 절대적인 효과이다. 우리가 가장 최신 기기를 원하는 것이 아니라, 우리가 그것을 원한다고 믿도록 유도된 것이다. 최신 트렌드를 유지하는 것을 선호하는 쪽으로 우리의 재정적인 우선순위를 바꾸면서, 원하는 것과 필요한 것 사이의 구분이 흐릿해진다. 이런 끊임없는 업그레이드를 하는 것에 대한 논리적인 논쟁에도 불구하고, 매력은 여전히 강력하다.

## 2024_H2_11_29

C_____115) Place Preference is a way of finding out what animals want. R_____116) train them to a_____117) one place with an experience such as food or a loud noise and another place with something completely different, usually where nothing happens. The two places are made o_____118) different to make it as easy as possible for the animal to associate each place with what happened to it there. The animal's p_____119) for being in one place or another is measured both before and after its experiences in the two places. If there is a s_____120) in where the animal chooses to spend its time for the reward, this suggests that it liked the experience and is trying to repeat it. C_____121) , if it now a_____122) the place the s_____123) appeared and starts to prefer the place it did not experience it, then this suggests that it found the stimulus unpleasant. For example, mice with c_____124) show a preference for the place where they have been given morphine, a drug used to r_____125) pain, rather than where they have received s_____126) whereas healthy mice developed no such preference. This suggests that the mice with cancer wanted the morphine.

조건부 장소 선호도는 동물들이 무엇을 원하는지 알아내는 하나의 방법이다. 연구자들은 그것들이 한 장소를 음식이나 시끄러운 소리와 같은 경험과 연관시키고 또 다른 장소를 완벽히 다른 어떤 것과 연관시키도록 훈련시키는데 대개 그곳에서는 아무것도 일어나지 않는다. 그 두 장소는 그 동물이 각 장소를 거기에서 그것에게 일어난 일과 연관시키는 것을 가능한한 쉽게 만들기 위해 명백히 다르게 만들어진다. 한 장소나 다른 장소에 있는 것에 대한 그 동물의 선호도는 두 장소에서 경험하기 전과 후에 모두 측정된다. 만약 동물이 보상을 위해 어디에서 시간을 보내기로 선택하는지에 변화가 있다면, 이것은 그것이 그 경험을 좋아했고 그것을 반복하려고 노력하는 중이라는 것을 시사한다. 반대로, 만약 그것이 이제 자극이 나타났던 장소를 피하고 그것이 그것을 경험하지 않았던 장소를 선호하기 시작한다면, 그러면 이것은 그것이 그 자극을 불쾌하게 느꼈다는 것을 시사한다. 예를 들어, 암에 걸린 쥐가 식염수를 받아 왔었던 곳보다 통증을 완화시키는 데 사용되는 약인 모르핀이 주어졌었던 장소에 대한 선호를 보여 준 반면, 건강한 쥐는 그러한 선호가 생기지 않았다. 이것은 암에 걸린 쥐가 그 모르핀을 원했음을 시사한다.

2024_H2_11_30

Near the e_____127) , many species of bird b_____128) all year round. But in t_____129) and p_____130) regions, the breeding seasons of birds are often sharply defined. They are t_____131) mainly by changes in day length. If all goes well, the outcome is that birds raise their young when the food supply is at its p_____132) . Most birds are not simply r_____133) to breed at other times but they are also p_____134) incapable of doing so. This is because their r_____135) system s_____136) , which helps flying birds save weight. The main exception to this rule are n_____137) desert species. These can i_____138) their breeding cycle within days of rain. It's for making the most of the sudden breeding opportunity. Also, different species divide the breeding season up in different ways. Most seabirds raise a single b_____139) . In warm regions, however, songbirds may r_____140) several families in a few months. In an e_____141) good year, a pair of House Sparrows, a kind of songbird, can raise s_____142) broods through a marathon r_____143) effort.

적도 근처에서, 새의 많은 종들은 일 년 내내번식한다. 하지만 온대와 극지방에서는 새들의 번식기들이 대개 뚜렷하게 정해진다. 그것들은 주로 낮의 길이의 변화에 의해 촉발된다. 만약에 모든 것이 잘 진행된다면, 결과는 새들이 먹이 공급이 최고조에 이를 때 새끼들을 기르는 것이다. 대부분의 새들은 다른 때에 번식하기를 단지 꺼리는 것뿐만 아니라 또한 신체적으로 그렇게 할 수 없는 것이다. 이것은 왜냐하면 그들의 번식 기관이 줄어들기 때문이고, 이 사실은 나는 새들이 몸무게를 줄일 수 있도록 도와준다. 유목성 사막 종은 이 규칙의 주요 예외이다. 이들은 비가 오는 날들에 번식 주기를 시작할 수 있다. 그것은 갑작스러운 번식 기회를 최대한으로 활용하기 위한 것이다. 또한, 다른 종들은 번식기간을 다른 방식으로 나눈다. 대부분의 바닷새들은 한 무리의 함께 태어난 새끼를 기른다. 그러나, 따뜻한 지역에서는, 명금(鳴禽)들이 몇 달 안에 여러 자녀들을 기를 수도 있다. 유난히 좋은 해에는 명금(鳴禽)의 한 종류인 참새 한 쌍은 마라톤과 같은 번식 노력을 통해 잇따라 태어난 여러 무리의 함께 태어난 새끼들을 기를 수 있다.

2024_H2_11_31

One factor that may h_____144) creativity is u_____145) of the resources required in each activity in students' learning. Often students are unable to identify the resources they need to perform the task required of them. Different resources may be c_____146) for specific learning tasks, and recognizing them may s_____147) the activity's performance. For example, it may be that students desire to conduct some experiments in their projects. There must be a p_____148) investigation of whether the students will have a_____149) to the laboratory, equipment, and chemicals required for the experiment. It means preparation is v_____150) for the students to succeed, and it may be about human and f_____151) resources such as laboratory t_____152) , money to purchase chemicals, and equipment for their learning where a_____153) . Even if some of the resources required for a task may not be available, identifying them in advance may help students' creativity. It may even lead to changing the topic, finding a_____154) resources, and other means.

창의성을 방해할 수도 있는 한 가지 요소는 학생들의 학습에서 각 활동에 요구되는 자원에 대한 인식이 없다는 것이다. 종종 학생들은 그들에게 요구되는 과제를 수행하는 데 필요한 자원들을 식별할 수 없다. 여러 가지의 자원들이 특정 학습 과제들에 대해 필수적일 수 있어서 그것들을 인식하는 것은 활동의 수행을 평이하게 해 줄 수도 있다. 예를 들어, 학생들이 프로젝트에서 어떤 실험을 수행하기를 원할 수도 있다. 학생들이 실험에 요구되는 실험실, 장비, 그리고 화학 물질에 접근할 수 있을지 여부에대한 사전 조사가 있어야 한다. 그것은 학생들이 성공하기 위해 준비가 필수적이라는 것을 의미하며, 그들의 학습을 위해 적용할 수 있는 경우에 그것은 실험실 기술자, 화학 물질 구입 자금, 그리고 장비와 같은 인적 그리고 재정적 자원에 대한 것일 수도 있다. 과제에 요구되는 자원들 중 일부가 이용 가능하지 않을 수도 있지만, 사전에 그것들을 식별하는 것은 학생들의 창의성에 도움이 될 수도 있다. 그것은 심지어 주제 변경, 대체 자원들 찾기, 그리고 다른 방법으로 이어질 수도 있다.

2024_H2_11_32

All translators feel some pressure from the community of readers for whom they are doing their work. And all translators arrive at their i_____ 155) in d_____ 156) with other people. The English poet Alexander Pope had pretty good Greek, but when he set about translating Homer's *Iliad* in the early 18th century he was not on his own. He had Greek c_____ 157) to refer to, and translations that had already been done in English, Latin, and French — and of course he had dictionaries. Translators always draw on more than one s_____ 158) text. Even when the scene of translation c_____ _159) just one person with a pen, paper, and the book that is being translated, or even when it is just one person translating o_____ 160) for another, that person's l_____ 161) knowledge a_____ 162) from lots of other texts and other conversations. And then his or her idea of the translation's purpose will be influenced by the e_____ 163) of the person or people it is for. In both these s_____ 164) every translation is a crowd translation.

모든 번역가들은 그들이 대상으로 작업하고 있는 독자들의 공동체로부터 약간의 압박을 느낀다. 그리고 모든 번역가들은 다른 사람들과의 대화에서 그들의 해석에 도달한다. 영국의 시인 알렉산더 포프는 그리스어를 꽤 잘했지만, 18세기 초에 호머의 'Iliad'를 번역하는 것에 대해 착수했을 때 그는 혼자한 것이 아니었다. 그는 참고할 그리스어 해설과 이미 영어, 라틴어, 프랑스어로 된 번역본을 가지고 있었고, 물론 사전도 가지고 있었다. 번역가들은 항상 한 가지 이상의 원문을 활용한다. 심지어 번역 현장이 하나의 펜, 종이, 그리고 번역 중인 책을 가진 단 한 사람으로 구성되어 있거나, 한 사람이 다른 사람을 위해 구두로 번역 중일 때에도, 그 사람의 언어적 지식은 많은 다른 텍스트와 다른 대화에서 발생한다. 그러고 나서 번역의 목적에 대한 그 또는 그녀의 생각은 이것의 대상이 되는 사람 또는 사람들의 기대에 의해 영향을 받는다. 이 두 가지 의미에서 모든 번역은 군중 번역이다.

2024_H2_11_33

Some people argue that there is a single, l_____ 165) c_____ 166) concept known as reading that can be neatly set apart from everything else people do with books. Is reading really that simple? The most p_____ 167) way to think about reading is as a loosely related set of behaviors that belong together owing to family r_____ 168) , as Ludwig Wittgenstein used the p_____ 169) , without having in common a single defining t_____ 170) . Consequently, efforts to d_____ 171) reading from nonreading are d_____ 172) to fail because there is no agreement on what q_____ 173) as reading in the first place. The more one tries to figure out where the border lies between reading and not-reading, the more edge cases will be found to s_____ 174) the term's f_____ 175) boundaries. Thus, it is worth attempting to collect together these exceptional forms of reading into a single f_____ 176) , one highlighting the challenges f_____ 177) by anyone wishing to establish the boundaries where reading begins and ends. The attempt moves toward an understanding of reading as a s_____ 178) that is e_____ 179) enough to a_____ 180) the distinct reading activities.

몇몇 사람들은 사람들이 책을 가지고 하는 모든 다른 행동들로부터 깔끔하게 분리될 수 있는, 읽기로 알려진 유일하고 논리적으로 일관성 있는 개념이 있다고 주장한다. 읽기는 정말로 그렇게 단순할까? 읽기에 대해 생각하는 가장 생산적인 방식은 하나의 명백한 특성을 공통적으로 가지지 않은 채 Ludwig Wittgenstein이 그 어구를 사용한 것처럼 가족 유사성 때문에 함께 속하게 되는 헐겁게 연결된 행동의 묶음으로서이다. 결론적으로, 읽기와 읽기가 아닌 것을 구분하려는 노력은 실패로 돌아가는데, 왜냐하면 애초에 무엇이 읽기로서의 자격을 주는가에 대한 동의가 없기 때문이다. 읽기와 읽기가 아닌 것 사이의 경계가 어디에 있는가를 알려고 하면 할수록, 더욱 많은 특이 사례들이 그 용어의 유연한 경계를 확장하고 있다는 것이 밝혀질 것이다. 그러므로, 이러한 예외적인 읽기의 형태들을 모두 함께 하나의 토론의 장으로 모으려는 시도는 해 볼 가치가 있으며, 그 토론의 장은 어디서 읽기가 시작되고 끝나는가에 대한 경계를 정하기를 원하는 누구나에 의해 마주하게 될 어려움들을 돋보이게 한다. 그러한 시도는 별개의 읽기 활동들을 다 수용할 만큼 충분히 광 범위한 스펙트럼으로서 읽기를 이해하는 것으로 발전한다.

2024_H2_11_34

Weber's law c_____181) the perception of difference between two stimuli. It suggests that we might not be able to d_____182) a 1-mm difference when we are looking at lines 466 mm and 467 mm in length, but we may be able to d_____183) a 1-mm difference when we are comparing a line 2 mm long with one 3 mm long. Another example of this p_____184) is that we can d_____185) 1 candle when it is lit in an otherwise dark room. But when 1 candle is lit in a room in which 100 candles are already burning, we may not notice the light from this candle. Therefore, the Just-noticeable difference (JND) v_____186) as a function of the strength of the signals. For example, the JND is greater for very loud noises than it is for much more quiet sounds. When a sound is very w_____187) , we can tell that another sound is louder, even if it is b_____188) louder. When a sound is very loud, to tell that another sound is even louder, it has to be much louder. Thus, Weber's law means that it is harder to d_____189) between two samples when those samples are larger or stronger levels of the stimuli.

베버의 법칙은 두 자극 사이의 차이에 대한 감지에 관한 것이다. 이것은 우리가 466mm와 467mm 길이인 선들을 볼 때 1mm의 차이를 감지할 수 없지만, 우리가 2mm 길이와 3mm 길이인 선을 비교할 때는 1mm의 차이를 감지할 수 있을지도 모른다는 것을 암시한다. 이 원리의 또 다른 예는 촛불이 켜지지 않았으면 어두웠을 방안에 하나의 촛불이 켜졌을 때 이것을 감지할 수 있다는 것이다. 그러나 100개의 촛불이 이미 타고 있는 방에 하나의 촛불이 켜졌을 때, 우리는 이 촛불의 빛을 알아차리지 못할지도 모른다. 그러므로, 겨우 알아차릴 수 있는 차이 (JND)는 신호의 세기에 대한 함수에 의해 달라진다. 예를 들어, JND는 훨씬 더 작은 소리에 대한 것보다 매우 큰 소음에 대해 더 크다. 한 소리가 매우 약할 때, 우리는 그것이 간신히 더 클지라도, 또 다른 소리가 더 크다는 것을 구분할 수 있다. 어떤 소리가 매우 클 때, 다른 소리가 훨씬 더 크다는 것을 구분하기 위해서는, 그 소리는 훨씬 더 커야 한다. 그러므로, 베버의 법칙은 그 표본들이 자극의 수준이 더 크거나 강할 때 두 표본을 구별하기가 더 어렵다는 것을 의미한다.

2024_H2_11_35

Any new resource (e.g., a new airport, a new mall) always opens with people b_____190) individually by s_____191) a common resource (e.g., the city or state budget). Soon, at some point, the amount of traffic grows too large for the "commons" to support. Traffic jams, overcrowding, and o_____192) lessen the benefits of the common resource for everyone —the tragedy of the commons! If the new resource cannot be e_____193) or provided with additional space, it becomes a problem, and you cannot solve the problem on your own, in i_____194) from your fellow drivers or walkers or competing users. The total activity on this new r_____195) keeps increasing, and so does individual activity; but if the dynamic of common use and o_____196) continues too long, both begin to fall after a peak, leading to a c_____197) . What makes the "_____198) of commons" tragic is the crash dynamic —the destruction or d_____199) of the common resource's ability to r_____200) itself.

어떤 새로운 자원(예를 들어, 새로운 공항, 새로운 쇼핑센터)은 항상 공동의 자원(예를 들어, 시 또는 주 예산)을 공유함으로써 사람들이 개별적으로 이익을 얻으면서 시작된다. 곧, 어느 시점에서, 교통량은 '공유지'가 견디기에 너무 커진다. 교통 체증, 과밀, 그리고 과도한 사용은 모두를 위한 공유 자원의 혜택을 줄이는데, 이것은 즉 공유지의 비극이다! 만약 새로운 자원이 확장될 수 없거나 추가적인 공간이 제공될 수 없다면, 이것은 문제가 되고, 여러분은 여러분의 동료 운전자나 보행자 또는 경쟁 사용자들로부터 고립된 상태로 혼자서 문제를 해결할 수 없다. 이 새로운 자원에 대한 총활동은 계속 증가하고, 개인 활동도 증가한다. 그러나 만약 공동 사용과 과도한 사용의 역학이 너무 오래 지속되면, 둘 다 정점 이후에 떨어지기 시작하고, 몰락으로 이어진다. (마찬가지로, 지식 그리고 정보와 같은 공동의 자원은 사용자의 수가 증가할 때 상대적 가치가 떨어지는 무한한 것이지만, 과도하게 사용된다고 할지라도 완전히 소모되지는 않을 것이다.) '공유지의 비극'을 더 비극적이게 만드는 것은 몰락 역학, 즉 그 스스로를 재생산할 수 있는 공동 자원의 능력의 파괴 또는 퇴보이다.

## 2024_H2_11_36

T_____201) , our brain would have the c_____202) to s_____203) all experiences throughout life, reaching the quality of a DVD. However, this theoretical capacity is o_____204) by the energy demand associated with the process of storing and r_____205) information in memory. As a result, the brain develops e_____206) strategies, becoming d_____207) on shortcuts. When we o_____208) a face, the visual image captured by the eyes is highly v_____209) , depending on the point of view, lighting conditions and other c_____210) factors. Nevertheless, we are able to recognize the face as the same, maintaining the u_____211) identity. The brain, rather than focusing on the details of v_____212) , creates and stores g_____213) patterns that allow for consistent recognition across d_____214) circumstances. This ability to match what we see with general v_____215) memory patterns serves as an effective mechanism for o_____216) brain performance and saving energy. The brain, being n_____217) against unnecessary effort, constantly seeks to simplify and generalize information to f_____218) the c_____219) process.

이론적으로는 우리의 뇌는 DVD의 품질에 도달할 정도로, 삶의 모든 경험들을 저장할 수 있는 수용력을 가지고 있을 것이다. 그러나, 이 이론상의 수용력은 기억에 정보를 저장하고 상기하는 과정과 관련된 에너지 수요로 인해 상쇄된다. 그 결과, 뇌는 효율적인 전략들을 수립하고, 지름길에 의존하게 된다. 우리가 얼굴을 관찰할 때, 눈에 의해 포착되는 시각적 이미지는 시점, 조명 조건 및 기타 상황적 요인들에 따라 매우 다양하다. 그럼에도 불구하고, 우리는 근본적인 정체성을 유지하면서 얼굴을 같은 것으로 인식할 수 있다. 뇌는 시각화의 세부 사항에 집중하기보다 다양한 상황들에서 일관된 인식을 가능하게 하는 일반적인 패턴을 생성하고 저장한다. 우리가 보는 것과 일반적인 시각 기억 패턴을 일치시키는 이 능력은 뇌의 수행을 최적화하고 에너지를 절약하는 효과적인 기제로 작용한다. 불필요한 노력에 자연스럽게 대항하는 뇌는 인지 과정을 돕기 위해서 끊임없이 정보를 단순화하고 일반화하는 것을 추구한다.

## 2024_H2_11_37

Where scientific research is c_____220) , e_____221) t_____222) are expected to a_____223) closely to experimental data and to i_____224) the regular and p_____225) features of experience. However, this p_____226) sometimes c_____227) the fact that theories are deeply loaded with creative elements that shape the c_____228) of research projects and the interpretations of evidence. Scientific explanations do not just relate a c_____229) of facts. They construct frameworks for s_____230) chosen data in order to provide a consistent and m_____231) explanation of what is observed. Such constructions lead us to imagine specific kinds of subject matter in particular sorts of relations, and the s_____232) they i_____233) will prove more effective for analyzing some features of experience over others. When we n_____234) the creative contributions of such scientific imagination and treat models and interpretive explanations as s_____235) facts — even worse, as facts including all of reality — we can b_____236) ourselves to the l_____237) of a given model and fail to note its p_____238) for m_____239) a situation to which it ill applies.

과학 연구에 관해서는, 설명하는 이야기들이 실험의 데이터에 엄밀히 충실할 것으로 기대되고 경험의 규칙적이고 예측 가능한 특징들을 밝힐 것으로 기대된다. 그러나, 이러한 패러다임은 때때로 이론들이 연구 프로젝트의 구성과 증거의 해석을 형성하는 창의적인 요소들로 철저히 채워져 있다는 사실을 감춘다. 과학적 설명들은 단순히 사실들의 연대기를 말하는 것은 아니다. 그것들은 관찰된 것에 대한 일관적이고 의미 있는 설명을 제공하기 위해 체계적으로 선택된 데이터에 대한 틀을 구축한다. 그러한 구성들은 우리가 특정한 유형의 관계에서 구체적인 종류의 주제를 상상하도록 하며, 그것들이 고취하는 줄거리는 다른 것들보다 경험의 일부 특징을 분석하는 데 더 효과적일 것으로 판명될 것이다. 우리가 그러한 과학적 상상의 창의적 기여를 무시하고 모델과 해석적 설명을 단순한 사실, 훨씬 더 심하게는 현실을 전부 포괄하는 사실로 간주할 때, 우리는 주어진 모델의 한계에 대해 우리 스스로를 눈멀게 하며 그것이 잘못 적용되는 상황에 대해 오해할 가능성을 알아차리지 못할 수 있다.

2024_H2_11_38

We e_____240) c_____241) claims about the relation of l_____242) to action. Theorists have maintained that literature e_____243) s_____244) reading and reflection as the way to engage with the world and thus counters the social and political activities that might produce social change. At best it encourages d_____245) or appreciation of complexity, and at worst p_____246) and acceptance of what is. But on the other hand, literature has historically been seen as dangerous: it p_____247) the questioning of a_____248) and social a_____249) . Plato b_____250) poets from his ideal republic because they could only do harm, and n_____251) have long been c_____252) with making people d_____253) with their lives and eager for something new. By promoting identification across d_____254) of class, gender, and race, books may promote a f_____255) that d_____256) struggle; but they may also produce a keen sense of i_____257) that makes progressive struggles possible. Historically, works of literature are credited with producing change: *Uncle Tom's Cabin*, a best-seller in its day, helped create a r_____258) against s_____259) that made possible the American Civil War.

우리는 문학과 행동의 관계에 대한 상반된 주장들과 마주한다. 이론가들은 문학이 세상과 관계를 맺는 방법으로써 고독한 독서와 성찰을 장려하고 따라서 사회 변화를 일으킬 수 있을지도 모르는 사회적이고 정치적인 활동들에 거스른다고 주장해 왔다. 기껏해야 이것은 단절 또는 복잡성에 대한 인정을, 최악의 경우 수동성과 있는 그대로에 대한 수용을 조장한다. 그러나 다른 한편으로, 문학은 역사적으로 권위와 사회적 합의에 대한 의문을 제기하는 것을 조장하므로 위험하다고 여겨져 왔다. 플라톤은 그들이 해를 끼치는 것만 할 수 있기 때문에 그의 이상적인 공화국으로부터 시인들을 추방했고, 소설은 사람들이 그들의 삶에 불만을 품게 만들고 새로운 무언가를 갈망하도록 하는 것으로 오랫동안 믿어져 왔다. 계급, 성별, 그리고 인종의 경계를 넘어 동일시를 촉진함으로써, 책들은 투쟁을 단념시키는 동료 의식을 장려할 수 있을지 모르지만, 이것들은 또한 진보적인 투쟁들을 가능하게 만드는 강한 불의의 감정을 일으킬 수 있다. 역사적으로, 문학 작품은 변화를 만드는 것으로 믿어져 왔는데 그 시대의 베스트셀러인 '톰 아저씨의 오두막'은 미국 남북 전쟁을 가능하게 만든 노예제에 대한 혐오감을 조성하는 것을 도왔다.

2024_H2_11_39

According to Hobbes, man is not a being who can act morally in s_____260) his instinct to protect his existence in the state of nature. Hence, the only place where morality and moral l_____261) will begin to find an application begins in a place where a s_____262) power, namely the state, emerges. Hobbes thus describes the state of nature as a c_____263) in which man's life is "solitary, poor, nasty, brutish and short". It means when people live without a general power to control them all, they are indeed in a s_____264) of war. In other words, Hobbes, who a_____265) that human beings are not social and political beings in the state of nature, believes that without the power human beings in the state of nature are "_____266) and r_____267) based on their selfishness". Moreover, since society is not a natural p_____268) and there is no natural f_____269) bringing people together, what will bring them together as a society is not m_____270) a_____271) according to Hobbes. It is, rather, mutual fear of men's present and future that assembles them, since the cause of fear is a common drive among people in the state of nature.

홉스에 따르면, 인간은 자연 상태에서 자신의 존재를 보호하려는 그의 본능을 무릅쓰고 도덕적으로 행동할 수 있는 존재가 아니다. 따라서, 도덕과 도덕적 자유가 적용을 찾기 시작하는 유일한 곳은 군림하는 권력, 즉 국가가 출현하는 곳에서 나타난다. 따라서 홉스는 자연 상태를 인간의 삶이 '고독하고, 가난하며, 불결하고, 잔인하고, 짧은' 상황으로 묘사한다. 그것은 사람들이 그들 모두를 통제할 일반적인 권력 없이 살아갈 때, 그들은 실로 전쟁 상태에 놓여 있는 것임을 의미한다. 즉 다시 말해, 자연 상태에 있는 인간은 사회적이고 정치적인 존재가 아니라는 것을 인정한 홉스는 그 권력이 없이 자연 상태에 있는 인간은 '이기심에 기초해 반사회적이고 이성적'이라고 믿는다. 게다가, 사회는 자연적인 현상이 아니며 사람들을 하나로 모으는 자연적인 힘도 없기 때문에, 홉스에 따르면 그들을 사회로 함께 모이게 하는 것은 상호 간의 애정이 아니다. 두려움으로부터의 동기가 자연 상태에 있는 사람들 사이의 공통된 추진력이기 때문에, 오히려, 그들을 모으는 것은 인간의 현재와 미래에 대한 상호 간의 두려움이다.

2024_H2_11_40

There is research that supports the idea that **c**_____**272)** factors influence the phenomenology of the **p**_____**273)** world. Delk and Fillenbaum asked participants to match the color of figures with the color of their background. Some of the figures **d**_____**274)** objects associated with a **p**_____**275)** color. These included **t**_____**276)** red objects such as an apple, lips, and a **s**_____**277)** heart. Other objects were **p**_____**278)** that are not usually associated with red, such as a mushroom or a bell. However, all the figures were made out of the same red-orange cardboard. Participants then had to match the figure to a background **v**_____**279)** from dark to light red. They had to make the background color match the color of the figures. The researchers found that red-associated objects **r**_____**280)** more red in the background to be judged a match than did the objects that are not associated with the color red. This **i**_____**281)** that the cognitive association of objects to color influences how we perceive that color.

인지적 요인들이 지각된 세계의 현상학에 영향을 미친다는 생각을 뒷받침하는 연구가 있다. Delk와 Fillenbaum은 참가자들에게 형상들의 색상을 배경 색상과 맞추도록 요청했다. 몇몇 형상들은 특정 색상과 연관된 물체들을 묘사했다. 그것들은 사과, 입술, 상징적인 하트 모양과 같이 전형적인 빨간색 물체를 포함했다. 버섯이나 종과 같이 빨간색과 일반적으로 연관이 되지 않는 다른 물체들도 제시되었다. 그러나, 모든 형상들은 동일한 다홍색 판지로 만들어졌다. 그러고 나서 참가자들은 그 형상을 진한 빨간색에서 연한 빨간색까지 다양한 배경색과 맞춰야 했다. 그들은 배경색이 형상들의 색과 일치하게 해야 했다. 연구자들은 빨간색과 연관된 물체들이 빨간색과 연관이 없는 물체가 그러한 것보다 배경과 일치한다고 판단되기 위해서 배경에서 더 빨간색을 요구한다는 것을 발견했다. 이것은 색과 물체의 인지적 연관성이 우리가 그 색을 어떻게 지각하는가에 영향을 미친다는 것을 함의한다. 한 연구에서, 참가자들은 일반적으로 빨간색인 물체의 색상과 같은 색상의 배경을 일치시키도록 요청받았을 때, 더 진한 빨강을 선택했는데, 이는 물체들의 색상에 대한 그들의 지식이 그들의 지각적 판단에 영향을 미쳤다는 것을 보여준다.

2024_H2_11_41~42

In each round of **g**_____**282)** copying in our body, there is still about a 70 percent chance that at least one pair of **c**_____**283)** will have an error. With each round of genome copying, errors **a**_____**284)** . This is similar to **a**_____**285)** in **m**_____**286)** books. Each time a copy was made by hand, some changes were introduced accidentally; as changes **s**_____**287)** up, the copies may have acquired meanings at **v**_____**288)** with the original. Similarly, genomes that have **u**_____**289)** more copying processes will have **g**_____**290)** more mistakes. To make things worse, **m**_____**291)** may damage genes responsible for error checking and repair of genomes, further **a**_____**292)** the introduction of mutations. Most genome mutations do not have any **n**_____**293)** effects. It is just like changing the *i* for a *y* in "kingdom" would not **d**_____**294)** the word's **r**_____**295)** . But sometimes a mutation to a human gene results in, for example, an eye whose **i**_____**296)** is of two different colors. **S**_____**297)** , almost everyone has **b**_____**298)** , which are **d**_____**299)** to mutations that occurred as our body's cells **m**_____**300)** to form skin. If mutations are changes to the genome of one **p**_____**301)** cell, how can a patch of cells in an iris or a whole **p**_____**302)** of skin, consisting of many individual cells, be affected **s**_____**303)** ? The answer lies in the cell **l**_____**304)** , the developmental history of a tissue from particular cells through to their fully **d**_____**305)** state. If the mutation occurred early on in the **l**_____**306)** of the developing iris, then all cells in that patch have **i**_____**307)** that change.

우리 몸속 게놈 복제의 각 과정마다, 적어도 한 쌍의 염색체들이 오류를 가질 확률이 여전히 약 70%이다. 게놈 복제의 각 과정마다, 오류들이 쌓인다. 이것은 중세 서적에 있어서의 변화와 유사하다. 하나의 복사본이 사람 손으로 만들어질 때마다, 일부 변화들이 우연히 도입되었고, 변화들이 쌓이면서, 복사본은 원본과 불일치하는 의미를 축적했을 것이다. 마찬가지로, 더 많은 복제 과정들을 거친 게놈은 더 많은 실수들을 축적하게 될 것이다. 설상가상으로, 변이들은 게놈의 오류 확인과 복구를 책임지는 유전자를 훼손해 변이들의 도입을 더욱 가속할 수도 있다.

대부분의 게놈 변이들은 어떠한 뚜렷한 영향이 없다. 그것은 마치 'kingdom'에서 'i'를 'y'로 변경하는 것이 그 단어의 가독성을 보장하지(→왜곡하지) 않는 것과 같다. 그러나 예를 들어, 때때로 인간 유전자에 대한 변이는 홍채가 두 가지 다른 색을 띠는 눈을 초래하기도 한다. 마찬가지로, 거의 모두가 모반이 있는데, 이는 우리 몸의 세포가 피부를 형성하기 위하여 증식하면서 발생한 변이들 때문이다. 만약 변이들이 하나의 특정 세포의 게놈에 대한 변화라면, 많은 개별적인 세포들로 구성된 홍채의 세포 집단이나 피부 전체 세포 집단이 어떻게 동시에 영향을 받을 수 있을까? 그 대답은 세포 계보, 즉 특정 세포에서 그들의 완전히 차별화된 상태까지의 조직 발달 변천에 있다. 만약 발달 중인 홍채의 계보 초기에 변이가 발생했다면, 그렇다면 그 세포 집단의 모든 세포는 그 변화를 물려받아 왔을 것이다.

2024_H2_11_43~45

Max awoke to the gentle sunlight of an a_____308) day. Right on schedule, he swung his legs off the bed and took a deep, satisfying breath. He began his morning the same way he usually did, getting dressed and going to school. Today was going to be another perfect day until he ran into Mr. Kapoor, his science teacher. "Just to remind you. Science fair projects are d_____309) next Wednesday. Don't forget to s_____310) your final draft on time," Mr. Kapoor said. Max froze. *What? It can't be! It was due next Friday!* After school, he came home worrying that his whole perfectly planned week was going to be ruined. Without his usual greeting, Max headed to his room in haste. "What's wrong Max?," Jeremy, his dad, followed Max, worrying about him. Max furiously b_____311) through his planner without answering him, only to find the wrong date written in it. Fighting through tears, Max finally m_____312) to explain the u_____313) pressure to be perfect to his dad. To his surprise, Jeremy laughed. "Max, guess what? Perfect is a great goal, but nobody gets there all the time. What matters is what we do when things get messy." That made him feel a little better. "You are saying I can fix this?" "Absolutely, try to deal with problems in a l_____314) way," Jeremy said. Max thought for a moment. "I guess.... I can do that by r_____315) tonight's baseball lesson." Jeremy b_____316) . "See? That's you finding a solution." Max felt a g_____317) smile spreading. The next Wednesday, he successfully handed in the final d_____318) on time with satisfaction. From then on, he still loved order and r_____319) , but also e_____320) the messy, unpredictable bits of life too.

Max는 가을날의 부드러운 햇빛에 잠에서 깼다. 시간에 맞추어 그는 다리를 침대 밖으로 휙 내려놓았고 깊고 만족스러운 숨을 내쉬었다. 그는 평소와 똑같은 방식으로 아침을 시작했고 옷을 입고 학교에갔다. 오늘은 과학 선생님인 Kapoor 선생님을 만나기 전까지는 또 다른 완벽한 날이 될 예정이었다. "그냥 너에게 알려 주는 거야. 과학 박람회 프로젝트가 다음 주 수요일까지야. 제 시간에 최종안을 제출하는 것을 잊어버리지 마."라고 Kapoor 선생님이 말했다. Max는 얼어붙었다. '뭐라고? 그럴 순 없어! 이건 다음 주 금요일까지였다고!' 학교를 마친 후에, 그는 그의 완벽히 계획된 일주일이 망쳐질 것을 걱정하며 집으로 돌아왔다. 그의 일상적인 인사 없이, Max는 급하게 그의 방으로 향했다. "무슨 일이니 Max?" 그의 아버지인 Jeremy는 그를 걱정하며 Max를 따라갔다. Max는 그에게 대답하지 않고 열성적으로 그의 일정표를 뒤적거렸지만, 거기에 잘못 적힌 날짜를 발견할 뿐이었다. 울음을 참으며, Max는 마침내 가까스로 그의 아버지에게 완벽해야 한다는 끝나지 않는 압박에 대해 설명했다. 놀랍게도, Jeremy는 웃었다. "Max, 있잖아? 완벽은 훌륭한 목표지만, 누구도 항상 거기에 도달할 수는 없단다. 중요한 건 일이 어질러졌을 때 우리가 무엇을 하는가야." 그것이 그의 기분을 조금 더 나아지게 만들어 주었다. "아빠는 제가 이것을 해결할 수 있다고 말씀하시는 거예요?" "물론이지. 논리적인 방식으로 문제를 처리해봐."라고 Jeremy가 말했다. Max는 잠시동안 생각했다. "아마.... 제가 오늘 밤 야구 레슨 일정을 변경함으로써 그렇게 할 수 있을 것 같아요." Jeremy가 활짝 웃었다. "봤지? 네가 해결책을 찾아냈잖니." Max는 진심 어린 미소가 퍼지는 것을 느꼈다. 다음 주 수요일에 그는 만족하며 성공적으로 최종안을 제시간에 제출했다. 그 이후로 그는 여전히 순서와 정해진 일과를 좋아했지만, 또한 어지럽고 예측 불가능한 삶의 부분들도 기꺼이 맞이했다.

# 2024 고2 11월 모의고사 ❷ 회차 : 점 / 350점

❶ voca  ❷ text  ❸ [ / ]  ④ ____  ❺ quiz 1  ❻ quiz 2  ❼ quiz 3  ❽ quiz 4  ❾ quiz 5

2024_H2_11_18

Dear Executive Manager Schulz,
It is a week before the i_____1) program starts. I am writing to bring your a_____2) to a matter that requires immediate c_____3) regarding the issue my department has. As the c_____4) , it is becoming a_____5) to me that the b_____6) , previously a_____7) by your department, needs some a_____8) in order to meet the emerging m_____9) . Since my department has h_____10) three more interns than planned initially, the most expensive need is for additional f_____11) to cover their w_____12) , training costs, and materials. I kindly request an additional budget a_____13) for these e_____14) . Please refer to the attachment for details. Thank you for your attention.
Best regards, Matt Perry

2024_H2_11_19

Katie a_____15) the hotel front desk to check-in but an unexpected event u_____16) . The r_____17) couldn't find her r_____18) under the name 'Katie'. "I'm sorry, but I can't seem to locate a reservation under that name," the receptionist said. "No way, I definitely made a reservation on the phone," Katie said, p_____19) . The receptionist asked, "Can you tell me your phone number?" and Katie told it to him, thinking 'What happened? Did I make a mistake?' "Just a moment," the receptionist said, typing d_____20) on the keyboard. "I found it! It seems there was a small m_____21) . Your reservation is under 'K-A-T-Y'," the receptionist explained. With a sense of ease, Katie watched her reservation a_____22) on the screen. With her heart slowing to a gentle rhythm, she p_____23) with her check-in, thinking that a simple misspelling might have r_____24) her plans.

2024_H2_11_20

To be mathematically l_____25) means to be able to think c_____26) about s_____27) issues on which mathematics has b_____28) so as to make i_____29) decisions about how to solve these problems. Dealing with such c_____30) problems through i_____31) approaches, m_____32) real-world problems requires i_____33) ways of planning and organizing mathematical teaching methods. N_____34) our world means being able to q_____35) , measure, estimate, classify, compare, find patterns, c_____36) , justify, prove, and generalize within critical thinking and when using critical thinking. Therefore, making decisions, even q_____37) is not possible without using mathematics and c_____38) thinking. Thus, teaching mathematics should be done in i_____39) with critical thinking along with a decision-making process. They can be d_____40) into the mathematical context, so that there is no excuse to not e_____41) support students to develop them.

## 2024_H2_11_21

Imagine that your usually **s**_____42) friend **d**_____43) in buying you a Christmas present after taking a **g**_____44) booster. How would you feel? **U**_____45) there is something **p**_____46) about the action. You'd be **p**_____47) to receive the gift. You'd say 'thank you', and mean it. But his change of heart is not entirely satisfying. According to Zagzebski, an American philosopher, he is not really **g**_____48) . When we praise someone's character, we use words for **v**_____49) **v**_____50) : 'generous', 'kind', ' **c**_____51) ', etc. A person who gives one gift isn't generous. Instead, generosity is a stable part of a person's 'moral **i**_____52) ', an emotional habit that is part of who you are. Thus **v**_____53) , as opposed to **n**_____54) **i**_____55) , are the result of your personal history. They are part of who you are, as they are part of how your character was formed. **I**_____56) virtue is therefore impossible. **P**_____57) a **p**_____58) cannot make you a better person.

## 2024_H2_11_22

To **d**_____59) the mass of my bowling ball, I might put it onto a balance and compare it with a known **m**_____60) , such as a number of metal cubes each weighing 1, 10, or 100 grams. Things get much more **c**_____61) if I want to know the **m**_____62) of a **d**_____63) star. How do I measure it? We can **r**_____64) say that measuring the mass of a star **i**_____65) various theories. If we want to measure the mass of a **b**_____66) star, we first determine a center of mass between the two stars, then their distance from that center **w**_____67) we can then use, together with a value for the period and a certain instance of Kepler's Third Law, to calculate the mass. In other words, in order to " **m**_____68) " the star mass, we measure other **q**_____69) and use those values, together with certain **e**_____70) , to calculate the mass. Measurement is not a simple and **u**_____71) estimation of independently existing **p**_____72) , but a determination of certain **m**_____73) before the background of a number of accepted theories.

## 2024_H2_11_23

Based on discoveries in **n**_____74) , pain and pleasure are formed and processed in the same **a**_____75) of the brain. Our bodies constantly **s**_____76) for **h**_____77) , which is **d**_____78) as the balance of **b**_____79) functions. Without the body's effective **c**_____80) mechanisms, which may cushion potential highs and lows, we would not be **c**_____81) of surviving. **P**_____82) and pain are like two sides of the same coin; they seem to work together and are heavily **r**_____83) on one another and keep **b**_____84) . If you imagine **p**_____85) and pain as the two opposite points on a scale, you can easily understand that as one of the two points rises, the other must **c**_____86) fall. We've all heard the **e**_____87) , "No pain, no gain." Well, according to **p**_____88) Dr. Anna Lembke, there may be some truth to these words. She says that our attempts to escape being **m**_____89) are in fact making us even more **m**_____90) . This is because pain is actually an **e**_____91) **c**_____92) of our ability to maintain a **n**_____93) state, and allowing it will in turn reset our **i**_____94) scale back to balance.

2024_H2_11_24

M_____95) m_____96) sow seeds of doubt about the a_____97) of our current devices. Suddenly, the phone that was your lifeline a year ago is now a museum piece, unable to keep pace with your digital demands. And thus, the i_____98) to u_____99) begins, often before there's a g_____100) need. This cycle isn't just c_____101) to our digital c_____102) . It s_____103) over into almost every a_____104) of consumer electronics, from the self-driving car to the smart fridge. Every product seems to be on an u_____105) march towards the next version, the next g_____106) that promises to r_____107) your life. What's fascinating, or perhaps disturbing, is the utter e_____108) of this c_____109) in shaping our desires. It's not so much that we want the newest device; we're led to believe we need it. The d_____110) between want and need b_____111) , shifting our f_____112) p_____113) in favor of staying c_____114) with trends. For all the l_____115) arguments against this c_____116) upgrading, the t_____117) remains c_____118) .

2024_H2_11_29

C_____119) Place Preference is a way of finding out what animals want. R_____120) train them to a_____121) one place with an experience such as food or a loud noise and another place with something completely different, usually w_____122) nothing happens. The two places are made o_____123) different to make it as easy as possible for the animal to a_____124) each place with what happened to it there. The animal's p_____125) for being in one place or another is measured both before and after its experiences in the two places. If there is a s_____126) in where the animal chooses to spend its time for the reward, this suggests that it liked the experience and is trying to repeat it. C_____127) , if it now a_____128) the place the s_____129) appeared and starts to prefer the place it did not experience it, then this suggests that it found the stimulus unpleasant. For example, mice with c_____130) show a p_____131) for the place where they have been given morphine, a drug used to r_____132) pain, rather than where they have received s_____133) whereas healthy mice developed no such p_____134) . This suggests that the mice with cancer wanted the morphine.

2024_H2_11_30

Near the e_____135) , many species of bird b_____136) all year round. But in t_____137) and p_____138) regions, the breeding seasons of birds are often sharply defined. They are t_____139) mainly by changes in day length. If all goes well, the outcome is that birds raise their young when the food supply is at its p_____140) . Most birds are not simply r_____141) to breed at other times but they are also p_____142) incapable of doing so. This is because their r_____143) system s_____144) , which helps flying birds save weight. The main exception to this rule are n_____145) desert species. These can i_____146) their breeding cycle within days of rain. It's for making the most of the sudden breeding opportunity. Also, different species divide the b_____147) season up in different ways. Most seabirds raise a single b_____148) . In warm regions, however, songbirds may raise several families in a few months. In an e_____149) good year, a pair of House Sparrows, a kind of songbird, can raise s_____150) broods through a marathon r_____151) effort.

2024_H2_11_31

One factor that may **h**_____152) creativity is **u**_____153) of the resources required in each activity in students' learning. Often students are unable to identify the resources they need to perform the task required of them. Different resources may be **c**_____154) for specific learning tasks, and recognizing them may **s**_____155) the activity's performance. For example, it may be that students desire to conduct some experiments in their projects. There must be a **p**_____156) investigation of whether the students will have **a**_____157) to the laboratory, equipment, and chemicals required for the experiment. It means preparation is **v**_____158) for the students to succeed, and it may be about human and **f**_____159) resources such as laboratory **t**_____160) , money to purchase chemicals, and equipment for their learning where **a**_____161) . Even if some of the resources required for a task may not be available, **i**_____162) them in advance may help students' creativity. It may even lead to changing the topic, finding **a**_____163) resources, and other means.

2024_H2_11_32

All translators feel some **p**_____164) from the community of readers for whom they are doing their work. And all translators arrive at their **i**_____165) in **d**_____166) with other people. The English poet Alexander Pope had pretty good Greek, but when he set about translating Homer's *Iliad* in the early 18th century he was not on his own. He had Greek **c**_____167) to refer to, and **t**_____168) that had already been done in English, Latin, and French — and of course he had dictionaries. Translators always draw on more than one **s**_____169) text. Even when the scene of translation **c**_____170) just one person with a pen, paper, and the book that is being translated, or even when it is just one person translating **o**_____171) for another, that person's **l**_____172) knowledge **a**_____173) from lots of other texts and other conversations. And then his or her idea of the translation's purpose will be influenced by the **e**_____174) of the person or people it is for. In both these **s**_____175) every translation is a crowd translation.

2024_H2_11_33

Some people argue that there is a single, **l**_____176) **c**_____177) concept known as reading that can be neatly set apart from everything else people do with books. Is reading really that simple? The most **p**_____178) way to think about reading is as a loosely **r**_____179) set of behaviors that belong together owing to family **r**_____180) , as Ludwig Wittgenstein used the **p**_____181) , without having in common a single defining **t**_____182) . Consequently, efforts to **d**_____183) reading from nonreading are **d**_____184) to fail because there is no agreement on what **q**_____185) as reading in the first place. The more one tries to figure out where the border lies between reading and not-reading, the more edge cases will be found to **s**_____186) the term's **f**_____187) boundaries. Thus, it is worth **a**_____188) to collect together these exceptional forms of reading into a single **f**_____189) , one highlighting the challenges **f**_____190) by anyone wishing to establish the boundaries where reading begins and ends. The attempt moves toward an understanding of reading as a **s**_____191) that is **e**_____192) enough to **a**_____193) the **d**_____194) reading activities.

## 2024_H2_11_34

Weber's law c_____195) the perception of difference between two stimuli. It suggests that we might not be able to d_____196) a 1-mm difference when we are looking at lines 466 mm and 467 mm in length, but we may be able to d_____197) a 1-mm difference when we are comparing a line 2 mm long with one 3 mm long. Another example of this p_____198) is that we can d_____199) 1 candle when it is lit in an otherwise dark room. But when 1 candle is l_____200) in a room in which 100 candles are already burning, we may not notice the light from this candle. Therefore, the Just-noticeable difference (JND) v_____201) as a function of the s_____202) of the signals. For example, the JND is greater for very loud noises than it is for much more quiet sounds. When a sound is very weak, we can tell that another sound is l_____203) , even if it is b_____204) louder. When a sound is very loud, to tell that another sound is even louder, it has to be much louder. Thus, Weber's l_____205) means that it is harder to d_____206) between two samples when those samples are larger or stronger levels of the s_____207) .

## 2024_H2_11_35

Any new resource (e.g., a new airport, a new mall) always opens with people b_____208) individually by sharing a common resource (e.g., the city or state budget). Soon, at some point, the amount of traffic grows too large for the "commons" to support. Traffic jams, overcrowding, and o_____209) lessen the b_____210) of the common resource for everyone —the tragedy of the commons! If the new resource cannot be e_____211) or provided with additional space, it becomes a problem, and you cannot solve the problem on your own, in i_____212) from your fellow drivers or walkers or c_____213) users. The total activity on this new r_____214) keeps increasing, and so does individual activity; but if the dynamic of common use and o_____215) continues too long, both begin to fall after a peak, leading to a c_____216) . What makes the "_____217) of commons" t_____218) is the crash dynamic —the destruction or d_____219) of the common resource's ability to r_____220) itself.

## 2024_H2_11_36

T_____221) , our brain would have the c_____222) to s_____223) all experiences throughout life, reaching the quality of a DVD. However, this theoretical capacity is o_____224) by the energy demand associated with the process of storing and r_____225) information in memory. As a result, the brain develops e_____226) strategies, becoming d_____227) on shortcuts. When we o_____228) a face, the visual image captured by the eyes is highly v_____229) , depending on the point of view, lighting conditions and other c_____230) factors. Nevertheless, we are able to recognize the face as the same, maintaining the u_____231) identity. The brain, rather than focusing on the details of v_____232) , creates and stores g_____233) patterns that allow for consistent recognition across d_____234) circumstances. This ability to match what we see with general v_____235) memory patterns serves as an effective mechanism for o_____236) brain performance and saving energy. The brain, being n_____237) against unnecessary effort, constantly seeks to s_____238) and g_____239) information to f_____240) the c_____241) process.

## 2024_H2_11_37

Where scientific research is c_____242), e_____243) t_____244) are expected to a_____245) closely to experimental data and to i_____246) the regular and p_____247) features of experience. However, this p_____248) sometimes c_____249) the fact that theories are deeply loaded with creative elements that shape the c_____250) of research projects and the interpretations of evidence. Scientific explanations do not just relate a c_____251) of facts. They construct frameworks for s_____252) chosen data in order to provide a consistent and m_____253) explanation of what is observed. Such constructions lead us to imagine specific kinds of subject matter in particular sorts of relations, and the s_____254) they i_____255) will prove more effective for analyzing some features of experience over others. When we n_____256) the creative c_____257) of such scientific i_____258) and treat models and interpretive explanations as s_____259) facts — even worse, as facts including all of reality — we can b_____260) ourselves to the l_____261) of a given model and fail to note its p_____ _262) for m_____263) a situation to which it ill applies.

## 2024_H2_11_38

We e_____264) c_____265) claims about the relation of l_____266) to action. Theorists have maintained that literature e_____267) s_____268) reading and reflection as the way to engage with the world and thus counters the social and political activities that might produce social change. At best it encourages d_____269) or appreciation of complexity, and at worst p_____ _270) and acceptance of what is. But on the other hand, literature has historically been seen as dangerous: it p_____271) the questioning of a_____272) and social a_____273). Plato b_____ _274) poets from his ideal republic because they could only do harm, and n_____275) have long been c_____276) with making people d_____277) with their lives and eager for something new. By promoting identification across d_____278) of class, gender, and race, books may promote a f_____279) that d_____280) struggle; but they may also produce a keen sense of i_____281) that makes progressive struggles possible. Historically, works of literature are c_____282) with producing change: *Uncle Tom's Cabin*, a best-seller in its day, helped create a r_____283) against s_____284) that made possible the American Civil War.

## 2024_H2_11_39

According to Hobbes, man is not a being who can act morally in s_____285) his instinct to protect his existence in the state of nature. Hence, the only place where morality and moral l_____286) will begin to find an application begins in a place where a s_____287) power, namely the state, e_____288). Hobbes thus describes the state of nature as a c_____289) in which man's life is "solitary, poor, nasty, brutish and short". It means when people live without a general power to control them all, they are indeed in a s_____290) of war. In other words, Hobbes, who a_____291) that human beings are not social and political beings in the state of nature, believes that without the power human beings in the state of nature are "_____292) and r_____293) based on their selfishness". Moreover, since society is not a natural p_____294) and there is no natural f_____295) bringing people together, what will bring them together as a society is not m_____296) a_____297) according to Hobbes. It is, rather, m_____298) fear of men's present and future that a_____299) them, since the cause of fear is a common d_____300) among people in the state of nature.

## 2024_H2_11_40

There is research that supports the idea that **c**_____**301)** factors influence the phenomenology of the **p**_____**302)** world. Delk and Fillenbaum asked participants to match the color of figures with the color of their background. Some of the figures **d**_____**303)** objects associated with a **p**_____**304)** color. These included **t**_____**305)** red objects such as an apple, lips, and a **s**_____**306)** heart. Other objects were **p**_____**307)** that are not usually associated with red, such as a mushroom or a bell. However, all the figures were made out of the same red-orange cardboard. Participants then had to match the figure to a background **v**_____**308)** from dark to light red. They had to make the background color match the color of the figures. The researchers found that red-associated objects **r**_____**309)** more red in the background to be judged a **m**_____**_310)** than did the objects that are not associated with the color red. This **i**_____**311)** that the cognitive association of objects to color influences how we perceive that color.

## 2024_H2_11_41~42

In each round of **g**_____**312)** copying in our body, there is still about a 70 percent chance that at least one pair of **c**_____**313)** will have an error. With each round of genome copying, errors **a**_____**314)** . This is similar to **a**_____**315)** in **m**_____**316)** books. Each time a copy was made by hand, some changes were introduced accidentally; as changes **s**_____**317)** up, the copies may have acquired meanings at **v**_____**318)** with the original. Similarly, genomes that have **u**_____**319)** more copying processes will have **g**_____**320)** more mistakes. To make things worse, **m**_____**321)** may damage genes responsible for error checking and repair of genomes, further **a**_____**322)** the introduction of mutations. Most genome mutations do not have any **n**_____**323)** effects. It is just like changing the *i* for a *y* in "kingdom" would not **d**_____**324)** the word's **r**_____**325)** . But sometimes a **m**_____**326)** to a human gene results in, for example, an eye whose **i**_____**327)** is of two different colors. Similarly, almost everyone has **b**_____**328)** , which are **d**_____**329)** to mutations that occurred as our body's cells **m**_____**330)** to form skin. If mutations are changes to the genome of one **p**_____**331)** cell, how can a patch of cells in an iris or a whole **p**_____**332)** of skin, consisting of many individual cells, be affected **s**_____**333)** ? The answer lies in the cell **l**_____**334)** , the developmental history of a tissue from particular cells through to their fully **d**_____**335)** state. If the mutation occurred early on in the **l**_____**336)** of the developing iris, then all cells in that patch have inherited that change.

2024_H2_11_43~45

Max awoke to the gentle sunlight of an **a**_____ 337) day. Right on schedule, he swung his legs off the bed and took a deep, satisfying breath. He began his morning the same way he usually did, getting dressed and going to school. Today was going to be another perfect day until he ran into Mr. Kapoor, his science teacher. "Just to remind you. Science fair projects are **d**_____ 338) next Wednesday. Don't forget to **s**_____ 339) your final draft on time," Mr. Kapoor said. Max froze. *What? It can't be! It was due next Friday!* After school, he came home worrying that his whole perfectly planned week was going to be ruined. Without his usual greeting, Max headed to his room in haste. "What's wrong Max?," Jeremy, his dad, followed Max, worrying about him. Max furiously **b**_____ 340) through his planner without answering him, only to find the wrong date written in it. Fighting through tears, Max finally **m**_____ 341) to explain the **u**_____ 342) pressure to be perfect to his dad. To his surprise, Jeremy laughed. "Max, guess what? Perfect is a great goal, but nobody gets there all the time. What matters is what we do when things get messy." That made him feel a little better. "You are saying I can fix this?" "Absolutely, try to deal with problems in a **l**_____ 343) way," Jeremy said. Max thought for a moment. "I guess…. I can do that by **r**_____ 344) tonight's baseball lesson." Jeremy **b**_____ 345) . "See? That's you finding a solution." Max felt a **g**_____ 346) smile spreading. The next Wednesday, he successfully handed in the final **d**_____ 347) on time with satisfaction. From then on, he still loved order and **r**_____ 348) , but also **e**_____ 349) the messy, **u**_____ 350) bits of life too.

# 2024 고2 11월 모의고사

❶ voca    ❷ text    ❸ [ / ]    ❹ ____    ❺ quiz 1    ❻ quiz 2    ❼ quiz 3    ❽ quiz 4    ❾ quiz 5

1. 18[1)]

(A) Thank you for your attention. Best regards, Matt Perry

(B) As the coordinator, it is becoming apparent to me that the budget, previously approved by your department, needs some adjustments in order to meet the emerging modifications. Since my department has hired three more interns than planned initially, the most expensive need is for additional funding to cover their wages, training costs, and materials.

(C) Dear Executive Manager Schulz,

(D) It is a week before the internship program starts. I am writing to bring your attention to a matter that requires immediate consideration regarding the issue my department has.

(E) I kindly request an additional budget allocation for these expenses. Please refer to the attachment for details.

2. 19[2)]

(A) The receptionist couldn't find her reservation under the name 'Katie'. "I'm sorry, but I can't seem to locate a reservation under that name," the receptionist said.

(B) "Just a moment," the receptionist said, typing deliberately on the keyboard. "I found it! It seems there was a small misspelling. Your reservation is under 'K-A-T-Y'," the receptionist explained.

(C) With a sense of ease, Katie watched her reservation appearing on the screen. With her heart slowing to a gentle rhythm, she proceeded with her check-in, thinking that a simple misspelling might have ruined her plans.

(D) "No way, I definitely made a reservation on the phone," Katie said, puzzled. The receptionist asked, "Can you tell me your phone number?" and Katie told it to him, thinking 'What happened? Did I make a mistake?'

(E) Katie approached the hotel front desk to check-in but an unexpected event unfolded.

3. 20[3)]

(A) To be mathematically literate means to be able to think critically about societal issues on which mathematics has bearing so as to make informed decisions about how to solve these problems.

(B) Therefore, making decisions, even qualitatively, is not possible without using mathematics and critical thinking.

(C) Navigating our world means being able to quantify, measure, estimate, classify, compare, find patterns, conjecture, justify, prove, and generalize within critical thinking and when using critical thinking.

(D) Dealing with such complex problems through interdisciplinary approaches, mirroring real-world problems requires innovative ways of planning and organizing mathematical teaching methods.

(E) Thus, teaching mathematics should be done in interaction with critical thinking along with a decision-making process. They can be developed into the mathematical context, so that there is no excuse to not explicitly support students to develop them.

4. p3-no.21[4)]

(A) But his change of heart is not entirely satisfying. According to Zagzebski, an American philosopher, he is not really generous. When we praise someone's character, we use words for various virtues: 'generous', 'kind', 'courageous', etc.

(B) Undoubtedly, there is something praiseworthy about the action. You'd be pleased to receive the gift. You'd say 'thank you', and mean it.

(C) Imagine that your usually stingy friend delights in buying you a Christmas present after taking a generosity booster. How would you feel?

(D) A person who gives one gift isn't generous. Instead, generosity is a stable part of a person's 'moral identity', an emotional habit that is part of who you are. Thus virtues, as opposed to nontypical impulse, are the result of your personal history.

(E) They are part of who you are, as they are part of how your character was formed. Instant virtue is therefore impossible. Popping a pill cannot make you a better person.

5. p3-no.22[5)]

(A) Things get much more complicated if I want to know the mass of a distant star.

(B) We can roughly say that measuring the mass of a star involves various theories. If we want to measure the mass of a binary star, we first determine a center of mass between the two stars, then their distance from that center which we can then use, together with a value for the period and a certain instance of Kepler's Third Law, to calculate the mass.

(C) In other words, in order to "measure" the star mass, we measure other quantities and use those values, together with certain equations, to calculate the mass. Measurement is not a simple and unmediated estimation of independently existing properties, but a determination of certain magnitudes before the background of a number of accepted theories.

(D) To determine the mass of my bowling ball, I might put it onto a balance and compare it with a known mass, such as a number of metal cubes each weighing 1, 10, or 100 grams.

(E) How do I measure it?

6. 23<sup>6)</sup>

(A) We've all heard the expression, "No pain, no gain." Well, according to psychiatrist Dr. Anna Lembke, there may be some truth to these words.

(B) Pleasure and pain are like two sides of the same coin; they seem to work together and are heavily reliant on one another and keep balance. If you imagine pleasure and pain as the two opposite points on a scale, you can easily understand that as one of the two points rises, the other must correspondingly fall.

(C) Our bodies constantly strive for homeostasis, which is defined as the balance of bodily functions. Without the body's effective compensatory mechanisms, which may cushion potential highs and lows, we would not be capable of surviving.

(D) She says that our attempts to escape being miserable are in fact making us even more miserable. This is because pain is actually an essential component of our ability to maintain a neutral state, and allowing it will in turn reset our internal scale back to balance.

(E) Based on discoveries in neuroscience, pain and pleasure are formed and processed in the same area of the brain.

7. 24<sup>7)</sup>

(A) Manufacturers masterfully sow seeds of doubt about the adequacy of our current devices. Suddenly, the phone that was your lifeline a year ago is now a museum piece, unable to keep pace with your digital demands.

(B) And thus, the itch to upgrade begins, often before there's a genuine need. This cycle isn't just confined to our digital companions.

(C) What's fascinating, or perhaps disturbing, is the utter efficacy of this cycle in shaping our desires. It's not so much that we want the newest device; we're led to believe we need it.

(D) The distinction between want and need blurs, shifting our financial priorities in favor of staying current with trends. For all the logical arguments against this ceaseless upgrading, the temptation remains compelling.

(E) It spills over into almost every aspect of consumer electronics, from the self-driving car to the smart fridge. Every product seems to be on an unstoppable march towards the next version, the next generation that promises to revolutionize your life.

8. 26<sup>8)</sup>

(A) Helen Suzman was an activist against apartheid, a racist political and social system in the Republic of South Africa.

(B) While working as a lecturer on economic history at Witwatersrand University, she joined the South African Institute of Race Relations.

(C) Even after her retirement in 1989, she continued to advocate for a multi-racial democracy in the Republic of South Africa and influenced the drafting of the country's new constitution after the end of apartheid. She remained an active voice for human rights and democracy until her death in 2009.

(D) Suzman was born to Jewish immigrant parents in Germiston in the Union of South Africa in 1917.

(E) In 1953, she joined the United Party and was elected to Parliament, but when the United Party adopted a more moderate stance on apartheid, Suzman and other progressive members left it and formed the Progressive Party in 1959. Suzman tirelessly fought against apartheid, exposing the government's abuses and challenging its laws for a total of 36 years in Parliament.

9. 29⁹⁾

(A) Researchers train them to associate one place with an experience such as food or a loud noise and another place with something completely different, usually where nothing happens.

(B) If there is a shift in where the animal chooses to spend its time for the reward, this suggests that it liked the experience and is trying to repeat it. Conversely, if it now avoids the place the stimulus appeared and starts to prefer the place it did not experience it, then this suggests that it found the stimulus unpleasant.

(C) The two places are made obviously different to make it as easy as possible for the animal to associate each place with what happened to it there. The animal's preference for being in one place or another is measured both before and after its experiences in the two places.

(D) For example, mice with cancer show a preference for the place where they have been given morphine, a drug used to relieve pain, rather than where they have received saline whereas healthy mice developed no such preference. This suggests that the mice with cancer wanted the morphine.

(D) For example, mice with cancer show a preference for the place where they have been given morphine, a drug used to relieve pain, rather than where they have received saline whereas healthy mice developed no such preference. This suggests that the mice with cancer wanted the morphine.

10. 30¹⁰⁾

(A) These can initiate their breeding cycle within days of rain. It's for making the most of the sudden breeding opportunity. Also, different species divide the breeding season up in different ways.

(B) Most birds are not simply reluctant to breed at other times but they are also physically incapable of doing so. This is because their reproductive system shrinks, which helps flying birds save weight. The main exception to this rule are nomadic desert species.

(C) They are triggered mainly by changes in day length. If all goes well, the outcome is that birds raise their young when the food supply is at its peak.

(D) Near the equator, many species of bird breed all year round. But in temperate and polar regions, the breeding seasons of birds are often sharply defined.

(E) Most seabirds raise a single brood. In warm regions, however, songbirds may raise several families in a few months. In an exceptionally good year, a pair of House Sparrows, a kind of songbird, can raise successive broods through a marathon reproductive effort.

11. 31¹¹⁾

(A) Often students are unable to identify the resources they need to perform the task required of them.

(B) Even if some of the resources required for a task may not be available, identifying them in advance may help students' creativity. It may even lead to changing the topic, finding alternative resources, and other means.

(C) Different resources may be compulsory for specific learning tasks, and recognizing them may simplify the activity's performance. For example, it may be that students desire to conduct some experiments in their projects.

(D) There must be a prior investigation of whether the students will have access to the laboratory, equipment, and chemicals required for the experiment. It means preparation is vital for the students to succeed, and it may be about human and financial resources such as laboratory technicians, money to purchase chemicals, and equipment for their learning where applicable.

(E) One factor that may hinder creativity is unawareness of the resources required in each activity in students' learning.

12. 32[12]

(A) Translators always draw on more than one source text. Even when the scene of translation consists of just one person with a pen, paper, and the book that is being translated, or even when it is just one person translating orally for another, that person's linguistic knowledge arises from lots of other texts and other conversations.

(B) And then his or her idea of the translation's purpose will be influenced by the expectations of the person or people it is for. In both these senses every translation is a crowd translation.

(C) And all translators arrive at their interpretations in dialogue with other people.

(D) All translators feel some pressure from the community of readers for whom they are doing their work.

(E) The English poet Alexander Pope had pretty good Greek, but when he set about translating Homer's Iliad in the early 18th century he was not on his own. He had Greek commentaries to refer to, and translations that had already been done in English, Latin, and French — and of course he had dictionaries.

13. 33[13]

(A) Some people argue that there is a single, logically consistent concept known as reading that can be neatly set apart from everything else people do with books.

(B) Consequently, efforts to distinguish reading from nonreading are destined to fail because there is no agreement on what qualifies as reading in the first place. The more one tries to figure out where the border lies between reading and not-reading, the more edge cases will be found to stretch the term's flexible boundaries.

(C) Is reading really that simple?

(D) The most productive way to think about reading is as a loosely related set of behaviors that belong together owing to family resemblances, as Ludwig Wittgenstein used the phrase, without having in common a single defining trait.

(E) Thus, it is worth attempting to collect together these exceptional forms of reading into a single forum, one highlighting the challenges faced by anyone wishing to establish the boundaries where reading begins and ends. The attempt moves toward an understanding of reading as a spectrum that is expansive enough to accommodate the distinct reading activities.

14. 34[14]

(A) Weber's law concerns the perception of difference between two stimuli.

(B) But when 1 candle is lit in a room in which 100 candles are already burning, we may not notice the light from this candle. Therefore, the Just-noticeable difference (JND) varies as a function of the strength of the signals.

(C) For example, the JND is greater for very loud noises than it is for much more quiet sounds. When a sound is very weak, we can tell that another sound is louder, even if it is barely louder.

(D) It suggests that we might not be able to detect a 1-mm difference when we are looking at lines 466 mm and 467 mm in length, but we may be able to detect a 1-mm difference when we are comparing a line 2 mm long with one 3 mm long. Another example of this principle is that we can detect 1 candle when it is lit in an otherwise dark room.

(E) When a sound is very loud, to tell that another sound is even louder, it has to be much louder. Thus, Weber's law means that it is harder to distinguish between two samples when those samples are larger or stronger levels of the stimuli.

**15. 35¹⁵⁾**

(A) The total activity on this new resource keeps increasing, and so does individual activity; but if the dynamic of common use and overuse continues too long, both begin to fall after a peak, leading to a crash. What makes the "tragedy of commons" tragic is the crash dynamic — the destruction or degeneration of the common resource's ability to regenerate itself.

(B) Soon, at some point, the amount of traffic grows too large for the "commons" to support.

(C) Traffic jams, overcrowding, and overuse lessen the benefits of the common resource for everyone — the tragedy of the commons!

(D) If the new resource cannot be expanded or provided with additional space, it becomes a problem, and you cannot solve the problem on your own, in isolation from your fellow drivers or walkers or competing users.

(E) Any new resource (e.g., a new airport, a new mall) always opens with people benefiting individually by sharing a common resource (e.g., the city or state budget).

**16. 36¹⁶⁾**

(A) Theoretically, our brain would have the capacity to store all experiences throughout life, reaching the quality of a DVD.

(B) However, this theoretical capacity is offset by the energy demand associated with the process of storing and retrieving information in memory.

(C) Nevertheless, we are able to recognize the face as the same, maintaining the underlying identity. The brain, rather than focusing on the details of visualization, creates and stores general patterns that allow for consistent recognition across diverse circumstances.

(D) This ability to match what we see with general visual memory patterns serves as an effective mechanism for optimizing brain performance and saving energy. The brain, being naturally against unnecessary effort, constantly seeks to simplify and generalize information to facilitate the cognitive process.

(E) As a result, the brain develops efficient strategies, becoming dependent on shortcuts. When we observe a face, the visual image captured by the eyes is highly variable, depending on the point of view, lighting conditions and other contextual factors.

**17. 37¹⁷⁾**

(A) However, this paradigm sometimes conceals the fact that theories are deeply loaded with creative elements that shape the construction of research projects and the interpretations of evidence.

(B) They construct frameworks for systematically chosen data in order to provide a consistent and meaningful explanation of what is observed.

(C) Where scientific research is concerned, explanatory tales are expected to adhere closely to experimental data and to illuminate the regular and predictable features of experience.

(D) Such constructions lead us to imagine specific kinds of subject matter in particular sorts of relations, and the storylines they inspire will prove more effective for analyzing some features of experience over others. When we neglect the creative contributions of such scientific imagination and treat models and interpretive explanations as straightforward facts — even worse, as facts including all of reality — we can blind ourselves to the limitations of a given model and fail to note its potential for misunderstanding a situation to which it ill applies.

(E) Scientific explanations do not just relate a chronology of facts.

18. 38[18)]

(A) Theorists have maintained that literature encourages solitary reading and reflection as the way to engage with the world and thus counters the social and political activities that might produce social change.

(B) We encounter contrary claims about the relation of literature to action.

(C) By promoting identification across divisions of class, gender, and race, books may promote a fellowship that discourages struggle; but they may also produce a keen sense of injustice that makes progressive struggles possible. Historically, works of literature are credited with producing change: Uncle Tom's Cabin, a best-seller in its day, helped create a revulsion against slavery that made possible the American Civil War.

(D) But on the other hand, literature has historically been seen as dangerous: it promotes the questioning of authority and social arrangements. Plato banned poets from his ideal republic because they could only do harm, and novels have long been credited with making people dissatisfied with their lives and eager for something new.

(E) At best it encourages detachment or appreciation of complexity, and at worst passivity and acceptance of what is.

19. 39[19)]

(A) Moreover, since society is not a natural phenomenon and there is no natural force bringing people together, what will bring them together as a society is not mutual affection according to Hobbes. It is, rather, mutual fear of men's present and future that assembles them, since the cause of fear is a common drive among people in the state of nature.

(B) Hence, the only place where morality and moral liberty will begin to find an application begins in a place where a sovereign power, namely the state, emerges.

(C) According to Hobbes, man is not a being who can act morally in spite of his instinct to protect his existence in the state of nature.

(D) Hobbes thus describes the state of nature as a circumstance in which man's life is "solitary, poor, nasty, brutish and short".

(E) It means when people live without a general power to control them all, they are indeed in a state of war. In other words, Hobbes, who accepted that human beings are not social and political beings in the state of nature, believes that without the power human beings in the state of nature are "antisocial and rational based on their selfishness".

20. 40[20)]

(A) Some of the figures depicted objects associated with a particular color. These included typically red objects such as an apple, lips, and a symbolic heart.

(B) The researchers found that red-associated objects required more red in the background to be judged a match than did the objects that are not associated with the color red. This implies that the cognitive association of objects to color influences how we perceive that color. —> In one study, participants chose greater redness when asked to match the color of objects that are usually red to a background with the same color, which showed that their knowledge about the colors of objects influenced their perceptual judgment.

(C) Other objects were presented that are not usually associated with red, such as a mushroom or a bell. However, all the figures were made out of the same red-orange cardboard.

(D) There is research that supports the idea that cognitive factors influence the phenomenology of the perceived world. Delk and Fillenbaum asked participants to match the color of figures with the color of their background.

(E) Participants then had to match the figure to a background varying from dark to light red. They had to make the background color match the color of the figures.

**21.** 41~42[21)]

(A) In each round of genome copying in our body, there is still about a 70 percent chance that at least one pair of chromosomes will have an error. With each round of genome copying, errors accumulate.

(B) If mutations are changes to the genome of one particular cell, how can a patch of cells in an iris or a whole patch of skin, consisting of many individual cells, be affected simultaneously? The answer lies in the cell lineage, the developmental history of a tissue from particular cells through to their fully differentiated state. If the mutation occurred early on in the lineage of the developing iris, then all cells in that patch have inherited that change.

(C) Similarly, genomes that have undergone more copying processes will have gathered more mistakes. To make things worse, mutations may damage genes responsible for error checking and repair of genomes, further accelerating the introduction of mutations. Most genome mutations do not have any noticeable effects.

(D) This is similar to alterations in medieval books. Each time a copy was made by hand, some changes were introduced accidentally; as changes stacked up, the copies may have acquired meanings at variance with the original.

(E) It is just like changing the i for a y in "kingdom" would not distort the word's readability. But sometimes a mutation to a human gene results in, for example, an eye whose iris is of two different colors. Similarly, almost everyone has birthmarks, which are due to mutations that occurred as our body's cells multiplied to form skin.

**22.** 43~45[22)]

(A) "I guess…. I can do that by rescheduling tonight's baseball lesson." Jeremy beamed. "See? That's you finding a solution." Max felt a genuine smile spreading. The next Wednesday, he successfully handed in the final draft on time with satisfaction. From then on, he still loved order and routines, but also embraced the messy, unpredictable bits of life too.

(B) Don't forget to submit your final draft on time," Mr. Kapoor said. Max froze. What? It can't be! It was due next Friday! After school, he came home worrying that his whole perfectly planned week was going to be ruined. Without his usual greeting, Max headed to his room in haste.

(C) "What's wrong Max?," Jeremy, his dad, followed Max, worrying about him. Max furiously browsed through his planner without answering him, only to find the wrong date written in it. Fighting through tears, Max finally managed to explain the unending pressure to be perfect to his dad. To his surprise, Jeremy laughed. "Max, guess what? Perfect is a great goal, but nobody gets there all the time.

(D) Max awoke to the gentle sunlight of an autumn day. Right on schedule, he swung his legs off the bed and took a deep, satisfying breath. He began his morning the same way he usually did, getting dressed and going to school. Today was going to be another perfect day until he ran into Mr. Kapoor, his science teacher. "Just to remind you. Science fair projects are due next Wednesday.

(E) What matters is what we do when things get messy." That made him feel a little better. "You are saying I can fix this?" "Absolutely, try to deal with problems in a logical way," Jeremy said. Max thought for a moment.

# 2024 고2 11월 모의고사

❶ voca  ❷ text  ❸ [ / ]  ❹ ____  ❺ quiz 1  ❻ quiz 2  ❼ quiz 3  ❽ quiz 4  ❾ quiz 5

**1.** 1)**밑줄 친 부분 중, 어법, 혹은 문맥상 어색한 곳을 고르시오.** 2024_H2_11_18

Dear Executive Manager Schulz,It is a week before the internship program starts. I am writing to bring your attention to a matter that ①**requires** immediate consideration regarding the issue my department has. As the coordinator, it is becoming ②**apparent** to me that the budget, previously ③**approved** by your department, ④**needs** some adjustments in order to meet the emerging modifications. Since my department has ⑤**been hired** three more interns than planned initially, the most expensive need is for additional funding to cover their wages, training costs, and materials. I kindly request an additional budget allocation for these expenses. Please refer to the attachment for details. Thank you for your attention.Best regards,Matt Perry

**2.** 2)**밑줄 친 부분 중, 어법, 혹은 문맥상 어색한 곳을 고르시오.** 2024_H2_11_19

Katie ①**approached** the hotel front desk to check-in but an unexpected event unfolded. The receptionist couldn't find her reservation under the name 'Katie'. "I'm sorry, but I can't seem to locate a reservation under that name," the receptionist said. "No way, I definitely made a reservation on the phone," Katie said, puzzled. The receptionist asked, "Can you tell me your phone number?" and Katie told ②**it** to him, ③**thought** 'What happened? Did I make a mistake?' "Just a moment," the receptionist said, typing deliberately on the keyboard. "I found it! It seems there was a small misspelling. Your reservation is under 'K-A-T-Y'," the receptionist explained. With a sense of ease, Katie watched her reservation appearing on the screen. With her heart slowing to a gentle rhythm, she ④**proceeded** with her check-in, thinking that a simple misspelling might have ⑤**ruined** her plans.

**3.** 3)**밑줄 친 부분 중, 어법, 혹은 문맥상 어색한 곳을 고르시오.** 2024_H2_11_20

To be mathematically ①**literate** means to be able to think critically about societal issues on ②**which** mathematics has bearing so as to make ③**informed** decisions about how to solve these problems. Dealing with such complex problems through interdisciplinary approaches, mirroring real-world problems requires innovative ways of planning and organizing mathematical teaching methods. Navigating our world means being able to quantify, measure, estimate, classify, compare, find patterns, ④**conjecture**, justify, prove, and generalize within critical thinking and when using critical thinking. Therefore, making decisions, even qualitatively, is not possible without using mathematics and critical thinking. Thus, teaching mathematics should be done in interaction with critical thinking along with a decision-making process. They can ⑤**develop** into the mathematical context, so that there is no excuse to not explicitly support students to develop them.

**4.** ⁴⁾**밑줄 친 부분 중, 어법, 혹은 문맥상 어색한 곳을 고르시오.** 2024_H2_11_21

Imagine that your usually stingy friend delights in buying you a Christmas present after taking a generosity booster. How would you feel? Undoubtedly, there is ①**something praiseworthy** about the action. You'd be pleased to receive the gift. You'd say 'thank you', and mean it. But his change of heart is not entirely satisfying. According to Zagzebski, an American philosopher, he is not really generous. When we praise someone's character, we use words for various virtues: 'generous', 'kind', 'courageous', etc. A person who gives one gift isn't generous. Instead, generosity is a stable part of a person's 'moral identity', an emotional ②**habitat** that is part of who you are. Thus virtues, as opposed to nontypical ③**impulse**, ④**are** the result of your personal history. They are part of who you are, as they are part of ⑤**how** your character was formed. Instant virtue is therefore impossible. Popping a pill cannot make you a better person.

**5.** ⁵⁾**밑줄 친 부분 중, 어법, 혹은 문맥상 어색한 곳을 고르시오.** 2024_H2_11_22

To determine the mass of my bowling ball, I might put it onto a balance and compare it with a ①**known** mass, such as a number of metal cubes each ②**weighing** 1, 10, or 100 grams. Things get ③**much** more complicated if I want to know the mass of a distant star. How do I measure it? We can roughly say that measuring the mass of a star involves various theories. If we want to measure the mass of a binary star, we first determine a center of mass between the two stars, then their distance from that center which we can then use, together with a value for the period and a certain instance of Kepler's Third Law, to calculate the mass. In other words, in order to "measure" the star mass, we measure other quantities and use those values, together with certain equations, to calculate the mass. Measurement is not a simple and ④**unmediated** estimation of ⑤**interdependently** existing properties, but a determination of certain magnitudes before the background of a number of accepted theories.

**6.** ⁶⁾**밑줄 친 부분 중, 어법, 혹은 문맥상 어색한 곳을 고르시오.** 2024_H2_11_23

Based on discoveries in neuroscience, pain and pleasure are formed and processed in the same area of the brain. Our bodies constantly strive for homeostasis, ①**which** is defined as the balance of bodily functions. Without the body's effective ②**compensatory** mechanisms, which may cushion potential highs and lows, we would not be capable of surviving. Pleasure and pain are like two sides of the same coin; they seem to work together and are heavily reliant on one another and keep balance. If you imagine pleasure and pain as the two ③**similar** points on a scale, you can easily understand that as one of the two points rises, the other must correspondingly fall. We've all heard the expression, "No pain, no gain." Well, according to psychiatrist Dr. Anna Lembke, there may be some truth to these words. She says that our attempts to escape ④**being** miserable are in fact making us even more miserable. This is because pain is actually an essential component of our ability to maintain a neutral state, and allowing ⑤**it** will in turn reset our internal scale back to balance.

**7.** 7)**밑줄 친 부분 중, 어법, 혹은 문맥상 어색한 곳을 고르시오.** 2024_H2_11_24

Manufacturers masterfully ①**saw** seeds of doubt about the adequacy of our current devices. Suddenly, the phone that was your lifeline a year ago is now a museum piece, unable to keep pace with your digital demands. And thus, the itch to upgrade begins, often before there's a genuine need. This cycle isn't just confined to our digital companions. It spills over into almost every aspect of consumer electronics, from the self-driving car to the smart fridge. Every product seems to be on an unstoppable march towards the next version, the next generation that promises to ② **revolutionize** your life. What's ③**fascinating**, or perhaps disturbing, is the utter efficacy of this cycle in shaping our desires. It's not so much that we want the newest device; we're led to believe we need it. The distinction between want and need blurs, ④**shifting** our financial priorities in favor of staying current with trends. For all the logical arguments against this ceaseless upgrading, the temptation ⑤**remains** compelling.

**8.** 8)**밑줄 친 부분 중, 어법, 혹은 문맥상 어색한 곳을 고르시오.** 2024_H2_11_29

Conditioned Place Preference is a way of finding out ①**that** animals want. Researchers train them to associate one place with an experience such as food or a loud noise and another place with something completely different, usually where nothing ②**happens**. The two places are made obviously different to make it as easy as possible for the animal to associate each place with what happened to it there. The animal's preference for being in one place or another is measured both before and after its experiences in the two places.

If there is a shift in where the animal chooses to spend its time for the reward, this suggests that it liked the experience and is trying to repeat it. Conversely, if it now avoids the place the stimulus ③**appeared** and starts to prefer the place it did not experience it, then this suggests that it found the stimulus ④**unpleasant**. For example, mice with cancer show a preference for the place where they have been given morphine, a drug used to relieve pain, rather than where they have ⑤**received** saline whereas healthy mice developed no such preference. This suggests that the mice with cancer wanted the morphine.

**9.** 9)**밑줄 친 부분 중, 어법, 혹은 문맥상 어색한 곳을 고르시오.** 2024_H2_11_30

Near the equator, many species of bird breed all year round. But in temperate and polar regions, the breeding seasons of birds are often sharply ①**defined**. They are triggered mainly by changes in day length. If all goes well, the outcome is that birds ②**raise** their young when the food supply is at ③**their** peak. Most birds are not simply reluctant to breed at other times but they are also physically incapable of doing so. This is ④**because** their reproductive system shrinks, which helps flying birds save weight. The main exception to this rule are nomadic desert species. These can initiate their breeding cycle within days of rain. It's for making the most of the sudden breeding opportunity. Also, different species divide the breeding season up in different ways. Most seabirds raise a single brood. In warm regions, however, songbirds may raise several families in a few months. In an exceptionally good year, a pair of House Sparrows, a kind of songbird, can raise ⑤**successive** broods through a marathon reproductive effort.

**10.** 10)**밑줄 친 부분 중, 어법, 혹은 문맥상 어색한 곳을 고르시오.** 2024_H2_11_31

One factor that may hinder creativity is ① **awareness** of the resources required in each activity in students' learning. Often students are unable to identify the resources they need to perform the task required of them. Different resources may be compulsory for specific learning tasks, and recognizing ②**them** may simplify the activity's performance. For example, it may be that students desire to conduct some experiments in their projects. There must be a prior investigation of whether the students will have ③**access** to the laboratory, equipment, and chemicals required for the experiment. It means preparation is vital for the students to succeed, and it may be about human and financial resources such as laboratory technicians, money to purchase chemicals, and equipment for their learning where applicable. Even if some of the resources required for a task may not be available, identifying ④**them** in advance may help students' creativity. It may even lead to ⑤**changing** the topic, finding alternative resources, and other means.

**11.** 11)**밑줄 친 부분 중, 어법, 혹은 문맥상 어색한 곳을 고르시오.** 2024_H2_11_32

All translators feel some pressure from the community of readers for whom they are doing their work. And all translators ①**arrive** at their interpretations in dialogue with other people. The English poet Alexander Pope had pretty good Greek, but when he set about ②**translating** Homer's Iliad in the early 18th century he was not on his own. He had Greek commentaries to refer to, and translations that had already been done in English, Latin, and French — and of course he had dictionaries. Translators always draw on more than one source text. Even when the scene of translation ③**consists of** just one person with a pen, paper, and the book that is being translated, or even when it is just one person translating orally for another, that person's linguistic knowledge ④**arouses** from lots of other texts and other conversations. And then his or her idea of the translation's purpose will ⑤**be influenced** by the expectations of the person or people it is for. In both these senses every translation is a crowd translation.

**12.** 12)**밑줄 친 부분 중, 어법, 혹은 문맥상 어색한 곳을 고르시오.** 2024_H2_11_33

Some people argue that there is a single, logically consistent concept known as reading that can be neatly set apart from everything else people do with books. Is reading really that simple? The most productive way to think about reading is as a loosely ①**related** set of behaviors that belong together owing to family resemblances, as Ludwig Wittgenstein used the phrase, without having in common a single ②**defining** trait. Consequently, efforts to distinguish reading from nonreading are ③**destined** to fail because there is no agreement on what qualifies as reading in the first place. The more one tries to figure out where the border ④**lies** between reading and not-reading, the more edge cases will be found to stretch the term's ⑤**fixed** boundaries. Thus, it is worth attempting to collect together these exceptional forms of reading into a single forum, one highlighting the challenges faced by anyone wishing to establish the boundaries where reading begins and ends. The attempt moves toward an understanding of reading as a spectrum that is expansive enough to accommodate the distinct reading activities.

**13.** 13)**밑줄 친 부분 중, 어법, 혹은 문맥상 어색한 곳을 고르시오.** 2024_H2_11_34

Weber's law concerns the perception of difference between two stimuli. It suggests that we might not be able to detect a 1-mm difference when we are looking at lines 466 mm and 467 mm in length, but we may be able to detect a 1-mm difference when we are comparing a line 2 mm long with one 3 mm long. Another example of this ① **principle** is that we can detect 1 candle when it ② **is lit** in an otherwise dark room. But when 1 candle is lit in a room in which 100 candles are already burning, we may not notice the light from this candle. Therefore, the Just-noticeable difference (JND) ③**varies** as a function of the strength of the signals. For example, the JND is greater for very loud noises than it is for much more quiet sounds. When a sound is very weak, we can tell that another sound is louder, even if it is barely louder. When a sound is very loud, ④**telling** that another sound is even louder, it has to be ⑤**much** louder. Thus, Weber's law means that it is harder to distinguish between two samples when those samples are larger or stronger levels of the stimuli.

**14.** 14)**밑줄 친 부분 중, 어법, 혹은 문맥상 어색한 곳을 고르시오.** 2024_H2_11_35

Any new resource (e.g., a new airport, a new mall) always opens with people ①**benefiting** individually by sharing a common resource (e.g., the city or state budget). Soon, at some point, the amount of traffic grows too large for the "commons" to support. Traffic jams, overcrowding, and overuse lessen the benefits of the common resource for everyone —the tragedy of the commons! If the new resource cannot be ②**expanded** or provided with additional space, it becomes a problem, and you cannot solve the problem on your own, in isolation from your fellow drivers or walkers or ③ **competitive** users. The total activity on this new resource keeps ④**increasing**, and so does individual activity; but if the dynamic of common use and overuse continues too long, both begin to fall after a peak, leading to a crash. What makes the "tragedy of commons" tragic is the crash dynamic —the destruction or degeneration of the common resource's ability to regenerate ⑤**itself**.

**15.** 15)**밑줄 친 부분 중, 어법, 혹은 문맥상 어색한 곳을 고르시오.** 2024_H2_11_36

Theoretically, our brain would have the capacity to store all experiences throughout life, ①**reaching** the quality of a DVD. However, this theoretical capacity is offset by the energy demand associated with the process of storing and retrieving information in memory. As a result, the brain develops efficient strategies, becoming dependent on shortcuts. When we observe a face, the visual image captured by the eyes is ②**highly** variable, depending on the point of view, lighting conditions and ③**the other** contextual factors. Nevertheless, we are able to recognize the face as the same, ④ **maintaining** the underlying identity. The brain, rather than focusing on the details of visualization, creates and stores general patterns that allow for consistent recognition across diverse circumstances. This ability to match what we see with general visual memory patterns serves as an effective mechanism for optimizing brain performance and saving energy. The brain, being naturally against unnecessary effort, constantly ⑤**seeks** to simplify and generalize information to facilitate the cognitive process.

**16.** 16)밑줄 친 부분 중, 어법, 혹은 문맥상 어색한 곳을 고르시오. 2024_H2_11_37

Where scientific research is concerned, explanatory tales are expected to adhere closely to experimental data and to illuminate the regular and predictable features of experience. However, this paradigm sometimes ①**conceals** the fact that theories are deeply loaded with creative elements that shape the construction of research projects and the interpretations of evidence. Scientific explanations do not just relate a chronology of facts. They construct frameworks for systematically chosen data in order to provide a consistent and meaningful explanation of what is observed. Such constructions lead us to imagine specific kinds of subject matter in particular sorts of relations, and the storylines they inspire will prove more ② **effective** for analyzing some features of experience over others. When we neglect the creative contributions of such scientific imagination and treat models and ③**interruptive** explanations as straightforward facts — even worse, as facts including all of reality — we can blind ourselves to the limitations of a given model and fail to note ④**its** potential for misunderstanding a situation to ⑤**which** it ill applies.

.

**17.** 17)밑줄 친 부분 중, 어법, 혹은 문맥상 어색한 곳을 고르시오. 2024_H2_11_38

We encounter contrary claims about the relation of literature to action. Theorists have maintained that literature encourages solitary reading and reflection as the way to engage with the world and thus counters the social and political activities that might produce social change. At best it encourages detachment or appreciation of complexity, and at worst passivity and acceptance of what is. But on the other hand, literature has historically been seen as dangerous: it promotes the questioning of authority and social arrangements. Plato banned poets from his ideal republic because they could only do harm, and novels have long been credited with making people ①**dissatisfied** with their lives and eager for something new. By promoting identification across divisions of class, gender, and race, books may promote a fellowship that discourages struggle; but they may also produce a ②**keen** sense of injustice that makes progressive struggles ③**impossible**. Historically, works of literature are credited with producing change: Uncle Tom's Cabin, a best-seller in its day, helped ④**create** a ⑤**revulsion** against slavery that made possible the American Civil War.

**18.** 18)밑줄 친 부분 중, 어법, 혹은 문맥상 어색한 곳을 고르시오. 2024_H2_11_39

According to Hobbes, man is not a being who can act morally in spite of his instinct to protect his existence in the state of nature. Hence, the only place where morality and moral liberty will begin to find an application begins in a place where a sovereign power, namely the state, ①**emerges**. Hobbes thus ②**describes** the state of nature as a circumstance in ③**what** man's life is "solitary, poor, nasty, brutish and short". It means when people live without a general power to control ④**them** all, they are indeed in a state of war. In other words, Hobbes, who accepted that human beings are not social and political beings in the state of nature, believes that without the power human beings in the state of nature are "antisocial and rational based on their selfishness". Moreover, since society is not a natural phenomenon and there is no natural force bringing people together, what will bring them together as a society is not mutual affection according to Hobbes. It is, rather, mutual fear of men's present and future that assembles ⑤ **them**, since the cause of fear is a common drive among people in the state of nature.

## 19. 19)밑줄 친 부분 중, 어법, 혹은 문맥상 어색한 곳을 고르시오. 2024_H2_11_40

There is research that supports the idea that cognitive factors influence the phenomenology of the perceived world. Delk and Fillenbaum asked participants to match the color of figures with the color of their background. Some of the figures depicted objects associated with a particular color. These ①**included** typically red objects such as an apple, lips, and a symbolic heart. Other objects were presented that are not usually associated with red, such as a mushroom or a bell. However, all the figures were made out of the same red-orange cardboard. Participants then had to match the figure to a background varying from dark to light red. They had to make the background color ②**to match** the color of the figures. The researchers ③**found** that red-associated objects required more red in the background to be judged a match than did the objects that are not associated with the color red. This ④**implies** that the cognitive association of objects to color influences ⑤**how** we perceive that color.

## 20. 20)밑줄 친 부분 중, 어법, 혹은 문맥상 어색한 곳을 고르시오. 2024_H2_11_41~42

In each round of genome copying in our body, there is still about a 70 percent chance that at least one pair of chromosomes will have an error. With each round of genome copying, errors accumulate. This is ①**similar to** ②**alterations** in medieval books. Each time a copy was made by hand, some changes were introduced accidentally; as changes stacked up, the copies may have acquired meanings at variance with the original. Similarly, genomes that have undergone more copying processes will have gathered more mistakes. To make things worse, mutations may damage genes responsible for error checking and repair of genomes, further accelerating the introduction of mutations. Most genome mutations do not have any noticeable effects. It is just like changing the i for a y in "kingdom" would not distort the word's readability. But sometimes a mutation to a human gene results in, for example, an eye whose iris is of two different colors. Similarly, almost everyone has birthmarks, which are due to mutations that occurred as our body's cells multiplied to form skin. If mutations are changes to the genome of one particular cell, how can a patch of cells in an iris or a whole patch of skin, ③**consisted** of many individual cells, ④**be affected** simultaneously? The answer ⑤**lies** in the cell lineage, the developmental history of a tissue from particular cells through to their fully differentiated state. If the mutation occurred early on in the lineage of the developing iris, then all cells in that patch have inherited that change.

21. 21)밑줄 친 부분 중, 어법, 혹은 문맥상 어색한 곳을 고르시오. 2024_H2_11_43~45

Max awoke to the gentle sunlight of an autumn day. Right on schedule, he swung his legs off the bed and took a deep, satisfying breath. He began his morning the same way he usually did, getting dressed and going to school. Today was going to be another perfect day until he ran into Mr. Kapoor, his science teacher. "Just to ①**recommend** you. Science fair projects are due next Wednesday. Don't forget ②**to submit** your final draft on time," Mr. Kapoor said. Max froze. What? It can't be! It was due next Friday! After school, he came home ③**worrying** that his whole perfectly planned week was going to ④**be ruined**. Without his usual greeting, Max headed to his room in haste. "What's wrong Max?," Jeremy, his dad, followed Max, worrying about him. Max furiously browsed through his planner without answering him, only to find the wrong date written in ⑤**it**. Fighting through tears, Max finally managed to explain the unending pressure to be perfect to his dad. To his surprise, Jeremy laughed. "Max, guess what? Perfect is a great goal, but nobody gets there all the time. What matters is what we do when things get messy." That made him feel a little better. "You are saying I can fix this?" "Absolutely, try to deal with problems in a logical way," Jeremy said. Max thought for a moment. "I guess···. I can do that by rescheduling tonight's baseball lesson." Jeremy beamed. "See? That's you finding a solution." Max felt a genuine smile spreading. The next Wednesday, he successfully handed in the final draft on time with satisfaction. From then on, he still loved order and routines, but also embraced the messy, unpredictable bits of life too.

# 2024 고2 11월 모의고사

❶ voca  ❷ text  ❸ [ / ]  ❹ ____  ❺ quiz 1  ❻ quiz 2  ❼ quiz 3  ❽ quiz 4  ❾ quiz 5

**1.** ¹⁾**밑줄 친 ⓐ~ⓖ 중 어법, 혹은 문맥상 어휘의 사용이 어색한 것끼리 짝지어진 것을 고르시오.** ²⁰²⁴_H2_11_18

Dear Executive Manager Schulz,It is a week before the internship program starts. I am writing to bring your attention to a matter that ⓐ**inquires** ⓑ**immediate** consideration regarding the issue my department has. As the coordinator, it is becoming ⓒ**apparent** to me that the budget, previously ⓓ**proved** by your department, ⓔ**needing** some adjustments in order to meet the emerging modifications. Since my department has ⓕ**hired** three more interns than planned initially, the most expensive need is for additional funding to cover their wages, training costs, and materials. I kindly request an additional budget ⓖ**allocation** for these expenses. Please refer to the attachment for details. Thank you for your attention.Best regards,Matt Perry

① ⓒ, ⓖ       ② ⓓ, ⓕ       ③ ⓐ, ⓒ, ⓓ
④ ⓐ, ⓓ, ⓔ    ⑤ ⓓ, ⓔ, ⓖ

**2.** ²⁾**밑줄 친 ⓐ~ⓘ 중 어법, 혹은 문맥상 어휘의 사용이 어색한 것끼리 짝지어진 것을 고르시오.** ²⁰²⁴_H2_11_19

Katie ⓐ**approached** the hotel front desk to check-in but an unexpected event unfolded. The receptionist couldn't find her ⓑ**reservation** under the name 'Katie'. "I'm sorry, but I can't seem to locate a reservation under that name," the receptionist said. "No way, I definitely made a reservation on the phone," Katie said, puzzled. The receptionist asked, "Can you tell me your phone number?" and Katie told ⓒ**it** to him, ⓓ**thinking** 'What happened? Did I make a mistake?' "Just a moment," the receptionist said, typing ⓔ**deliberately** on the keyboard. "I found it! It seems there was a small misspelling. Your reservation is under 'K-A-T-Y'," the receptionist explained. With a sense of ease, Katie watched her reservation ⓕ**appearing** on the screen. With her heart slowing to a gentle rhythm, she ⓖ**processed** with her check-in, ⓗ**thought** that a simple misspelling might have ⓘ**been ruined** her plans.

① ⓐ, ⓔ, ⓘ    ② ⓖ, ⓗ, ⓘ    ③ ⓒ, ⓔ
④ ⓒ, ⓓ, ⓗ    ⑤ ⓑ, ⓒ, ⓖ

**3.** ³⁾**밑줄 친 ⓐ~ⓘ 중 어법, 혹은 문맥상 어휘의 사용이 어색한 것끼리 짝지어진 것을 고르시오.** ²⁰²⁴_H2_11_20

To be mathematically ⓐ**literacy** means to be able to think ⓑ**critically** about societal issues on ⓒ**which** mathematics has bearing so as to make ⓓ**informed** decisions about how to solve these problems. Dealing with such complex problems through interdisciplinary approaches, mirroring real-world problems ⓔ**requires** innovative ways of planning and organizing mathematical teaching methods. Navigating our world means being able to quantify, measure, estimate, classify, compare, find patterns, ⓕ**conjunction**, justify, prove, and generalize within critical thinking and when ⓖ**using** critical thinking. Therefore, making decisions, even ⓗ**qualitatively**, is not possible without using mathematics and critical thinking. Thus, teaching mathematics should ⓘ**be done** in interaction with critical thinking along with a decision-making process. They can ⓙ**develop** into the mathematical context, so that there is no excuse to not ⓚ**explicitly** support students to develop ⓛ**them**.

① ⓒ, ⓔ       ② ⓐ, ⓕ, ⓙ    ③ ⓙ, ⓛ
④ ⓑ, ⓙ       ⑤ ⓗ, ⓘ

**4.** <sup>4)</sup>**밑줄 친 ⓐ~ⓙ 중 어법, 혹은 문맥상 어휘의 사용이 어색한 것끼리 짝지어진 것을 고르시오.** 2024_H2_11_21

Imagine ⓐ**that** your usually stingy friend delights in buying you a Christmas present after taking a generosity booster. How would you feel? Undoubtedly, there is ⓑ**praiseworthy something** about the action. You'd be ⓒ**pleased** to receive the gift. You'd say 'thank you', and mean it. But his change of heart is not entirely ⓓ**satisfied**. According to Zagzebski, an American philosopher, he is not really generous. When we praise someone's character, we use words for various virtues: 'generous', 'kind', 'courageous', etc. A person who gives one gift isn't generous. Instead, generosity is a ⓔ**stable** part of a person's 'moral identity', an emotional ⓕ**habit** that is part of who you are. Thus virtues, as opposed to nontypical ⓖ**impulse**, ⓗ**is** the result of your personal history. They are part of who you are, as they are part of ⓘ**how** your character was formed. Instant virtue is therefore ⓙ**impossible**. Popping a pill cannot make you a better person.

① ⓔ, ⓙ        ② ⓔ, ⓕ, ⓘ        ③ ⓑ, ⓒ
④ ⓑ, ⓓ, ⓗ        ⑤ ⓕ, ⓘ, ⓙ

**5.** <sup>5)</sup>**밑줄 친 ⓐ~ⓙ 중 어법, 혹은 문맥상 어휘의 사용이 어색한 것끼리 짝지어진 것을 고르시오.** 2024_H2_11_22

To determine the mass of my bowling ball, I might put it onto a balance and compare it with a ⓐ**known** mass, such as ⓑ**a** number of metal cubes each ⓒ**weighing** 1, 10, or 100 grams. Things get ⓓ**much** more complicated if I want to know the mass of a distant star. How do I measure it? We can roughly say that measuring the mass of a star ⓔ**resolves** various theories. If we want to measure the mass of a binary star, we first determine a center of mass between the two stars, then their distance from that center ⓕ**where** we can then use, together with a value for the period and a

certain instance of Kepler's Third Law, to calculate the mass. In other words, in order to "measure" the star mass, we measure other ⓖ**quantities** and use those values, together with certain equations, to calculate the mass. Measurement is not a simple and ⓗ**unmediated** estimation of ⓘ**independently** existing properties, but a determination of certain magnitudes before the background of ⓙ**a** number of accepted theories.

① ⓐ, ⓒ        ② ⓓ, ⓗ        ③ ⓔ, ⓕ
④ ⓑ, ⓖ        ⑤ ⓑ, ⓒ, ⓕ

**6.** <sup>6)</sup>**밑줄 친 ⓐ~ⓛ 중 어법, 혹은 문맥상 어휘의 사용이 어색한 것끼리 짝지어진 것을 고르시오.** 2024_H2_11_23

Based on discoveries in neuroscience, pain and pleasure are formed and processed in the same area of the brain. Our bodies constantly strive for homeostasis, ⓐ**which** is defined as the balance of bodily functions. Without the body's effective ⓑ**compensatory** mechanisms, ⓒ**which** may cushion potential highs and lows, we would not be capable of surviving. Pleasure and pain are ⓓ**like** two sides of the same coin; they seem to work together and are heavily ⓔ**reliable** on one another and keep balance. If you imagine pleasure and pain as the two ⓕ**opposite** points on a scale, you can easily understand that as one of the two points ⓖ**rises**, ⓗ**the other** must correspondingly fall. We've all heard the expression, "No pain, no gain." Well, according to psychiatrist Dr. Anna Lembke, there may be some truth to these words. She says that our attempts to escape ⓘ**being** miserable ⓙ**are** in fact making us even more ⓚ**miserably**. This is because pain is actually an essential component of our ability to maintain a neutral state, and allowing ⓛ**it** will in turn reset our internal scale back to balance.

① ⓕ, ⓘ        ② ⓑ, ⓓ        ③ ⓔ, ⓚ
④ ⓕ, ⓛ        ⑤ ⓐ, ⓚ, ⓛ

7. 7)밑줄 친 ⓐ~ⓘ 중 어법, 혹은 문맥상 어휘의 사용이 어색한 것끼리 짝지어진 것을 고르시오. 2024_H2_11_24

Manufacturers masterfully ⓐ**saw** seeds of doubt about the adequacy of our current devices. Suddenly, the phone that was your lifeline a year ago is now a museum piece, ⓑ**unable** to keep pace with your digital demands. And thus, the itch to upgrade begins, often before there's a genuine need. This cycle isn't just ⓒ**confined** to our digital companions. It spills over into almost every aspect of consumer electronics, from the self-driving car to the smart fridge. Every product seems to be on an unstoppable march towards the next version, the next generation that promises to ⓓ**revolutionize** your life. What's ⓔ**fascinating**, or perhaps disturbing, is the utter ⓕ**efficacy** of this cycle in shaping our desires. It's not so much that we want the newest device; we're led to believe we need it. The distinction between want and need blurs, ⓖ**shifting** our financial priorities in favor of staying current with trends. For all the logical arguments against this ⓗ**careless** upgrading, the temptation ⓘ**remains** compelling.

① ⓕ, ⓗ     ② ⓐ, ⓗ     ③ ⓓ, ⓗ
④ ⓒ, ⓗ, ⓘ     ⑤ ⓓ, ⓕ, ⓗ

8. 8)밑줄 친 ⓐ~ⓘ 중 어법, 혹은 문맥상 어휘의 사용이 어색한 것끼리 짝지어진 것을 고르시오. 2024_H2_11_29

Conditioned Place Preference is a way of finding out ⓐ**what** animals want. Researchers train them to associate one place with an experience such as food or a loud noise and another place with something completely different, usually where nothing ⓑ**happens**. The two places are made obviously ⓒ**different** to make it as ⓓ**easy** as possible for the animal to associate each place with ⓔ**what** happened to it there. The animal's preference for being in one place or another is measured both before and after its experiences in the two places. If there is a shift in where the animal chooses to spend its time for the reward,

this suggests that it liked the experience and is trying to repeat it. Conversely, if it now avoids the place the stimulus ⓕ**appeared** and starts to prefer the place it did not experience it, then this suggests that it found the stimulus ⓖ**unpleasant**. For example, mice with cancer show a preference for the place where they have ⓗ**given** morphine, a drug used to relieve pain, rather than where they have ⓘ**been received** saline whereas healthy mice developed no such preference. This suggests that the mice with cancer ⓙ**wanted** the morphine.

① ⓒ, ⓔ, ⓗ     ② ⓑ, ⓒ     ③ ⓐ, ⓑ, ⓖ
④ ⓗ, ⓘ     ⑤ ⓑ, ⓕ

9. 9)밑줄 친 ⓐ~ⓘ 중 어법, 혹은 문맥상 어휘의 사용이 어색한 것끼리 짝지어진 것을 고르시오. 2024_H2_11_30

Near the equator, many species of bird breed all year round. But in temperate and polar regions, the breeding seasons of birds are often sharply ⓐ**defined**. They are triggered mainly by changes in day length. If all goes well, the outcome is that birds ⓑ**raise** their young when the food supply is at ⓒ**its** peak. Most birds are not simply ⓓ**willing** to breed at other times but they are also ⓔ**physically** incapable of doing so. This is ⓕ**because** their reproductive system shrinks, which helps flying birds save weight. The main exception to this rule ⓖ**are** nomadic ⓗ**dessert** species. These can initiate their breeding cycle within days of rain. It's for making the most of the sudden breeding opportunity. Also, different species divide the breeding season up in different ways. Most seabirds ⓘ**raise** a single brood. In warm regions, however, songbirds may raise several families in a few months. In an exceptionally good year, a pair of House Sparrows, a kind of songbird, can raise ⓙ**successful** broods through a marathon reproductive effort.

① ⓓ, ⓗ, ⓙ     ② ⓑ, ⓗ, ⓙ     ③ ⓑ, ⓕ
④ ⓒ, ⓘ     ⑤ ⓐ, ⓔ

**10.** <sup>10)</sup>밑줄 친 ⓐ~ⓘ 중 어법, 혹은 문맥상 어휘의 사용이 어색한 것끼리 짝지어진 것을 고르시오.

2024_H2_11_31

One factor that may hinder creativity is ⓐ**unawareness** of the resources required in each activity in students' learning. Often students are unable to identify the resources they need to perform the task required of them. Different resources may be ⓑ**impulsive** for specific learning tasks, and recognizing ⓒ**them** may simplify the activity's performance. For example, it may be that students desire to conduct some experiments in their projects. There must be a ⓓ**prior** ⓔ**investment** of whether the students will have ⓕ**access** to the laboratory, equipment, and chemicals ⓖ**required** for the experiment. It means preparation is vital for the students to succeed, and it may be about human and financial resources such as laboratory technicians, money to purchase chemicals, and equipment for their learning where ⓗ**applicable**. Even if some of the resources required for a task may not be available, identifying ⓘ**them** in advance may help students' creativity. It may even lead to ⓙ**changing** the topic, finding alternative resources, and other means.

① ⓐ, ⓓ, ⓘ     ② ⓔ, ⓕ, ⓗ     ③ ⓑ, ⓔ
④ ⓒ, ⓗ         ⑤ ⓐ, ⓑ, ⓗ

**11.** <sup>11)</sup>밑줄 친 ⓐ~ⓗ 중 어법, 혹은 문맥상 어휘의 사용이 어색한 것끼리 짝지어진 것을 고르시오.

2024_H2_11_32

All translators feel some pressure from the community of readers for ⓐ**whom** they are doing their work. And all translators ⓑ**arrive** at their interpretations in dialogue with other people. The English poet Alexander Pope had pretty good Greek, but when he set about ⓒ**transferring** Homer's Iliad in the early 18th century he was not on his own. He had Greek commentaries to refer to, and translations that had already ⓓ**done** in English, Latin, and French — and of course he had dictionaries. Translators always draw on more than one source text. Even when the scene of translation ⓔ**consists of** just one person with a pen, paper, and the book that is ⓕ**translating**, or even when it is just one person translating orally for another, that person's linguistic knowledge ⓖ**arises** from lots of other texts and other conversations. And then his or her idea of the translation's purpose will ⓗ**be influenced** by the expectations of the person or people it is for. In both these senses every translation is a crowd translation.

① ⓐ, ⓑ     ② ⓒ, ⓓ, ⓕ     ③ ⓓ, ⓕ
④ ⓑ, ⓒ, ⓗ     ⑤ ⓐ, ⓓ

**12.** <sup>12)</sup>밑줄 친 ⓐ~ⓘ 중 어법, 혹은 문맥상 어휘의 사용이 어색한 것끼리 짝지어진 것을 고르시오.

2024_H2_11_33

Some people argue that there is a single, logically consistent concept known ⓐ**for** reading that can be neatly set apart from everything else people do with books. Is reading really that simple? The most productive way to think about reading is as a loosely ⓑ**related** set of behaviors that ⓒ**are belonged** together owing to family resemblances, as Ludwig Wittgenstein used the phrase, without having in common a single ⓓ**confining** trait. Consequently, efforts to distinguish reading from nonreading are ⓔ**destined** to fail because there is no agreement on what qualifies as reading in the first place. The more one tries to figure out where the border ⓕ**lies** between reading and not-reading, the more edge cases will be found to stretch the term's ⓖ**flexible** boundaries. Thus, it is worth ⓗ**attempting** to collect together these exceptional forms of reading into a single forum, one highlighting the challenges ⓘ**faced** by anyone wishing to establish the boundaries where reading begins and ends. The attempt moves toward an understanding of reading as a spectrum that is ⓙ**expansive** enough to accommodate the distinct reading activities.

① ⓐ, ⓒ, ⓖ     ② ⓐ, ⓒ     ③ ⓒ, ⓘ
④ ⓒ, ⓕ, ⓙ     ⑤ ⓐ, ⓒ, ⓓ

**13.** 13)밑줄 친 ⓐ~ⓗ 중 어법, 혹은 문맥상 어휘의 사용이 어색한 것끼리 짝지어진 것을 고르시오.

2024_H2_11_34

Weber's law concerns the ⓐ**inception** of difference between two stimuli. It suggests that we ⓑ**might** not be able to detect a 1-mm difference when we are looking at lines 466 mm and 467 mm in length, but we may be able to detect a 1-mm difference when we are comparing a line 2 mm long with one 3 mm long. Another example of this ⓒ**principal** is that we can detect 1 candle when it ⓓ**is lit** in an otherwise dark room. But when 1 candle is lit in a room in ⓔ**which** 100 candles are already burning, we may not notice the light from this candle. Therefore, the Just-noticeable difference (JND) ⓕ**is varied** as a function of the strength of the signals. For example, the JND is greater for very loud noises than it is for much more quiet sounds. When a sound is very weak, we can tell that another sound is louder, even if it is barely louder. When a sound is very loud, ⓖ**to tell** that another sound is even louder, it has to be ⓗ**much** louder. Thus, Weber's law means that it is harder to distinguish between two samples when those samples are larger or stronger levels of the stimuli.

① ⓐ, ⓒ, ⓕ    ② ⓐ, ⓗ    ③ ⓐ, ⓔ, ⓖ
④ ⓑ, ⓗ    ⑤ ⓔ, ⓕ, ⓗ

**14.** 14)밑줄 친 ⓐ~ⓗ 중 어법, 혹은 문맥상 어휘의 사용이 어색한 것끼리 짝지어진 것을 고르시오.

2024_H2_11_35

Any new resource (e.g., a new airport, a new mall) always opens with people ⓐ**benefiting** individually by sharing a common resource (e.g., the city or state budget). Soon, at some point, the amount of traffic grows too large for the "commons" to ⓑ**support**. Traffic jams, overcrowding, and overuse lessen the benefits of the common resource for everyone —the tragedy of the commons! If the new resource cannot be ⓒ**expended** or provided with additional space, it becomes a problem, and you cannot solve the problem on your own, in isolation from your fellow drivers or walkers or ⓓ**competitive** users. The total activity on this new resource keeps ⓔ**decreasing**, and so ⓕ**does** individual activity; but if the dynamic of common use and overuse continues too long, both begin to fall after a peak, leading to a crash. What makes the "tragedy of commons" tragic is the crash dynamic —the ⓖ**destruction** or degeneration of the common resource's ability to regenerate ⓗ**itself**.

① ⓒ, ⓓ, ⓔ    ② ⓒ, ⓖ, ⓗ    ③ ⓐ, ⓒ
④ ⓔ, ⓗ    ⑤ ⓐ, ⓒ, ⓕ

**15.** 15)밑줄 친 ⓐ~ⓛ 중 어법, 혹은 문맥상 어휘의 사용이 어색한 것끼리 짝지어진 것을 고르시오.

2024_H2_11_36

Theoretically, our brain would have the capacity to store all experiences throughout life, ⓐ**reaching at** the quality of a DVD. However, this theoretical capacity ⓑ**is offset** by the energy demand associated with the process of storing and ⓒ**retrieving** information in memory. As a result, the brain develops efficient strategies, becoming ⓓ**independent** on shortcuts. When we observe a face, the visual image captured by the eyes is ⓔ**highly** variable, depending on the point of view, lighting conditions and ⓕ**other** contextual factors. Nevertheless, we are able to recognize the face as the same, ⓖ**maintaining** the underlying identity. The brain, rather than focusing on the details of visualization, creates and stores general patterns that allow for consistent recognition across diverse circumstances. This ability to match ⓗ**what** we see with general visual memory patterns ⓘ**serves** as an ⓙ**effective** mechanism for optimizing brain performance and saving energy. The brain, being naturally against unnecessary effort, constantly ⓚ**seeking** ⓛ**to simplify** and generalize information to facilitate the cognitive process.

① ⓒ, ⓔ    ② ⓐ, ⓓ, ⓚ    ③ ⓔ, ⓛ
④ ⓐ, ⓔ, ⓗ    ⑤ ⓑ, ⓖ, ⓗ

**16.** 16)밑줄 친 ⓐ~ⓙ 중 어법, 혹은 문맥상 어휘의 사용이 어색한 것끼리 짝지어진 것을 고르시오.
2024_H2_11_37

Where scientific research is concerned, explanatory tales are expected to adhere closely to experimental data and to illuminate the regular and predictable features of experience. However, this paradigm sometimes ⓐ**reveals** the fact that theories are deeply loaded with creative elements that shape the construction of research projects and the ⓑ**interpretations** of evidence. Scientific explanations do not just relate a chronology of facts. They construct frameworks for systematically chosen data in order to provide a ⓒ**consistent** and meaningful explanation of what is observed. Such constructions lead us ⓓ**to imagine** specific kinds of subject matter in particular sorts of relations, and the storylines they inspire will ⓔ**prove** more ⓕ**effective** for ⓖ**analyzing** some features of experience over others. When we neglect the creative contributions of such scientific imagination and treat models and ⓗ**interruptive** explanations as straightforward facts — even worse, as facts including all of reality — we can blind ourselves to the limitations of a given model and fail to note ⓘ**its** potential for misunderstanding a situation to ⓙ**which** it ill applies.

① ⓐ, ⓒ, ⓕ  ② ⓒ, ⓔ  ③ ⓗ, ⓘ
④ ⓐ, ⓗ  ⑤ ⓘ, ⓙ

**17.** 17)밑줄 친 ⓐ~ⓝ 중 어법, 혹은 문맥상 어휘의 사용이 어색한 것끼리 짝지어진 것을 고르시오.
2024_H2_11_38

We encounter contrary claims about the relation of ⓐ**literature** to action. Theorists have ⓑ**maintained** that literature encourages solitary reading and reflection as the way to engage ⓒ**with** the world and thus counters the social and political activities that might produce social change. At best it ⓓ**encourages** detachment or ⓔ**appreciation** of complexity, and at worst passivity and acceptance of what is. But on the other hand, literature has historically ⓕ**been seen** as dangerous: it promotes the questioning of authority and social arrangements. Plato banned poets from his ideal republic because they could only do harm, and novels have long ⓖ**been credited** with making people ⓗ**dissatisfy** with their lives and eager for something new. By promoting identification across divisions of class, gender, and race, books may promote a fellowship that ⓘ**encourages** struggle; but they may also produce a ⓙ**keen** sense of injustice that makes progressive struggles ⓚ**possible**. Historically, works of literature are credited with producing change: Uncle Tom's Cabin, a best-seller in its day, helped ⓛ**create** a ⓜ **revulsion** against slavery that made ⓝ**possible** the American Civil War.

① ⓚ, ⓜ, ⓝ  ② ⓜ, ⓝ  ③ ⓗ, ⓘ
④ ⓔ, ⓗ, ⓛ  ⑤ ⓑ, ⓓ, ⓕ

**18.** 18)밑줄 친 ⓐ~ⓙ 중 어법, 혹은 문맥상 어휘의 사용이 어색한 것끼리 짝지어진 것을 고르시오.
2024_H2_11_39

According to Hobbes, man is not a being who can act morally in ⓐ**spite** of his instinct to protect his existence in the state of nature. Hence, the only place where morality and moral liberty will begin to find an application begins in a place where a sovereign power, namely the state, ⓑ**emerges**. Hobbes thus ⓒ**describes** the state of nature as a circumstance in ⓓ**which** man's life is "solitary, poor, nasty, brutish and short". It means when people live without a general power to control ⓔ**themselves** all, they are indeed in a state of war. In other words, Hobbes, who accepted that human beings are not social and political beings in the state of nature, believes that without the power human beings in the state of nature ⓕ**is** "antisocial and rational based on their selfishness". Moreover, since society is not a natural phenomenon and there is no natural force bringing people together, ⓖ**that** will bring them together as a society is not mutual ⓗ**affection** according to Hobbes. It is, rather, mutual fear of men's present and future that ⓘ**assembles** ⓙ**them**, since the cause of fear is a common drive among people in the state of nature.

① ⓒ, ⓓ, ⓘ  ② ⓔ, ⓕ, ⓖ  ③ ⓒ, ⓓ, ⓙ
④ ⓐ, ⓖ  ⑤ ⓓ, ⓗ, ⓙ

## 19. 19)밑줄 친 ⓐ~ⓚ 중 어법, 혹은 문맥상 어휘의 사용이 어색한 것끼리 짝지어진 것을 고르시오.
2024_H2_11_40

There is research that supports the idea that cognitive factors ⓐ**influence** the phenomenology of the perceived world. Delk and Fillenbaum asked participants to match the color of figures with the color of their background. Some of the figures ⓑ**depicted** objects associated with a particular color. These ⓒ**excluded** typically red objects such as an apple, lips, and a symbolic heart. Other objects were presented that are not usually associated with red, such as a mushroom or a bell. However, all the figures ⓓ**were made** out of the same red-orange cardboard. Participants then had to match the figure to a background ⓔ**varying** from dark to light red. They had to make the background color ⓕ**match** the color of the figures. The researchers ⓖ**found** that red-associated objects ⓗ**required** more red in the background to ⓘ**be judged** a match than did the objects that are not associated with the color red. This ⓙ**implies** that the cognitive association of objects to color influences ⓚ**what** we perceive that color.

① ⓔ, ⓘ      ② ⓒ, ⓚ      ③ ⓒ, ⓔ, ⓕ
④ ⓔ, ⓗ      ⑤ ⓐ, ⓒ, ⓖ

## 20. 20)밑줄 친 ⓐ~ⓝ 중 어법, 혹은 문맥상 어휘의 사용이 어색한 것끼리 짝지어진 것을 고르시오.
2024_H2_11_41~42

In each round of genome copying in our body, there is still about a 70 percent chance that at least one pair of chromosomes will have an error. With each round of genome copying, errors ⓐ**circulate**. This is ⓑ**different from** ⓒ**alternatives** in medieval books. Each time a copy was made by hand, some changes ⓓ**were introduced** accidentally; as changes stacked up, the copies may have acquired meanings at variance with the original. Similarly, genomes that have undergone more copying processes will have gathered more mistakes. To make things ⓔ**worse**, mutations may damage genes responsible for error checking and repair of genomes, further ⓕ**accelerating** the introduction of mutations. Most genome mutations do not have any noticeable effects. It is just like changing the i for a y in "kingdom" would not distort the word's readability. But sometimes a mutation to a human gene results ⓖ**in**, for example, an eye ⓗ**whose** iris is of two different colors. Similarly, almost everyone has birthmarks, which are due to mutations that ⓘ**occurred** as our body's cells multiplied to form skin. If mutations are changes to the genome of one particular cell, how can a patch of cells in an iris or a whole patch of skin, ⓙ**consisting** of many individual cells, ⓚ**be affected** simultaneously? The answer ⓛ**lies** in the cell lineage, the developmental history of a tissue from particular cells through to their fully differentiated state. If the mutation ⓜ**occurred** early on in the lineage of the developing iris, then all cells in that patch have ⓝ**inherited** that change.

① ⓐ, ⓜ      ② ⓕ, ⓘ, ⓛ      ③ ⓚ, ⓝ
④ ⓐ, ⓓ, ⓔ      ⑤ ⓐ, ⓑ, ⓒ

21. 21)밑줄 친 @~ⓚ 중 어법, 혹은 문맥상 어휘의 사용이 어색한 것끼리 짝지어진 것을 고르시오.

2024_H2_11_43~45

Max awoke to the gentle sunlight of an autumn day. Right on schedule, he swung his legs off the bed and took a deep, ⓐ**satisfied** breath. He began his morning the same way he usually ⓑ**did**, getting dressed and going to school. Today was going to be another perfect day until he ran into Mr. Kapoor, his science teacher. "Just to ⓒ**recommend** you. Science fair projects are due next Wednesday. Don't forget ⓓ**to submit** your final draft on time," Mr. Kapoor said. Max froze. What? It can't be! It was due next Friday! After school, he came home ⓔ**worrying** that his whole perfectly planned week was going to ⓕ**be ruined**. Without his usual greeting, Max headed to his room in haste. "What's wrong Max?," Jeremy, his dad, ⓖ**followed** Max, worrying about him. Max furiously browsed through his planner without answering him, only to find the wrong date written in ⓗ**them**. Fighting through tears, Max finally managed to ⓘ**explain** the unending pressure to be perfect to his dad. To his surprise, Jeremy laughed. "Max, guess what? Perfect is a great goal, but nobody gets there all the time. What matters is what we do when things get messy." That made him ⓙ**feel** a little better. "You are saying I can fix this?" "Absolutely, try to deal with problems in a logical way," Jeremy said. Max thought for a moment. "I guess···. I can do that by rescheduling tonight's baseball lesson." Jeremy beamed. "See? That's you finding a solution." Max felt a genuine smile ⓚ**spreading**. The next Wednesday, he successfully handed in the final draft on time with satisfaction. From then on, he still loved order and routines, but also embraced the messy, unpredictable bits of life too.

① ⓐ, ⓒ, ⓗ   ② ⓐ, ⓓ, ⓖ   ③ ⓑ, ⓙ
④ ⓑ, ⓔ, ⓗ   ⑤ ⓐ, ⓒ

# 2024 고2 11월 모의고사

❶ voca　　❷ text　　❸ [ / ]　　❹ _____　　❺ quiz 1　　❻ quiz 2　　❼ quiz 3　　⑧ quiz 4　　❾ quiz 5

**1. ¹⁾밑줄 부분 중 어법, 혹은 문맥상 어휘의 쓰임이 어색한 것을 올바르게 고쳐 쓰시오. (5개)** <sup>2024_H2_11_18</sup>

Dear Executive Manager Schulz,It is a week before the internship program starts. I am writing to bring your attention to a matter that ①**requires** ②intermediate consideration regarding the issue my department has. As the coordinator, it is becoming ③**apparent** to me that the budget, previously ④**proved** by your department, ⑤**needing** some adjustments in order to meet the emerging modifications. Since my department has ⑥**been hired** three more interns than planned initially, the most expensive need is for additional funding to cover their wages, training costs, and materials. I kindly request an additional budget ⑦**alterating** for these expenses. Please refer to the attachment for details. Thank you for your attention.Best regards,Matt Perry

| 기호 | 어색한 표현 | | 올바른 표현 |
|------|-------------|---|-------------|
| ( ) | _____ | => | _____ |
| ( ) | _____ | => | _____ |
| ( ) | _____ | => | _____ |
| ( ) | _____ | => | _____ |
| ( ) | _____ | => | _____ |

**2. ²⁾밑줄 부분 중 어법, 혹은 문맥상 어휘의 쓰임이 어색한 것을 올바르게 고쳐 쓰시오. (5개)** <sup>2024_H2_11_19</sup>

Katie ①**approached** the hotel front desk to check-in but an unexpected event unfolded. The receptionist couldn't find her ②**conservation** under the name 'Katie'. "I'm sorry, but I can't seem to locate a reservation under that name," the receptionist said. "No way, I definitely made a reservation on the phone," Katie said, puzzled. The receptionist asked, "Can you tell me your phone number?" and Katie told ③**it** to him, ④**thought** 'What happened? Did I make a mistake?' "Just a moment," the receptionist said, typing ⑤**delightfully** on the keyboard. "I found it! It seems there was a small misspelling. Your reservation is under 'K-A-T-Y'," the receptionist explained. With a sense of ease, Katie watched her reservation ⑥**to appear** on the screen. With her heart slowing to a gentle rhythm, she ⑦**processed** with her check-in, ⑧ **thinking** that a simple misspelling might have ⑨**ruined** her plans.

| 기호 | 어색한 표현 | | 올바른 표현 |
|------|-------------|---|-------------|
| ( ) | _____ | => | _____ |
| ( ) | _____ | => | _____ |
| ( ) | _____ | => | _____ |
| ( ) | _____ | => | _____ |
| ( ) | _____ | => | _____ |

**3.** 3)밑줄 부분 중 어법, 혹은 문맥상 어휘의 쓰임이 어색한 것을 올바르게 고쳐 쓰시오. **(5개)** 2024_H2_11_20

To be mathematically ①**literate** means to be able to think ②**critical** about societal issues on ③**which** mathematics has bearing so as to make ④**informing** decisions about how to solve these problems. Dealing with such complex problems through interdisciplinary approaches, mirroring real-world problems ⑤**requires** innovative ways of planning and organizing mathematical teaching methods. Navigating our world means being able to quantify, measure, estimate, classify, compare, find patterns, ⑥**conjunction**, justify, prove, and generalize within critical thinking and when ⑦**using** critical thinking. Therefore, making decisions, even ⑧**qualitatively**, is not possible without using mathematics and critical thinking. Thus, teaching mathematics should ⑨**do** in interaction with critical thinking along with a decision-making process. They can ⑩**develop** into the mathematical context, so that there is no excuse to not ⑪**explicitly** support students to develop ⑫**them**.

| 기호 | 어색한 표현 | | 올바른 표현 |
|---|---|---|---|
| ( ) | _____ | => | _____ |
| ( ) | _____ | => | _____ |
| ( ) | _____ | => | _____ |
| ( ) | _____ | => | _____ |
| ( ) | _____ | => | _____ |

**4.** 4)밑줄 부분 중 어법, 혹은 문맥상 어휘의 쓰임이 어색한 것을 올바르게 고쳐 쓰시오. **(5개)** 2024_H2_11_21

Imagine ①**that** your usually stingy friend delights in buying you a Christmas present after taking a generosity booster. How would you feel? Undoubtedly, there is ②**something praiseworthy** about the action. You'd be ③**pleased** to receive the gift. You'd say 'thank you', and mean it. But his change of heart is not entirely ④**satisfying**. According to Zagzebski, an American philosopher, he is not really generous. When we praise someone's character, we use words for various virtues: 'generous', 'kind', 'courageous', etc. A person who gives one gift isn't generous. Instead, generosity is a ⑤**stable** part of a person's 'moral identity', an emotional ⑥**habitat** that is part of who you are. Thus virtues, as opposed to nontypical ⑦**compulsory**, ⑧**is** the result of your personal history. They are part of who you are, as they are part of ⑨ **what** your character was formed. Instant virtue is therefore ⑩**possible**. Popping a pill cannot make you a better person.

| 기호 | 어색한 표현 | | 올바른 표현 |
|---|---|---|---|
| ( ) | _____ | => | _____ |
| ( ) | _____ | => | _____ |
| ( ) | _____ | => | _____ |
| ( ) | _____ | => | _____ |
| ( ) | _____ | => | _____ |

**5. 5)밑줄 부분 중 어법, 혹은 문맥상 어휘의 쓰임이 어색한 것을 올바르게 고쳐 쓰시오. (5개)** 2024_H2_11_22

To determine the mass of my bowling ball, I might put it onto a balance and compare it with a ①**known** mass, such as ②**the** number of metal cubes each ③**weighing** 1, 10, or 100 grams. Things get ④**very** more complicated if I want to know the mass of a distant star. How do I measure it? We can roughly say that measuring the mass of a star ⑤**resolves** various theories. If we want to measure the mass of a binary star, we first determine a center of mass between the two stars, then their distance from that center ⑥**where** we can then use, together with a value for the period and a certain instance of Kepler's Third Law, to calculate the mass. In other words, in order to "measure" the star mass, we measure other ⑦**quantities** and use those values, together with certain equations, to calculate the mass. Measurement is not a simple and ⑧**unmediated** estimation of ⑨**interdependently** existing properties, but a determination of certain magnitudes before the background of ⑩**a** number of accepted theories.

| 기호 | 어색한 표현 | | 올바른 표현 |
|---|---|---|---|
| ( ) | _____ | => | _____ |
| ( ) | _____ | => | _____ |
| ( ) | _____ | => | _____ |
| ( ) | _____ | => | _____ |
| ( ) | _____ | => | _____ |

**6. 6)밑줄 부분 중 어법, 혹은 문맥상 어휘의 쓰임이 어색한 것을 올바르게 고쳐 쓰시오. (5개)** 2024_H2_11_23

Based on discoveries in neuroscience, pain and pleasure are formed and processed in the same area of the brain. Our bodies constantly strive for homeostasis, ①**that** is defined as the balance of bodily functions. Without the body's effective ②**compensatory** mechanisms, ③**that** may cushion potential highs and lows, we would not be capable of surviving. Pleasure and pain are ④**like** two sides of the same coin; they seem to work together and are heavily ⑤**reliable** on one another and keep balance. If you imagine pleasure and pain as the two ⑥**opposite** points on a scale, you can easily understand that as one of the two points ⑦**rises**, ⑧**the other** must correspondingly fall. We've all heard the expression, "No pain, no gain." Well, according to psychiatrist Dr. Anna Lembke, there may be some truth to these words. She says that our attempts to escape ⑨**to be** miserable ⑩**are** in fact making us even more ⑪**miserable**. This is because pain is actually an essential component of our ability to maintain a neutral state, and allowing ⑫**them** will in turn reset our internal scale back to balance.

| 기호 | 어색한 표현 | | 올바른 표현 |
|---|---|---|---|
| ( ) | _____ | => | _____ |
| ( ) | _____ | => | _____ |
| ( ) | _____ | => | _____ |
| ( ) | _____ | => | _____ |
| ( ) | _____ | => | _____ |

**7.** 7)밑줄 부분 중 어법, 혹은 문맥상 어휘의 쓰임이 어색한 것을 올바르게 고쳐 쓰시오. **(5개)** 2024_H2_11_24

Manufacturers masterfully ①**sow** seeds of doubt about the adequacy of our current devices. Suddenly, the phone that was your lifeline a year ago is now a museum piece, ②**unable** to keep pace with your digital demands. And thus, the itch to upgrade begins, often before there's a genuine need. This cycle isn't just ③**refined** to our digital companions. It spills over into almost every aspect of consumer electronics, from the self-driving car to the smart fridge. Every product seems to be on an unstoppable march towards the next version, the next generation that promises to ④**revolutionize** your life. What's ⑤**fascinated**, or perhaps disturbing, is the utter ⑥**efficiency** of this cycle in shaping our desires. It's not so much that we want the newest device; we're led to believe we need it. The distinction between want and need blurs, ⑦**shifting** our financial priorities in favor of staying current with trends. For all the logical arguments against this ⑧**careless** upgrading, the temptation ⑨**is remained** compelling.

| 기호 | 어색한 표현 | | 올바른 표현 |
|---|---|---|---|
| ( ) | _____ | => | _____ |
| ( ) | _____ | => | _____ |
| ( ) | _____ | => | _____ |
| ( ) | _____ | => | _____ |
| ( ) | _____ | => | _____ |

**8.** 8)밑줄 부분 중 어법, 혹은 문맥상 어휘의 쓰임이 어색한 것을 올바르게 고쳐 쓰시오. **(5개)** 2024_H2_11_29

Conditioned Place Preference is a way of finding out ①**that** animals want. Researchers train them to associate one place with an experience such as food or a loud noise and another place with something completely different, usually where nothing ②**happens**. The two places are made obviously ③**different** to make it as ④**easily** as possible for the animal to associate each place with ⑤**what** happened to it there. The animal's preference for being in one place or another is measured both before and after its experiences in the two places. If there is a shift in where the animal chooses to spend its time for the reward, this suggests that it liked the experience and is trying to repeat it. Conversely, if it now avoids the place the stimulus ⑥**appearing** and starts to prefer the place it did not experience it, then this suggests that it found the stimulus ⑦**unpleasantly**. For example, mice with cancer show a preference for the place where they have ⑧**been given** morphine, a drug used to relieve pain, rather than where they have ⑨ **received** saline whereas healthy mice developed no such preference. This suggests that the mice with cancer ⑩**should want** the morphine.

| 기호 | 어색한 표현 | | 올바른 표현 |
|---|---|---|---|
| ( ) | _____ | => | _____ |
| ( ) | _____ | => | _____ |
| ( ) | _____ | => | _____ |
| ( ) | _____ | => | _____ |
| ( ) | _____ | => | _____ |

**9.** 9)밑줄 부분 중 어법, 혹은 문맥상 어휘의 쓰임이 어색한 것을 올바르게 고쳐 쓰시오. (5개) 2024_H2_11_30

Near the equator, many species of bird breed all year round. But in temperate and polar regions, the breeding seasons of birds are often sharply ①**defined**. They are triggered mainly by changes in day length. If all goes well, the outcome is that birds ②**rise** their young when the food supply is at ③**their** peak. Most birds are not simply ④**willing** to breed at other times but they are also ⑤**physically** incapable of doing so. This is ⑥**why** their reproductive system shrinks, which helps flying birds save weight. The main exception to this rule ⑦**are** nomadic ⑧**desert** species. These can initiate their breeding cycle within days of rain. It's for making the most of the sudden breeding opportunity. Also, different species divide the breeding season up in different ways. Most seabirds ⑨**rise** a single brood. In warm regions, however, songbirds may raise several families in a few months. In an exceptionally good year, a pair of House Sparrows, a kind of songbird, can raise ⑩**successive** broods through a marathon reproductive effort.

| 기호 | 어색한 표현 | | 올바른 표현 |
|---|---|---|---|
| ( ) | _____ | => | _____ |
| ( ) | _____ | => | _____ |
| ( ) | _____ | => | _____ |
| ( ) | _____ | => | _____ |
| ( ) | _____ | => | _____ |

**10.** 10)밑줄 부분 중 어법, 혹은 문맥상 어휘의 쓰임이 어색한 것을 올바르게 고쳐 쓰시오. (5개) 2024_H2_11_31

One factor that may hinder creativity is ①**unawareness** of the resources required in each activity in students' learning. Often students are unable to identify the resources they need to perform the task required of them. Different resources may be ②**compulsory** for specific learning tasks, and recognizing ③**them** may simplify the activity's performance. For example, it may be that students desire to conduct some experiments in their projects. There must be a ④**inferior** ⑤**investigation** of whether the students will have ⑥**assess** to the laboratory, equipment, and chemicals ⑦**were required** for the experiment. It means preparation is vital for the students to succeed, and it may be about human and financial resources such as laboratory technicians, money to purchase chemicals, and equipment for their learning where ⑧**application**. Even if some of the resources required for a task may not be available, identifying ⑨**them** in advance may help students' creativity. It may even lead to ⑩**change** the topic, finding alternative resources, and other means.

| 기호 | 어색한 표현 | | 올바른 표현 |
|---|---|---|---|
| ( ) | _____ | => | _____ |
| ( ) | _____ | => | _____ |
| ( ) | _____ | => | _____ |
| ( ) | _____ | => | _____ |
| ( ) | _____ | => | _____ |

**11.** 11)밑줄 부분 중 어법, 혹은 문맥상 어휘의 쓰임이 어색한 것을 올바르게 고쳐 쓰시오. (5개) ²⁰²⁴_H2_11_32

All translators feel some pressure from the community of readers for ①**who** they are doing their work. And all translators ②**reach** at their interpretations in dialogue with other people. The English poet Alexander Pope had pretty good Greek, but when he set about ③**translating** Homer's Iliad in the early 18th century he was not on his own. He had Greek commentaries to refer to, and translations that had already ④**done** in English, Latin, and French — and of course he had dictionaries. Translators always draw on more than one source text. Even when the scene of translation ⑤**consists of** just one person with a pen, paper, and the book that is ⑥**translating**, or even when it is just one person translating orally for another, that person's linguistic knowledge ⑦**arouses** from lots of other texts and other conversations. And then his or her idea of the translation's purpose will ⑧**be influenced** by the expectations of the person or people it is for. In both these senses every translation is a crowd translation.

| 기호 | 어색한 표현 | | 올바른 표현 |
|---|---|---|---|
| ( ) | _____ | => | _____ |
| ( ) | _____ | => | _____ |
| ( ) | _____ | => | _____ |
| ( ) | _____ | => | _____ |
| ( ) | _____ | => | _____ |

**12.** 12)밑줄 부분 중 어법, 혹은 문맥상 어휘의 쓰임이 어색한 것을 올바르게 고쳐 쓰시오. (5개) ²⁰²⁴_H2_11_33

Some people argue that there is a single, logically consistent concept known ①**as** reading that can be neatly set apart from everything else people do with books. Is reading really that simple? The most productive way to think about reading is as a loosely ②**related** set of behaviors that ③**belong** together owing to family resemblances, as Ludwig Wittgenstein used the phrase, without having in common a single ④**confining** trait. Consequently, efforts to distinguish reading from nonreading are ⑤**determined** to fail because there is no agreement on what qualifies as reading in the first place. The more one tries to figure out where the border ⑥**lays** between reading and not-reading, the more edge cases will be found to stretch the term's ⑦**flexible** boundaries. Thus, it is worth ⑧**attempting** to collect together these exceptional forms of reading into a single forum, one highlighting the challenges ⑨**were faced** by anyone wishing to establish the boundaries where reading begins and ends. The attempt moves toward an understanding of reading as a spectrum that is ⑩**expensive** enough to accommodate the distinct reading activities.

| 기호 | 어색한 표현 | | 올바른 표현 |
|---|---|---|---|
| ( ) | _____ | => | _____ |
| ( ) | _____ | => | _____ |
| ( ) | _____ | => | _____ |
| ( ) | _____ | => | _____ |
| ( ) | _____ | => | _____ |

**13.** 13)밑줄 부분 중 어법, 혹은 문맥상 어휘의 쓰임이 어색한 것을 올바르게 고쳐 쓰시오. (5개) <sup>2024_H2_11_34</sup>

Weber's law concerns the ①**perception** of difference between two stimuli. It suggests that we ②**should** not be able to detect a 1-mm difference when we are looking at lines 466 mm and 467 mm in length, but we may be able to detect a 1-mm difference when we are comparing a line 2 mm long with one 3 mm long. Another example of this ③**principle** is that we can detect 1 candle when it ④**is lit** in an otherwise dark room. But when 1 candle is lit in a room in ⑤**that** 100 candles are already burning, we may not notice the light from this candle. Therefore, the Just-noticeable difference (JND) ⑥**is varied** as a function of the strength of the signals. For example, the JND is greater for very loud noises than it is for much more quiet sounds. When a sound is very weak, we can tell that another sound is louder, even if it is barely louder. When a sound is very loud, ⑦**telling** that another sound is even louder, it has to be ⑧ **more** louder. Thus, Weber's law means that it is harder to distinguish between two samples when those samples are larger or stronger levels of the stimuli.

| 기호 | 어색한 표현 | | 올바른 표현 |
|---|---|---|---|
| ( ) | _____ | => | _____ |
| ( ) | _____ | => | _____ |
| ( ) | _____ | => | _____ |
| ( ) | _____ | => | _____ |
| ( ) | _____ | => | _____ |

**14.** 14)밑줄 부분 중 어법, 혹은 문맥상 어휘의 쓰임이 어색한 것을 올바르게 고쳐 쓰시오. (5개) <sup>2024_H2_11_35</sup>

Any new resource (e.g., a new airport, a new mall) always opens with people ①**benefitted** individually by sharing a common resource (e.g., the city or state budget). Soon, at some point, the amount of traffic grows too large for the "commons" to ②**be supported**. Traffic jams, overcrowding, and overuse lessen the benefits of the common resource for everyone —the tragedy of the commons! If the new resource cannot be ③**expended** or provided with additional space, it becomes a problem, and you cannot solve the problem on your own, in isolation from your fellow drivers or walkers or ④**competing** users. The total activity on this new resource keeps ⑤**decreasing**, and so ⑥**does** individual activity; but if the dynamic of common use and overuse continues too long, both begin to fall after a peak, leading to a crash. What makes the "tragedy of commons" tragic is the crash dynamic —the ⑦**destruction** or degeneration of the common resource's ability to regenerate ⑧**it**.

| 기호 | 어색한 표현 | | 올바른 표현 |
|---|---|---|---|
| ( ) | _____ | => | _____ |
| ( ) | _____ | => | _____ |
| ( ) | _____ | => | _____ |
| ( ) | _____ | => | _____ |
| ( ) | _____ | => | _____ |

**15.** <sup>15)</sup>밑줄 부분 중 어법, 혹은 문맥상 어휘의 쓰임이 어색한 것을 올바르게 고쳐 쓰시오. (5개) <sup>2024_H2_11_36</sup>

Theoretically, our brain would have the capacity to store all experiences throughout life, ①**reaching** the quality of a DVD. However, this theoretical capacity ②**offsets** by the energy demand associated with the process of storing and ③**reviving** information in memory. As a result, the brain develops efficient strategies, becoming ④**dependent** on shortcuts. When we observe a face, the visual image captured by the eyes is ⑤**highly** variable, depending on the point of view, lighting conditions and ⑥**the other** contextual factors. Nevertheless, we are able to recognize the face as the same, ⑦**maintaining** the underlying identity. The brain, rather than focusing on the details of visualization, creates and stores general patterns that allow for consistent recognition across diverse circumstances. This ability to match ⑧**that** we see with general visual memory patterns ⑨**serve** as an ⑩**effective** mechanism for optimizing brain performance and saving energy. The brain, being naturally against unnecessary effort, constantly ⑪**seeks** ⑫**to simplify** and generalize information to facilitate the cognitive process.

| 기호 | 어색한 표현 | | 올바른 표현 |
|---|---|---|---|
| ( ) | _____ | => | _____ |
| ( ) | _____ | => | _____ |
| ( ) | _____ | => | _____ |
| ( ) | _____ | => | _____ |
| ( ) | _____ | => | _____ |

**16.** <sup>16)</sup>밑줄 부분 중 어법, 혹은 문맥상 어휘의 쓰임이 어색한 것을 올바르게 고쳐 쓰시오. (5개) <sup>2024_H2_11_37</sup>

Where scientific research is concerned, explanatory tales are expected to adhere closely to experimental data and to illuminate the regular and predictable features of experience. However, this paradigm sometimes ①**reveals** the fact that theories are deeply loaded with creative elements that shape the construction of research projects and the ②**interpretations** of evidence. Scientific explanations do not just relate a chronology of facts. They construct frameworks for systematically chosen data in order to provide a ③**consistent** and meaningful explanation of what is observed. Such constructions lead us ④**to imagine** specific kinds of subject matter in particular sorts of relations, and the storylines they inspire will ⑤**prove** more ⑥**effectively** for ⑦**analysis** some features of experience over others. When we neglect the creative contributions of such scientific imagination and treat models and ⑧**interruptive** explanations as straightforward facts ─ even worse, as facts including all of reality ─ we can blind ourselves to the limitations of a given model and fail to note ⑨**their** potential for misunderstanding a situation to ⑩**which** it ill applies.

| 기호 | 어색한 표현 | | 올바른 표현 |
|---|---|---|---|
| ( ) | _____ | => | _____ |
| ( ) | _____ | => | _____ |
| ( ) | _____ | => | _____ |
| ( ) | _____ | => | _____ |
| ( ) | _____ | => | _____ |

**17.** 17)밑줄 부분 중 어법, 혹은 문맥상 어휘의 쓰임이 어색한 것을 올바르게 고쳐 쓰시오. (5개) <sup>2024_H2_11_38</sup>

We encounter contrary claims about the relation of ①**literature** to action. Theorists have ②**maintained** that literature encourages solitary reading and reflection as the way to engage ③**to** the world and thus counters the social and political activities that might produce social change. At best it ④**encourages** detachment or ⑤**appreciation** of complexity, and at worst passivity and acceptance of what is. But on the other hand, literature has historically ⑥**been seen** as dangerous: it promotes the questioning of authority and social arrangements. Plato banned poets from his ideal republic because they could only do harm, and novels have long ⑦**been credited** with making people ⑧**dissatisfy** with their lives and eager for something new. By promoting identification across divisions of class, gender, and race, books may promote a fellowship that ⑨**encourages** struggle; but they may also produce a ⑩**kin** sense of injustice that makes progressive struggles ⑪**possible**. Historically, works of literature are credited with producing change: Uncle Tom's Cabin, a best-seller in its day, helped ⑫**create** a ⑬**compulsion** against slavery that made ⑭**possible** the American Civil War.

| 기호 | 어색한 표현 | | 올바른 표현 |
|---|---|---|---|
| ( ) | _____ | => | _____ |
| ( ) | _____ | => | _____ |
| ( ) | _____ | => | _____ |
| ( ) | _____ | => | _____ |
| ( ) | _____ | => | _____ |

**18.** 18)밑줄 부분 중 어법, 혹은 문맥상 어휘의 쓰임이 어색한 것을 올바르게 고쳐 쓰시오. (5개) <sup>2024_H2_11_39</sup>

According to Hobbes, man is not a being who can act morally in ①**spite** of his instinct to protect his existence in the state of nature. Hence, the only place where morality and moral liberty will begin to find an application begins in a place where a sovereign power, namely the state, ②**emerges**. Hobbes thus ③**prescribes** the state of nature as a circumstance in ④**what** man's life is "solitary, poor, nasty, brutish and short". It means when people live without a general power to control ⑤**them** all, they are indeed in a state of war. In other words, Hobbes, who accepted that human beings are not social and political beings in the state of nature, believes that without the power human beings in the state of nature ⑥**is** "antisocial and rational based on their selfishness". Moreover, since society is not a natural phenomenon and there is no natural force bringing people together, ⑦**that** will bring them together as a society is not mutual ⑧**affection** according to Hobbes. It is, rather, mutual fear of men's present and future that ⑨**assembles** ⑩**themselves**, since the cause of fear is a common drive among people in the state of nature.

| 기호 | 어색한 표현 | | 올바른 표현 |
|---|---|---|---|
| ( ) | _____ | => | _____ |
| ( ) | _____ | => | _____ |
| ( ) | _____ | => | _____ |
| ( ) | _____ | => | _____ |
| ( ) | _____ | => | _____ |

**19.** 19)밑줄 부분 중 어법, 혹은 문맥상 어휘의 쓰임이 어색한 것을 올바르게 고쳐 쓰시오. (5개) 2024_H2_11_40

There is research that supports the idea that cognitive factors ①**influence on** the phenomenology of the perceived world. Delk and Fillenbaum asked participants to match the color of figures with the color of their background. Some of the figures ②**depicting** objects associated with a particular color. These ③**included** typically red objects such as an apple, lips, and a symbolic heart. Other objects were presented that are not usually associated with red, such as a mushroom or a bell. However, all the figures ④**made** out of the same red-orange cardboard. Participants then had to match the figure to a background ⑤**varied** from dark to light red. They had to make the background color ⑥**to match** the color of the figures. The researchers ⑦**found** that red-associated objects ⑧**required** more red in the background to ⑨**be judged** a match than did the objects that are not associated with the color red. This ⑩**implies** that the cognitive association of objects to color influences ⑪**how** we perceive that color.

| 기호 | 어색한 표현 | | 올바른 표현 |
|---|---|---|---|
| ( ) | _____ | => | _____ |
| ( ) | _____ | => | _____ |
| ( ) | _____ | => | _____ |
| ( ) | _____ | => | _____ |
| ( ) | _____ | => | _____ |

**20.** 20)밑줄 부분 중 어법, 혹은 문맥상 어휘의 쓰임이 어색한 것을 올바르게 고쳐 쓰시오. (5개) 2024_H2_11_41~42

In each round of genome copying in our body, there is still about a 70 percent chance that at least one pair of chromosomes will have an error. With each round of genome copying, errors ①**accumulate**. This is ②**similar to** ③**alternatives** in medieval books. Each time a copy was made by hand, some changes ④**were introduced** accidentally; as changes stacked up, the copies may have acquired meanings at variance with the original. Similarly, genomes that have undergone more copying processes will have gathered more mistakes. To make things ⑤**badly**, mutations may damage genes responsible for error checking and repair of genomes, further ⑥**accelerated** the introduction of mutations. Most genome mutations do not have any noticeable effects. It is just like changing the i for a y in "kingdom" would not distort the word's readability. But sometimes a mutation to a human gene results ⑦**from**, for example, an eye ⑧**whose** iris is of two different colors. Similarly, almost everyone has birthmarks, which are due to mutations that ⑨**occurred** as our body's cells multiplied to form skin. If mutations are changes to the genome of one particular cell, how can a patch of cells in an iris or a whole patch of skin, ⑩**consisting** of many individual cells, ⑪**be affected** simultaneously? The answer ⑫**lays** in the cell lineage, the developmental history of a tissue from particular cells through to their fully differentiated state. If the mutation ⑬**occurred** early on in the lineage of the developing iris, then all cells in that patch have ⑭**inherited** that change.

| 기호 | 어색한 표현 | | 올바른 표현 |
|---|---|---|---|
| ( ) | _____ | => | _____ |
| ( ) | _____ | => | _____ |
| ( ) | _____ | => | _____ |
| ( ) | _____ | => | _____ |
| ( ) | _____ | => | _____ |

**21.** 21)밑줄 부분 중 어법, 혹은 문맥상 어휘의 쓰임이 어색한 것을 올바르게 고쳐 쓰시오. (5개) 2024_H2_11_43~45

Max awoke to the gentle sunlight of an autumn day. Right on schedule, he swung his legs off the bed and took a deep, ①**satisfied** breath. He began his morning the same way he usually ②**did**, getting dressed and going to school. Today was going to be another perfect day until he ran into Mr. Kapoor, his science teacher. "Just to ③**remind** you. Science fair projects are due next Wednesday. Don't forget ④**to submit** your final draft on time," Mr. Kapoor said. Max froze. What? It can't be! It was due next Friday! After school, he came home ⑤**to worry** that his whole perfectly planned week was going to ⑥**ruin**. Without his usual greeting, Max headed to his room in haste. "What's wrong Max?," Jeremy, his dad, ⑦**followed** Max, worrying about him. Max furiously browsed through his planner without answering him, only to find the wrong date written in ⑧**them**. Fighting through tears, Max finally managed to ⑨**explain** the unending pressure to be perfect to his dad. To his surprise, Jeremy laughed. "Max, guess what? Perfect is a great goal, but nobody gets there all the time. What matters is what we do when things get messy." That made him ⑩**to feel** a little better. "You are saying I can fix this?" "Absolutely, try to deal with problems in a logical way," Jeremy said. Max thought for a moment. "I guess…. I can do that by rescheduling tonight's baseball lesson." Jeremy beamed. "See? That's you finding a solution." Max felt a genuine smile ⑪**spreading**. The next Wednesday, he successfully handed in the final draft on time with satisfaction. From then on, he still loved order and routines, but also embraced the messy, unpredictable bits of life too.

| 기호 | 어색한 표현 | | 올바른 표현 |
|---|---|---|---|
| (　　) | ＿＿＿＿＿＿＿＿ | => | ＿＿＿＿＿＿＿＿ |
| (　　) | ＿＿＿＿＿＿＿＿ | => | ＿＿＿＿＿＿＿＿ |
| (　　) | ＿＿＿＿＿＿＿＿ | => | ＿＿＿＿＿＿＿＿ |
| (　　) | ＿＿＿＿＿＿＿＿ | => | ＿＿＿＿＿＿＿＿ |
| (　　) | ＿＿＿＿＿＿＿＿ | => | ＿＿＿＿＿＿＿＿ |

# 2024 고2 11월 모의고사

❶ voca　　❷ text　　❸ [ / ]　　❹ ____　　❺ quiz 1　　❻ quiz 2　　❼ quiz 3　　❽ quiz 4　　❾ quiz 5

☑ **다음 글을 읽고 물음에 답하시오.** 2024_H2_11_18

Dear Executive Manager Schulz,It is a week before the internship program starts. I am writing to bring your attention to a matter that requires <sup>즉각적인</sup> _____ consideration regarding the issue my department has. As the coordinator, it is becoming apparent to me that the budget, previously approved by your department, needs some <sup>조정</sup> _____ in order to meet the emerging <sup>수정</sup> _____. ⓐ <u>Since my department has been hired three more interns as planned initially, the most expensive need is for additional funding to cover their wages, training costs, and materials.</u> I kindly request an additional budget <sup>배당</sup> _____ for these expenses. Please refer to the attachment for details. Thank you for your attention.Best regards,Matt Perry

1. <sup>1)</sup>힌트를 참고하여 각 <u>빈칸</u>에 알맞은 단어를 쓰시오.

2. <sup>2)</sup>밑줄 친 ⓐ에서, 어법 혹은 문맥상 어색한 부분을 찾아 올바르게 고쳐 쓰시오.

　ⓐ　　　잘못된 표현　　　　　　바른 표현
　( 　　　　　　　 ) ⇨ ( 　　　　　　　　 )
　( 　　　　　　　 ) ⇨ ( 　　　　　　　　 )

☑ **다음 글을 읽고 물음에 답하시오.** 2024_H2_11_19

Katie approached the hotel front desk to check-in but an <sup>예상하지 못한</sup> _____ event unfolded. The receptionist couldn't find her reservation under the name 'Katie'. "I'm sorry, but I can't seem to locate a reservation under that name," the receptionist said. "No way, I definitely made a reservation on the phone," Katie said, puzzled. The receptionist asked, "Can you tell me your phone number?" and Katie told it to him, thinking 'What happened? Did I make a mistake?' "Just a moment," the receptionist said, typing <sup>의도적으로</sup> _____ on the keyboard. "I found it! It seems there was a small misspelling. Your reservation is under 'K-A-T-Y'," the receptionist explained. (가) <u>편안한 기분으로</u> Katie watched her reservation appearing on the screen. With her heart slowing to a gentle rhythm, she proceeded with her check-in, thinking that a simple misspelling might have ruined her plans.

3. <sup>3)</sup>힌트를 참고하여 각 <u>빈칸</u>에 알맞은 단어를 쓰시오.

4. <sup>4)</sup>위 글에 주어진 (가)의 한글과 같은 의미를 가지도록, 각각의 주어진 단어들을 알맞게 배열하시오.

(가) a / sense / With / of / ease,

☑ **다음 글을 읽고 물음에 답하시오.** 2024_H2_11_20

To be mathematically <sup>문해력 있는</sup> _____ means to be able to think critically about societal issues on which mathematics has bearing so as to make informed decisions about how to solve these problems. Dealing with such complex problems through <sup>범교과적인</sup> _____ approaches, mirroring real-world problems requires innovative ways of planning and organizing mathematical teaching methods. ⓐ <u>Navigating our world means are able to quantify, measure, estimate, classify, compare, find patterns, conjecture, justify, prove, and generalize within critical thinking and when using critical thinking.</u> Therefore, making decisions, even <sup>질적으로</sup> _____, is not possible without using mathematics and critical thinking. Thus, (가) <u>수학을 가르치는 것은 의사 결정 과정과 함께 비판적 사고와의 상호 작용 안에서 이루어져야 한다.</u> They can be developed into the mathematical context, so that there is no <sup>변명</sup> _____ to not explicitly support students to develop them.

5. 5)힌트를 참고하여 각 빈칸에 알맞은 단어를 쓰시오.

6. 6)밑줄 친 ⓐ에서, 어법 혹은 문맥상 어색한 부분을 찾아 올바르게 고쳐 쓰시오.
   ⓐ       잘못된 표현        바른 표현
   (           ) ⇨ (            )

7. 7)위 글에 주어진 (가)의 한글과 같은 의미를 가지도록, 각각의 주어진 단어들을 알맞게 배열하시오.

> (가) along / with / with / teaching / done / be / critical / should / interaction / process. / thinking / in / mathematics / decision-making / a

☑ **다음 글을 읽고 물음에 답하시오.** 2024_H2_11_21

Imagine that your usually stingy friend delights in buying you a Christmas present after taking a <sup>관대함</sup> _____ booster. How would you feel? <sup>의심할 여지 없이</sup> _____, there is something praiseworthy about the action. ⓐ <u>You'd be pleasing to receive the gift.</u> You'd say 'thank you', and mean it. But his change of heart is not entirely satisfying. According to Zagzebski, an American philosopher, he is not really generous. When we praise someone's character, we use words for various virtues: 'generous', 'kind', 'courageous', etc. A person who gives one gift isn't generous. Instead, generosity is a <sup>안정된</sup> _____ part of a person's 'moral identity', an emotional habit that is part of who you are. Thus virtues, as opposed to nontypical <sup>충동</sup> _____, are the result of your personal history. (가) <u>그것들이 여러분의 인품이 형성되었던 방식의 일부이기 때문에 그것들은 여러분의 모습 중 일부이다</u> Instant virtue is therefore impossible. Popping a pill cannot make you a better person.

8. 8)힌트를 참고하여 각 빈칸에 알맞은 단어를 쓰시오.

9. 9)밑줄 친 ⓐ에서, 어법 혹은 문맥상 어색한 부분을 찾아 올바르게 고쳐 쓰시오.
   ⓐ       잘못된 표현        바른 표현
   (           ) ⇨ (            )

10. 10)위 글에 주어진 (가)의 한글과 같은 의미를 가지도록, 각각의 주어진 단어들을 알맞게 배열하시오.

> (가) of / was / character / who / of / how / are, / formed. / are / they / part / as / are / your / They / part / you

☑ **다음 글을 읽고 물음에 답하시오.** 2024_H2_11_22

To determine the mass of my bowling ball, I might put it onto a balance and compare it with a known mass, such as a number of metal cubes each weighing 1, 10, or 100 grams. (가) 만약 내가 먼 별의 질량을 알고 싶다면 상황은 훨씬 더 복잡해진다. How do I measure it? We can roughly say that measuring the mass of a star involves various theories. ⓐ <u>If we want to measuring the mass of a binary star, we first determine a center of mass between the two stars, then their distance from that center where we can then use, together with a value for the period and a certain instance of Kepler's Third Law, to calculate the mass.</u> <sup>들어갈 연결어</sup> _____, in order to "measure" the star mass, we measure other quantities and use those values, together with certain equations, to calculate the mass. Measurement is not a simple and <sup>중재되지 않은</sup> _____ estimation of independently existing properties, but a determination of certain magnitudes before the background of a number of accepted theories.

11. 11)힌트를 참고하여 각 빈칸에 알맞은 단어를 쓰시오.

12. 12)밑줄 친 ⓐ에서, 어법 혹은 문맥상 어색한 부분을 찾아 올바르게 고쳐 쓰시오.

  ⓐ      잘못된 표현          바른 표현
    (               ) ⇨ (              )
    (               ) ⇨ (              )

13. 13)위 글에 주어진 (가)의 한글과 같은 의미를 가지도록, 각각의 주어진 단어들을 알맞게 배열하시오.

(가) the / star. / to / a / I / Things / get / more / distant / know / mass / want / complicated / of / much / if

☑ **다음 글을 읽고 물음에 답하시오.** 2024_H2_11_23

Based on discoveries in neuroscience, pain and pleasure are formed and processed in the same area of the brain. Our bodies constantly <sup>-를 추구하다</sup> _____ homeostasis, which is defined as the balance of bodily functions. Without the body's effective <sup>보상의</sup> _____ mechanisms, which may cushion <sup>잠재적인</sup> _____ highs and lows, we would not be capable of surviving. Pleasure and pain are like two sides of the same coin; they seem to work together and are heavily reliant on one another and keep balance. If you imagine pleasure and pain as the two opposite points on a scale, you can easily understand that as one of the two points rises, the other must <sup>상응하여</sup> _____ fall. ⓐ <u>We've all hearing the expression, "No pain, no gain."</u> Well, according to psychiatrist Dr. Anna Lembke, there may be some truth to these words. (가) 그녀는 우리가 비참함에서 벗어나려는 우리의 시도가 사실 우리를 훨씬 더 비참하게 만들고 있다고 말한다. This is because pain is actually an essential component of our ability to maintain a neutral state, and allowing it will in turn reset our internal scale back to balance.

14. 14)힌트를 참고하여 각 빈칸에 알맞은 단어를 쓰시오.

**15.** <sup>15)</sup>밑줄 친 ⓐ에서, 어법 혹은 문맥상 어색한 부분을 찾아 올바르게 고쳐 쓰시오.

　　ⓐ　　　잘못된 표현　　　　　　바른 표현
　　(　　　　　　　　　) ⇨ (　　　　　　　　　　)

**16.** <sup>16)</sup>위 글에 주어진 (가)의 한글과 같은 의미를 가지도록, 각각의 주어진 단어들을 알맞게 배열하시오.

(가) She / in / even / miserable / us / being / fact / says / attempts / miserable. / more / escape / to / are / our / that / making

☑ **다음 글을 읽고 물음에 답하시오.** <sup>2024_H2_11_24</sup>

Manufacturers masterfully sow seeds of doubt about the <sup>적절성</sup> _____ of our current devices. Suddenly, the phone that was your lifeline a year ago is now a museum piece, unable to keep pace with your digital demands. ⓐ And thus, the itch to upgrade begins, often before there's a genuine need. This cycle isn't just defined to our digital companions. ⓑ It spills over into almost every aspects of consumer electronics, from the self-driving car to the smart fridge. ⓒ Every product seems to be on an unstoppable march towards the next version, the next generation that promise to revolutionize your life. (가) 흥미로운 점, 또는 어쩌면 당황스러운 점은 우리의 욕구를 형성하는 이 순환의 절대적인 효과이다 It's not so much that we want the newest device; we're led to believe we need it. The distinction between want and need <sup>흐릿해지다</sup> _____, shifting our financial <sup>우선순위</sup> _____ in favor of staying current with trends. For all the logical arguments against this <sup>끊임없는</sup> _____ upgrading, the <sup>매력</sup> _____ remains compelling.

**17.** <sup>17)</sup>힌트를 참고하여 각 빈칸에 알맞은 단어를 쓰시오.

**18.** <sup>18)</sup>밑줄 친 ⓐ에서, 어법 혹은 문맥상 어색한 부분을 찾아 올바르게 고쳐 쓰시오.

　　ⓐ　　　잘못된 표현　　　　　　바른 표현
　　(　　　　　　　　　) ⇨ (　　　　　　　　　　)

**19.** <sup>19)</sup>밑줄 친 ⓑ에서, 어법 혹은 문맥상 어색한 부분을 찾아 올바르게 고쳐 쓰시오.

　　ⓑ　　　잘못된 표현　　　　　　바른 표현
　　(　　　　　　　　　) ⇨ (　　　　　　　　　　)

**20.** <sup>20)</sup>밑줄 친 ⓒ에서, 어법 혹은 문맥상 어색한 부분을 찾아 올바르게 고쳐 쓰시오.

　　ⓒ　　　잘못된 표현　　　　　　바른 표현
　　(　　　　　　　　　) ⇨ (　　　　　　　　　　)

**21.** <sup>21)</sup>위 글에 주어진 (가)의 한글과 같은 의미를 가지도록, 각각의 주어진 단어들을 알맞게 배열하시오.

(가) cycle / shaping / desires. / perhaps / or / in / utter / the / What's / our / this / disturbing, / efficacy / fascinating, / of / is

☑ **다음 글을 읽고 물음에 답하시오.** 2024_H2_11_29

Conditioned Place Preference is a way of finding out what animals want. Researchers train them to <sup>연관시키다</sup> _____ one place with an experience such as food or a loud noise and another place with something completely different, usually where nothing happens. (가) 그 두 장소는 그 동물이 각 장소를 거기에서 그것에게 일어난 일과 연관시키는 것을 가능한 한 쉽게 만들기 위해 명백히 다르게 만들어진다. ⓐ <u>The animal's defence for being in one place or another is measured both before and after its experiences in the two places.</u> ⓑ <u>If there is a shift in which the animal chooses spending its time for the reward, this suggests what it liked the experience and is trying to repeat it.</u> <sup>들어갈 연결어</sup> _____, if it now avoids the place the stimulus appeared and starts to prefer the place it did not experience it, then this suggests that it found the stimulus <sup>불쾌한</sup> _____. For example, mice with cancer show a preference for the place where they have been given morphine, a drug used to <sup>완화하다</sup> _____ pain, rather than where they have received saline whereas healthy mice developed no such preference. This suggests that the mice with cancer wanted the morphine.

22. 22)힌트를 참고하여 각 빈칸에 알맞은 단어를 쓰시오.


23. 23)밑줄 친 ⓐ에서, 어법 혹은 문맥상 어색한 부분을 찾아 올바르게 고쳐 쓰시오.
   ⓐ       잘못된 표현         바른 표현
   (               ) ⇨ (               )


24. 24)밑줄 친 ⓑ에서, 어법 혹은 문맥상 어색한 부분을 찾아 올바르게 고쳐 쓰시오.
   ⓑ       잘못된 표현         바른 표현
   (               ) ⇨ (               )
   (               ) ⇨ (               )
   (               ) ⇨ (               )

25. 25)위 글에 주어진 (가)의 한글과 같은 의미를 가지도록, 각각의 주어진 단어들을 알맞게 배열하시오.

(가) to / it / The / easy / possible / different / as / associate / places / two / to / each / with / to / animal / what / there. / for / are / it / place / make / the / made / as / happened / obviously

☑ **다음 글을 읽고 물음에 답하시오.** 2024_H2_11_30

Near the ^적도 _____, many species of bird breed all year round. But in temperate and polar regions, the breeding seasons of birds are often sharply defined. They are ^촉발하다 _____ mainly by changes in day length. If all goes well, the outcome is that birds raise their young when the food supply is at its peak. (가) 대부분의 새들은 다른 때에 번식하기를 단지 꺼리는 것뿐만 아니라 또한 신체적으로 그렇게 할 수 없는 것이다 This is because their ^번식의 _____system shrinks, which helps flying birds save weight. The main exception to this rule are ^유목의 _____ desert species. These can initiate their breeding cycle within days of rain. ⓐ It's for making the most of the sudden breeding opportunity. Also, different species combine the breeding season up in different ways. Most seabirds raise a single brood. In warm regions, however, songbirds may raise several families in a few months. In an ^유난히 _____ good year, a pair of House Sparrows, a kind of songbird, can raise successive broods through a marathon reproductive effort.

26. 26)힌트를 참고하여 각 빈칸에 알맞은 단어를 쓰시오.

27. 27)밑줄 친 ⓐ에서, 어법 혹은 문맥상 어색한 부분을 찾아 올바르게 고쳐 쓰시오.
　　ⓐ　　　잘못된 표현　　　　　바른 표현
　　( 　　　　　　　) ⇨ ( 　　　　　　　)

28. 28)위 글에 주어진 (가)의 한글과 같은 의미를 가지도록, 각각의 주어진 단어들을 알맞게 배열하시오.

(가) Most / times / so. / of / but / they / at / incapable / doing / not / reluctant / breed / simply / birds / physically / other / are / also / are / to

☑ **다음 글을 읽고 물음에 답하시오.** 2024_H2_11_31

One factor that may ^방해하다 _____ creativity is unawareness of the resources required in each activity in students' learning. (가) 종종 학생들은 그들에게 요구되는 과제를 수행하는 데 필요한 자원들을 식별할 수 없다. Different resources may be ^필수적인 _____ for specific learning tasks, and recognizing them may simplify the activity's performance. For example, it may be that students desire to ^수행하다 _____ some experiments in their projects. ⓐ There must be a superior investigation of whether the students will have access to the laboratory, equipment, and chemicals inquired for the experiment. It means preparation is vital for the students to succeed, and it may be about human and financial resources such as laboratory technicians, money to purchase chemicals, and equipment for their learning where applicable. (나) 과제에 요구되는 자원들 중 일부가 이용 가능하지 않을 수도 있지만, 사전에 그것들을 식별하는 것은 학생들의 창의성에 도움이 될 수도 있다. It may even lead to changing the topic, finding ^대체 _____ resources, and other means.

29. 29)힌트를 참고하여 각 빈칸에 알맞은 단어를 쓰시오.

30. 30)밑줄 친 ⓐ에서, 어법 혹은 문맥상 어색한 부분을 찾아 올바르게 고쳐 쓰시오.
　　ⓐ　　　잘못된 표현　　　　　바른 표현
　　( 　　　　　　　) ⇨ ( 　　　　　　　)
　　( 　　　　　　　) ⇨ ( 　　　　　　　)

**31.** <sup>31)</sup>위 글에 주어진 (가) ~ (나)의 한글과 같은 의미를 가지도록, 각각의 주어진 단어들을 알맞게 배열하시오.

> (가) students / required / unable / perform / resources / are / they / identify / need / Often / the / task / to / to / of / the / them.

> (나) help / required / if / available, / some / advance / for / the / may / creativity. / resources / Even / students' / of / in / be / task / a / not / may / identifying / them

☑ **다음 글을 읽고 물음에 답하시오.** <sup>2024_H2_11_32</sup>

(가) <u>모든 번역가들은 그들이 대상으로 작업하고 있는 독자들의 공동체로부터 약간의 압박을 느낀다.</u> And all translators arrive at their <sup>해석</sup> _____ in <sup>대화</sup> _____ with other people. The English poet Alexander ⓐ <u>Pope had pretty good Greek, but when he set about transporting Homer's Iliad in the early 18th century he was not on his own. He had Greek commentaries to refer,</u> and translations that had already been done in English, Latin, and French — and of course he had dictionaries. Translators always draw on more than one source text. Even when the scene of translation consists of just one person with a pen, paper, and the book that is being translated, or even when it is just one person translating <sup>구두로</sup> _____ for another, that person's linguistic knowledge arises from lots of other texts and other conversations. And then (나) <u>번역의 목적에 대한 그 또는 그녀의 생각은 이것의 대상이 되는 사람 또는 사람들의 기대에 의해 영향을 받는다.</u> In both these senses every translation is a crowd translation.

**32.** <sup>32)</sup>힌트를 참고하여 각 <u>빈칸</u>에 알맞은 단어를 쓰시오.

**33.** <sup>33)</sup>밑줄 친 ⓐ에서, 어법 혹은 문맥상 어색한 부분을 찾아 올바르게 고쳐 쓰시오.

  ⓐ       잘못된 표현          바른 표현

    (           ) ⇨ (          )

    (           ) ⇨ (          )

**34.** <sup>34)</sup>위 글에 주어진 (가) ~ (나)의 한글과 같은 의미를 가지도록, 각각의 주어진 단어들을 알맞게 배열하시오.

> (가) doing / community / work. / feel / translators / pressure / All / some / of / their / readers / the / whom / they / for / are / from

> (나) is / translation's / for. / of / of / or / her / be / it / will / the person or people / purpose / the / influenced / the expectations / by / his / idea

☑ **다음 글을 읽고 물음에 답하시오.** 2024_H2_11_33

Some people argue that there is a single, logically consistent concept known as reading that can be neatly set apart from everything else people do with books. Is reading really that simple? The most 생산적인 _____ way to think about reading is as a loosely related set of behaviors that belong together owing to family 유사성 _____, as Ludwig Wittgenstein used the phrase, without having in common a single defining trait. ⓐ Consequently, efforts to distinguish reading from nonreading is destined to fail because there is no agreement on what quantifies as reading in the first place. (가) 읽기와 읽기가 아닌 것 사이의 경계가 어디에 있는가를 알려고 하면 할수록, 더욱 많은 특이 사례들이 그 용어의 유연한 경계를 확장하고 있다는 것이 밝혀질 것이다. ⓑ Thus, it is worthy attempting to collect together these exceptional forms of reading into a single forum, one highlighting the challenges faced by anyone wish to establish the boundaries where reading begins and ends. (나) 그러한 시도는 별개의 읽기 활동들을 다 수용할 만큼 충분히 광 범위한 스펙트럼으로서 읽기를 이해하는 것으로 발전한다.

35. 35)힌트를 참고하여 각 빈칸에 알맞은 단어를 쓰시오.

36. 36)밑줄 친 ⓐ에서, 어법 혹은 문맥상 어색한 부분을 찾아 올바르게 고쳐 쓰시오.

  ⓐ     잘못된 표현         바른 표현
  (            ) ⇨ (            )
  (            ) ⇨ (            )

37. 37)밑줄 친 ⓑ에서, 어법 혹은 문맥상 어색한 부분을 찾아 올바르게 고쳐 쓰시오.

  ⓑ     잘못된 표현         바른 표현
  (            ) ⇨ (            )
  (            ) ⇨ (            )

38. 38)위 글에 주어진 (가) ~ (나)의 한글과 같은 의미를 가지도록, 각각의 주어진 단어들을 알맞게 배열하시오.

(가) The / where / the / cases / more / will / not-reading, / more / and / the border / figure / found / lies / between / be / the term's flexible boundaries. / tries / out / one / to / to / reading / edge / stretch

(나) expansive / distinct / that / a spectrum / the / moves / is / of / as / activities. / toward / reading / The attempt / to / reading / understanding / enough / an / accommodate

☑ **다음 글을 읽고 물음에 답하시오.** 2024_H2_11_34

Weber's law concerns the <sup>감지</sup> _____ of difference between two stimuli. It suggests that we might not be able to detect a 1-mm difference when we are looking at lines 466 mm and 467 mm in length, but we may be able to detect a 1-mm difference when we are comparing a line 2 mm long with one 3 mm long. Another example of this principle is that we can detect 1 candle when it is lit in an <sup>그렇지 않았더라면</sup> _____ dark room. ⓐ <u>But when 1 candle is light in a room in where 100 candles are already burning, we may not notice the light from this candle.</u> Therefore, the Just-noticeable difference (JND) varies as a function of the strength of the signals. ⓑ <u>For example, the JND is greater for very loud noises than it is for much more quiet sounds. When a sound is very strong , we can tell that another sound is louder, even if it is very louder.</u> When a sound is very loud, to tell that another sound is even louder, it has to be much louder. Thus, (가) 베버의 법칙은 그 표본들이 자극의 수준이 더 크거나 강할 때 두 표본을 구별하기가 더 어렵다는 것을 의미한다.

39. <sup>39)</sup>힌트를 참고하여 각 빈칸에 알맞은 단어를 쓰시오.

40. <sup>40)</sup>밑줄 친 ⓐ에서, 어법 혹은 문맥상 어색한 부분을 찾아 올바르게 고쳐 쓰시오.

| ⓐ | 잘못된 표현 | | 바른 표현 |
|---|---|---|---|
| ( | ) | ⇨ ( | ) |
| ( | ) | ⇨ ( | ) |

41. <sup>41)</sup>밑줄 친 ⓑ에서, 어법 혹은 문맥상 어색한 부분을 찾아 올바르게 고쳐 쓰시오.

| ⓑ | 잘못된 표현 | | 바른 표현 |
|---|---|---|---|
| ( | ) | ⇨ ( | ) |
| ( | ) | ⇨ ( | ) |

42. <sup>42)</sup>위 글에 주어진 (가)의 한글과 같은 의미를 가지도록, 각각의 주어진 단어들을 알맞게 배열하시오.

(가) it / when / stimuli. / larger / samples / between / those / law / is / two / that / samples / distinguish / the / harder / Weber's / means / to / are / stronger / or / levels / of

☑ **다음 글을 읽고 물음에 답하시오.** 2024_H2_11_35

Any new resource (e.g., a new airport, a new mall) always opens with people benefiting individually by sharing a common resource (e.g., the city or state budget). Soon, at some point, the amount of 교통량 _____ grows too large for the "commons" to support. Traffic jams, overcrowding, and overuse lessen the benefits of the common resource for everyone —the tragedy of the 들어갈 적절한 단어 본문 활용 _____! If the new resource cannot be expanded or provided with additional space, it becomes a problem, and you cannot solve the problem on your own, in 고립 _____ from your fellow drivers or walkers or competing users. The total activity on this new resource keeps increasing, and so does individual activity; but if the dynamic of common use and overuse continues too long, both begin to fall after a peak, leading to a crash. What makes the "tragedy of 들어갈 적절한 단어 본문 활용 _____" tragic is the crash dynamic —the destruction or degeneration of the common resource's ability to 재생산하다 _____ itself.

43. 43)힌트를 참고하여 각 빈칸에 알맞은 단어를 쓰시오.

☑ **다음 글을 읽고 물음에 답하시오.** 2024_H2_11_36

Theoretically, our brain would have the 수용력 _____ to store all experiences throughout life, reaching the quality of a DVD. However, this theoretical capacity is offset by the energy demand associated with the process of storing and 상기하다 _____ information in memory. ⓐ As a result, the brain develops efficient strategies, becoming independent on shortcuts. When we observe a face, the visual image capturing the eyes is highly variable, depending on the point of view, lighting conditions and other contextual factors. Similarly, we are able to recognize the face as the same, maintaining the underlying identity. The brain, rather than focusing on the details of visualization, creates and stores general patterns that allow for 지속적인 _____ recognition across diverse circumstances. This ability to match what we see with general visual memory patterns serves as an effective mechanism for optimizing brain performance and saving energy. (가) 불필요한 노력에 자연스럽게 대항하는 뇌는 인지 과정을 돕기 위해서 끊임없이 정보를 단순화하고 일반화하는 것을 추구한다.

44. 44)힌트를 참고하여 각 빈칸에 알맞은 단어를 쓰시오.

45. 45)밑줄 친 ⓐ에서, 어법 혹은 문맥상 어색한 부분을 찾아 올바르게 고쳐 쓰시오.

| ⓐ | 잘못된 표현 | | 바른 표현 |
|---|---|---|---|
| ( | ) | ⇨ ( | ) |
| ( | ) | ⇨ ( | ) |
| ( | ) | ⇨ ( | ) |

46. 46)위 글에 주어진 (가)의 한글과 같은 의미를 가지도록, 각각의 주어진 단어들을 알맞게 배열하시오.

(가) information / to / the / to / effort, / constantly / naturally / being / process. / generalize / cognitive / and / unnecessary / simplify / against / seeks / The / facilitate / brain,

☑ **다음 글을 읽고 물음에 답하시오.** 2024_H2_11_37

Where scientific research is concerned, explanatory tales are expected to adhere closely to experimental data and to illuminate the regular and <sup>예측가능한</sup> _____ features of experience. However, this paradigm sometimes <sup>감추다</sup> _____ the fact that theories are deeply loaded with creative elements that shape the construction of research projects and the interpretations of evidence. Scientific explanations do not just relate a <sup>연대기</sup> _____ of facts. They construct frameworks for systematically chosen data in order to provide a consistent and meaningful explanation of what is observed. Such constructions lead us to imagine specific kinds of subject matter in particular sorts of relations, and the storylines they inspire will prove more effective for <sup>분석하다</sup> _____ some features of experience over others. When we <sup>무시하다</sup> _____ the creative contributions of such scientific imagination and treat models and interpretive explanations as straightforward facts — even worse, as facts including all of reality — (가) <u>우리는 주어진 모델의 한계에 대해 우리 스스로를 눈멀게 하며 그것이 잘못 적용되는 상황에 대해 오해할 가능성을 알아차리지 못할 수 있다.</u>

47. 47)힌트를 참고하여 각 <u>빈칸에 알맞은</u> 단어를 쓰시오.

48. 48)위 글에 주어진 (가)의 한글과 같은 의미를 가지도록, 각각의 주어진 단어들을 알맞게 배열하시오.

(가) which / the / to / of / situation / ourselves / can / misunderstanding / potential / limitations / and / given / it / for / a / applies. / its / to / fail / model / blind / we / a / ill / to / note

☑ **다음 글을 읽고 물음에 답하시오.** 2024_H2_11_38

We encounter contrary claims about the relation of literature to action. (가) <u>이론가들은 문학이 세상과 관계를 맺는 방법으로써 고독한 독서와 성찰을 장려하고 따라서 사회 변화를 일으킬 수 있을지도 모르는 사회적이고 정치적인 활동들에 거스른다고 주장해 왔다.</u> At best it encourages detachment or appreciation of complexity, and at worst passivity and acceptance of what is. But on the other hand, literature has historically been seen as dangerous: it promotes the questioning of <sup>권위</sup> _____ and social arrangements. ⓐ <u>Plato banned poets from his idle republic because they could only do harm, and novels have long credited with making people satisfied with their lives and eager for something new.</u> By promoting identification across divisions of class, gender, and race, books may promote a fellowship that discourages struggle; but they may also produce a keen sense of <sup>불의</sup> _____ that makes progressive struggles possible. Historically, works of literature are credited with producing change: Uncle Tom's Cabin, a best-seller in its day, helped create a <sup>혐오감</sup> _____ against slavery that made possible the American Civil War.

49. 49)힌트를 참고하여 각 <u>빈칸에 알맞은</u> 단어를 쓰시오.

50. 50)밑줄 친 ⓐ에서, 어법 혹은 문맥상 어색한 부분을 찾아 올바르게 고쳐 쓰시오.

| ⓐ | 잘못된 표현 | | 바른 표현 |
|---|---|---|---|
| | ( ) | ⇨ | ( ) |
| | ( ) | ⇨ | ( ) |
| | ( ) | ⇨ | ( ) |

51. 51)위 글에 주어진 (가)의 한글과 같은 의미를 가지도록, 각각의 주어진 단어들을 알맞게 배열하시오.

(가) counters / the way / and / might / Theorists / change. / that / maintained / as / encourages / the world / reading / the social and political activities / solitary / reflection / with / thus / and / to / engage / have / produce / that / literature / social

☑ **다음 글을 읽고 물음에 답하시오.** <sup>2024_H2_11_39</sup>

According to Hobbes, man is not a being who can act morally in spite of his instinct to protect his existence in the state of nature. Hence, the only place where morality and moral liberty will begin to find an application begins in a place where a <sup>군주 권력</sup> _____, namely the state, emerges. ⓐ <u>Hobbes thus describes the state of nature as a circumstance in which man's life is "solitary, poor, nasty, brutish and short".</u> It means when people live with a general power to control them all, they are indeed in a state of war. In other words, Hobbes, who accepted that human beings are not social and political beings in the state of nature, believing that without the power human beings in the state of nature are "antisocial and rational based on their selfishness". Moreover, since society is not a natural phenomenon and there is no natural force bringing people together, that will bring them together as a society is not mutual affection according to Hobbes. (가) 두려움으로부터의 동기가 자연 상태에 있는 사람들 사이의 공통된 추진력이기 때문에, 오히려, 그들을 모으는 것은 인간의 현재와 미래에 대한 상호 간의 두려움이다.

52. <sup>52)</sup>힌트를 참고하여 각 <u>빈칸</u>에 알맞은 단어를 쓰시오.

53. <sup>53)</sup>밑줄 친 ⓐ에서, 어법 혹은 문맥상 어색한 부분을 찾아 올바르게 고쳐 쓰시오.

| ⓐ | 잘못된 표현 | | 바른 표현 |
|---|---|---|---|
| ( | ) | ⇨ ( | ) |
| ( | ) | ⇨ ( | ) |
| ( | ) | ⇨ ( | ) |

54. <sup>54)</sup>위 글에 주어진 (가)의 한글과 같은 의미를 가지도록, 각각의 주어진 단어들을 알맞게 배열하시오.

(가) men's / the cause / that / in / them, / common / of / is / nature. / It / rather, / fear / and / people / drive / since / mutual / the state / among / of / present / a / future / of / is, / fear / assembles

☑ **다음 글을 읽고 물음에 답하시오.** 2024_H2_11_40

There is research that supports the idea that cognitive factors influence the phenomenology of the <sup>인지되는</sup> _____ world. ⓐ Delk and Fillenbaum asked participants match the color of figures with the color of their background. Some of the figures were depicted objects associated with a particular color. These included typically red objects such as an apple, lips, and a <sup>상징적인</sup> _____ heart. Other objects were presented that are not usually associated with red, such as a mushroom or a bell. However, all the figures were made out of the same red-orange cardboard. (가) 그러고 나서 참가자들은 그 형상을 진한 빨간색에서 연한 빨간색까지 다양한 배경색과 맞춰야 했다. They had to make the background color match the color of the figures. The researchers found that red-associated objects required more red in the background to be judged a match than did the objects that are not associated with the color red. (나) 이는 물체들의 색상에 대한 그들의 지식이 그들의 지각적 판단에 영향을 미쳤다는 것을 보여준다.

55. <sup>55)</sup>힌트를 참고하여 각 빈칸에 알맞은 단어를 쓰시오.

56. <sup>56)</sup>밑줄 친 ⓐ에서, 어법 혹은 문맥상 어색한 부분을 찾아 올바르게 고쳐 쓰시오.

   ⓐ       잘못된 표현             바른 표현

   (             ) ⇨ (             )

   (             ) ⇨ (             )

57. <sup>57)</sup>위 글에 주어진 (가) ~ (나)의 한글과 같은 의미를 가지도록, 각각의 주어진 단어들을 알맞게 배열하시오.

(가) match / to / from / light / then / background / had / figure / to / varying / the / red. / dark / a / to / Participants

(나) influences / how / This / that / we / color / to / color. / the / implies / cognitive / perceive / objects / that / of / association

☑ **다음 글을 읽고 물음에 답하시오.** 2024_H2_11_41~42

ⓐ In each round of genome copy in our body, there is still about a 70 percent chance that at least one pair of chromosomes will have an error. With each round of genome copy , errors accumulate. This is similar to alterations in 중세의 _____ books. Each time a copy was made by hand, some changes were introduced accidentally; as changes stacked up, the copies may have acquired meanings at variance with the original. Similarly, genomes that have undergone more copying processes will have gathered more mistakes. (가) 설상가상으로, 변이들은 게놈의 오류 확인과 복구를 책임지는 유전자를 훼손해 변이들의 도입을 더욱 가속할 수도 있다. Most genome mutations do not have any noticeable effects. It is just like changing the i for a y in "kingdom" would not distort the word's readability. But sometimes a mutation to a human gene results in, for example, an eye whose iris is of two different colors. 들어갈 연결어 _____, almost everyone has birthmarks, which are due to mutations that occurred as our body's cells multiplied to form skin. If mutations are changes to the genome of one particular cell, how can a patch of cells in an iris or a whole patch of skin, consisting of many individual cells, be affected 동시에 _____? The answer lies in the cell 계보 _____, the developmental history of a tissue from particular cells through to their fully differentiated state. (나) 만약 발달 중인 홍채의 계보 초기에 변이가 발생했다면, 그렇다면 그 세포 집단의 모든 세포는 그 변화를 물려받아 왔을 것이다.

58. 58)힌트를 참고하여 각 빈칸에 알맞은 단어를 쓰시오.

59. 59)밑줄 친 ⓐ에서, 어법 혹은 문맥상 어색한 부분을 찾아 올바르게 고쳐 쓰시오.

    ⓐ      잘못된 표현         바른 표현

    (              ) ⇨ (             )
    (              ) ⇨ (             )

60. 60)위 글에 주어진 (가) ~ (나)의 한글과 같은 의미를 가지도록, 각각의 주어진 단어들을 알맞게 배열하시오.

(가) error / of / introduction / mutations. / further / checking / make / mutations / repair / for / the / worse, / To / damage / responsible / and / may / things / accelerating / genes / of / genomes,

(나) of / iris, / that / inherited / lineage / the / have / all / then / change. / the mutation / the / occurred / in / that / on / cells / early / in / If / patch / developing

☑ **다음 글을 읽고 물음에 답하시오.** 2024_H2_11_43~45

ⓐ Max awoke to the gentle sunlight of an autumn day. Right on schedule, he swung his legs off the bed and took a deep, satisfying breath. He began his morning the same way he usually was , getting dressing and going to school. Today was going to be another perfect day until he ran into Mr. Kapoor, his science teacher. "Just to <sup>상기시키다</sup> _____ you. Science fair projects are due next Wednesday. Don't forget to submit your final draft on time," Mr. Kapoor said. Max froze. What? It can't be! It was due next Friday! After school, he came home worrying that his whole perfectly planned week was going to be ruined. Without his usual greeting, Max headed to his room <sup>급하게 2단어</sup> _____. "What's wrong Max?," Jeremy, his dad, followed Max, worrying about him. (가) <u>Max는 그에게 대답하지 않고 열성적으로 그의 일정표를 뒤적거렸지만, 거기에 잘못 적힌 날짜를 발견할 뿐이었다.</u> Fighting through tears, Max finally managed to explain the unending pressure to be perfect to his dad. To his surprise, Jeremy laughed. "Max, guess what? Perfect is a great goal, but nobody gets there all the time. (나) <u>중요한 건 일이 어질러졌을 때 우리가 무엇을 하는가야."</u> That made him feel a little better. "You are saying I can fix this?" "Absolutely, try to deal with problems in a logical way," Jeremy said. Max thought for a moment. "I guess…. I can do that by rescheduling tonight's baseball lesson." Jeremy beamed. "See? That's you finding a solution." Max felt a genuine smile spreading. The next Wednesday, he successfully handed in the final draft on time with <sup>만족감</sup> _____. From then on, he still loved order and routines, but also embraced the messy, <sup>예측 불가능한</sup> _____ bits of life too.

61. <sup>61)</sup>힌트를 참고하여 각 빈칸에 알맞은 단어를 쓰시오.

62. <sup>62)</sup>밑줄 친 ⓐ에서, 어법 혹은 문맥상 어색한 부분을 찾아 올바르게 고쳐 쓰시오.

| ⓐ 잘못된 표현 | | 바른 표현 |
|---|---|---|
| ( ) | ⇨ | ( ) |
| ( ) | ⇨ | ( ) |

63. <sup>63)</sup>위 글에 주어진 (가) ~ (나)의 한글과 같은 의미를 가지도록, 각각의 주어진 단어들을 알맞게 배열하시오.

(가) Max / his / wrong / browsed / find / him, / only / written / the / it. / without / planner / date / through / to / in / answering / furiously

(나) What / is / things / what / we / do / get / messy. / when / matters

보듬영어

# 정답

## WORK BOOK

——

**2024년 고2 11월 모의고사 내신대비용 WorkBook & 변형문제**

## Prac 1 Answers

1) attention
2) hired
3) more
4) attachment
5) attention
6) unfolded
7) puzzled
8) What
9) appearing
10) proceeded
11) literate
12) complex
13) requires
14) making
15) be done
16) critical
17) explicitly
18) something
19) pleased
20) entirely
21) moral
22) identity
23) nontypical
24) personal
25) impossible
26) more
27) that
28) other
29) independently
30) accepted
31) are
32) same
33) strive
34) which
35) effective
36) capable
37) same
38) opposite
39) that
40) theother
41) that
42) are
43) more
44) because
45) neutral
46) reset
47) doubt
48) devices
49) genuine
50) confined
51) aspect
52) seems
53) What
54) fascinating
55) distinction
56) blurs
57) compelling
58) Preference
59) what
60) associate
61) another
62) different
63) different
64) associate
65) what
66) preference
67) reward
68) to repeat
69) starts
70) unpleasant
71) preference
72) preference
73) breed

74) outcome
75) raise
76) other
77) because
78) exception
79) different
80) raise
81) warm
82) raise
83) raise
84) successive
85) hinder
86) Different
87) specific
88) access
89) vital
90) available
91) alternative
92) arrive
93) other
94) more
95) consists
96) translation
97) consistent
98) common
99) are
100) because
101) what
102) where
103) more
104) faced
105) attempt
106) expansive
107) distinct
108) that
109) Another
110) principle
111) dark
112) more
113) barely
114) distinguish
115) common
116) common
117) expanded
118) increasing
119) does
120) common
121) What
122) common
123) itself
124) reaching
125) storing
126) retrieving
127) dependent
128) highly
129) same
130) identity
131) what
132) effective
133) saving
134) seeks
135) facilitate
136) conceals
137) construction
138) provide
139) what
140) specific
141) effective
142) blind
143) encourages
144) social
145) social
146) encourages
147) complexity
148) what
149) social
150) ideal

151) because
152) dissatisfied
153) progressive
154) possible
155) moral
156) application
157) emerges
158) accepted
159) social
160) natural
161) natural
162) what
163) fear
164) fear
165) common
166) perceived
167) particular
168) were presented
169) same
170) dark
171) more
172) perceive
173) least
174) original
175) more
176) more
177) effects
178) distort
179) different
180) particular
181) simultaneously
182) particular
183) satisfying
184) same
185) perfect
186) fair
187) What
188) be ruined
189) What
190) wrong
191) wrong
192) explain
193) perfect
194) Perfect
195) What
196) what
197) feel
198) spreading
199) embraced
200) unpredictable

Prac 1   Answers

1) attention
2) hired
3) more
4) attachment
5) attention
6) unfolded
7) puzzled
8) What
9) appearing
10) proceeded
11) literate
12) complex
13) requires
14) making
15) be done
16) critical
17) explicitly
18) something
19) pleased
20) entirely
21) moral

22) identity
23) nontypical
24) personal
25) impossible
26) more
27) that
28) other
29) independently
30) accepted
31) are
32) same
33) strive
34) which
35) effective
36) capable
37) same
38) opposite
39) that
40) theother
41) that
42) are
43) more
44) because
45) neutral
46) reset
47) doubt
48) devices
49) genuine
50) confined
51) aspect
52) seems
53) What
54) fascinating
55) distinction
56) blurs
57) compelling
58) Preference
59) what
60) associate
61) another
62) different
63) different
64) associate
65) what
66) preference
67) reward
68) to repeat
69) starts
70) unpleasant
71) preference
72) preference
73) breed
74) outcome
75) raise
76) other
77) because
78) exception
79) different
80) raise
81) warm
82) raise
83) raise
84) successive
85) hinder
86) Different
87) specific
88) access
89) vital
90) available
91) alternative
92) arrive
93) other
94) more
95) consists
96) translation
97) consistent
98) common

99) are
100) because
101) what
102) where
103) more
104) faced
105) attempt
106) expansive
107) distinct
108) that
109) Another
110) principle
111) dark
112) more
113) barely
114) distinguish
115) common
116) common
117) expanded
118) increasing
119) does
120) common
121) What
122) common
123) itself
124) reaching
125) storing
126) retrieving
127) dependent
128) highly
129) same
130) identity
131) what
132) effective
133) saving
134) seeks
135) facilitate
136) conceals
137) construction
138) provide
139) what
140) specific
141) effective
142) blind
143) encourages
144) social
145) social
146) encourages
147) complexity
148) what
149) social
150) ideal
151) because
152) dissatisfied
153) progressive
154) possible
155) moral
156) application
157) emerges
158) accepted
159) social
160) natural
161) natural
162) what
163) fear
164) fear
165) common
166) perceived
167) particular
168) were presented
169) same
170) dark
171) more
172) perceive
173) least
174) original
175) more

176) more
177) effects
178) distort
179) different
180) particular
181) simultaneously
182) particular
183) satisfying
184) same
185) perfect
186) fair
187) What
188) be ruined
189) What
190) wrong
191) wrong
192) explain
193) perfect
194) Perfect
195) What
196) what
197) feel
198) spreading
199) embraced
200) unpredictable

Prac 2 **Answers**

1) internship
2) attention
3) consideration
4) coordinator
5) apparent
6) budget
7) approved
8) adjustments
9) modifications
10) hired
11) funding
12) wages
13) allocation
14) expenses
15) approached
16) unfolded
17) receptionist
18) reservation
19) puzzled
20) deliberately
21) proceeded
22) ruined
23) literate
24) critically
25) societal
26) bearing
27) informed
28) complex
29) interdisciplinary
30) mirroring
31) innovative
32) Navigating
33) quantify
34) conjecture
35) qualitatively,
36) interaction
37) developed
38) context
39) explicitly
40) stingy
41) delights
42) generosity
43) Undoubtedly,
44) praiseworthy
45) pleased
46) generous

47) various
48) virtues
49) courageous
50) identity
51) nontypical
52) impulse
53) Instant
54) Popping
55) pill
56) determine
57) mass
58) complicated
59) mass
60) distant
61) roughly
62) involves
63) binary
64) distance
65) quantities
66) equations
67) unmediated
68) properties
69) magnitudes
70) theories
71) neuroscience
72) area
73) strive
74) homeostasis
75) defined
76) bodily
77) compensator
78) capable
79) Pleasure
80) reliant
81) balance
82) correspondingly
83) expression
84) psychiatrist
85) miserable
86) miserable
87) essential
88) component
89) neutral
90) internal
91) Manufacturers
92) masterfully
93) adequacy
94) itch
95) upgrade
96) genuine
97) confined
98) companions
99) spills
100) aspect
101) unstoppable
102) generation
103) revolutionize
104) efficacy
105) cycle
106) distinction
107) blurs
108) financial
109) priorities
110) current
111) logical
112) ceaseless
113) temptation
114) compelling
115) Conditioned
116) Researchers
117) associate
118) obviously
119) preference
120) shift
121) Conversely
122) avoids
123) stimulus

124) cancer
125) relieve
126) saline
127) equator
128) breed
129) temperate
130) polar
131) triggered
132) peak
133) reluctant
134) physically
135) reproductive
136) shrinks
137) nomadic
138) initiate
139) brood
140) raise
141) exceptionally
142) successive
143) reproductive
144) hinder
145) unawareness
146) compulsory
147) simplify
148) prior
149) access
150) vital
151) financial
152) technicians
153) applicable
154) alternative
155) interpretations
156) dialogue
157) commentaries
158) source
159) consists of
160) orally
161) linguistic
162) arises
163) expectations
164) senses
165) logically
166) consistent
167) productive
168) resemblances
169) phrase
170) trait
171) distinguish
172) destined
173) qualifies
174) stretch
175) flexible
176) forum
177) faced
178) spectrum
179) expansive
180) accommodate
181) concerns
182) detect
183) detect
184) principle
185) detect
186) varies
187) weak
188) barely
189) distinguish
190) benefiting
191) sharing
192) overuse
193) expanded
194) isolation
195) resource
196) overuse
197) crash
198) tragedy
199) degeneration
200) regenerate

201) Theoretically
202) capacity
203) store
204) offset
205) retrieving
206) efficient
207) dependent
208) observe
209) variable
210) contextual
211) underlying
212) visualization
213) general
214) diverse
215) visual
216) optimizing
217) naturally
218) facilitate
219) cognitive
220) concerned
221) explanatory
222) tales
223) adhere
224) illuminate
225) predictable
226) paradigm
227) conceals
228) construction
229) chronology
230) systematically
231) meaningful
232) storylines
233) inspire
234) neglect
235) straightforward
236) blind
237) limitations
238) potential
239) misunderstanding
240) encounter
241) contrary
242) literature
243) encourages
244) solitary
245) detachment
246) passivity
247) promotes
248) authority
249) arrangements
250) banned
251) novels
252) credited
253) dissatisfied
254) divisions
255) fellowship
256) discourages
257) injustice
258) revulsion
259) slavery
260) spiteof
261) liberty
262) sovereign
263) circumstance
264) state
265) accepted
266) antisocial
267) rational
268) phenomenon
269) force
270) mutual
271) affection
272) cognitive
273) perceived
274) depicted
275) particular
276) typically
277) symbolic

278) presented
279) varying
280) required
281) implies
282) genome
283) chromosomes
284) accumulate
285) alterations
286) medieval
287) stacked
288) variance
289) undergone
290) gathered
291) mutations
292) accelerating
293) noticeable
294) distort
295) readability
296) iris
297) Similarly
298) birthmarks
299) due
300) multiplied
301) particular
302) patch
303) simultaneously
304) lineage
305) differentiated
306) lineage
307) inherited
308) autumn
309) due
310) submit
311) browsed
312) managed
313) unending
314) logical
315) rescheduling
316) beamed
317) genuine
318) draft
319) routines
320) embraced

Prac 2 Answers

1) internship
2) attention
3) consideration
4) coordinator
5) apparent
6) budget
7) approved
8) adjustments
9) modifications
10) hired
11) funding
12) wages
13) allocation
14) expenses
15) approached
16) unfolded
17) receptionist
18) reservation
19) puzzled
20) deliberately
21) misspelling
22) appearing
23) proceeded
24) ruined
25) literate
26) critically
27) societal
28) bearing

29) informed
30) complex
31) interdisciplinary
32) mirroring
33) innovative
34) Navigating
35) quantify
36) conjecture
37) qualitatively,
38) critical
39) interaction
40) developed
41) explicitly
42) stingy
43) delights
44) generosity
45) Undoubtedly,
46) praiseworthy
47) pleased
48) generous
49) various
50) virtues
51) courageous
52) identity
53) virtues
54) nontypical
55) impulse
56) Instant
57) Popping
58) pill
59) determine
60) mass
61) complicated
62) mass
63) distant
64) roughly
65) involves
66) binary
67) which
68) measure
69) quantities
70) equations
71) unmediated
72) properties
73) magnitudes
74) neuroscience
75) area
76) strive
77) homeostasis
78) defined
79) bodily
80) compensator
81) capable
82) Pleasure
83) reliant
84) balance
85) pleasure
86) correspondingly
87) expression
88) psychiatrist
89) miserable
90) miserable
91) essential
92) component
93) neutral
94) internal
95) Manufacturers
96) masterfully
97) adequacy
98) itch
99) upgrade
100) genuine
101) confined
102) companions
103) spills
104) aspect
105) unstoppable

106) generation
107) revolutionize
108) efficacy
109) cycle
110) distinction
111) blurs
112) financial
113) priorities
114) current
115) logical
116) ceaseless
117) temptation
118) compelling
119) Conditioned
120) Researchers
121) associate
122) where
123) obviously
124) associate
125) preference
126) shift
127) Conversely
128) avoids
129) stimulus
130) cancer
131) preference
132) relieve
133) saline
134) preference
135) equator
136) breed
137) temperate
138) polar
139) triggered
140) peak
141) reluctant
142) physically
143) reproductive
144) shrinks
145) nomadic
146) initiate
147) breeding
148) brood
149) exceptionally
150) successive
151) reproductive
152) hinder
153) unawareness
154) compulsory
155) simplify
156) prior
157) access
158) vital
159) financial
160) technicians
161) applicable
162) identifying
163) alternative
164) pressure
165) interpretations
166) dialogue
167) commentaries
168) translations
169) source
170) consists of
171) orally
172) linguistic
173) arises
174) expectations
175) senses
176) logically
177) consistent
178) productive
179) related
180) resemblances
181) phrase
182) trait

183) distinguish
184) destined
185) qualifies
186) stretch
187) flexible
188) attempting
189) forum
190) faced
191) spectrum
192) expansive
193) accommodate
194) distinct
195) concerns
196) detect
197) detect
198) principle
199) detect
200) lit
201) varies
202) strength
203) louder
204) barely
205) law
206) distinguish
207) stimuli
208) benefiting
209) overuse
210) benefits
211) expanded
212) isolation
213) competing
214) resource
215) overuse
216) crash
217) tragedy
218) tragic
219) degeneration
220) regenerate
221) Theoretically
222) capacity
223) store
224) offset
225) retrieving
226) efficient
227) dependent
228) observe
229) variable
230) contextual
231) underlying
232) visualization
233) general
234) diverse
235) visual
236) optimizing
237) naturally
238) simplify
239) generalize
240) facilitate
241) cognitive
242) concerned
243) explanatory
244) tales
245) adhere
246) illuminate
247) predictable
248) paradigm
249) conceals
250) construction
251) chronology
252) systematically
253) meaningful
254) storylines
255) inspire
256) neglect
257) contributions
258) imagination
259) straightforward

260) blind
261) limitations
262) potential
263) misunderstanding
264) encounter
265) contrary
266) literature
267) encourages
268) solitary
269) detachment
270) passivity
271) promotes
272) authority
273) arrangements
274) banned
275) novels
276) credited
277) dissatisfied
278) divisions
279) fellowship
280) discourages
281) injustice
282) credited
283) revulsion
284) slavery
285) spiteof
286) liberty
287) sovereign
288) emerges
289) circumstance
290) state
291) accepted
292) antisocial
293) rational
294) phenomenon
295) force
296) mutual
297) affection
298) mutual
299) assembles
300) drive
301) cognitive
302) perceived
303) depicted
304) particular
305) typically
306) symbolic
307) presented
308) varying
309) required
310) match
311) implies
312) genome
313) chromosomes
314) accumulate
315) alterations
316) medieval
317) stacked
318) variance
319) undergone
320) gathered
321) mutations
322) accelerating
323) noticeable
324) distort
325) readability
326) mutation
327) iris
328) birthmarks
329) due
330) multiplied
331) particular
332) patch
333) simultaneously
334) lineage
335) differentiated
336) lineage

337) autumn
338) due
339) submit
340) browsed
341) managed
342) unending
343) logical
344) rescheduling
345) beamed
346) genuine
347) draft
348) routines
349) embraced
350) unpredictable

## quiz 1 Answers

1) C-D-B-E-A
2) E-A-D-B-C
3) A-D-C-B-E
4) C-B-A-D-E
5) D-A-E-B-C
6) E-C-B-A-D
7) A-B-E-C-D
8) A-D-B-E-C
9) E-A-C-B-D
10) D-C-B-A-E
11) E-A-C-D-B
12) D-C-E-A-B
13) A-C-D-B-E
14) A-D-B-C-E
15) E-B-C-D-A
16) A-B-E-C-D
17) C-A-E-B-D
18) B-A-E-D-C
19) C-B-D-E-A
20) D-A-C-E-B
21) A-D-C-E-B
22) D-B-C-E-A

## quiz 2 Answers

1) [정답 및 해설] ⑤
been hired => hired

2) [정답 및 해설] ③
thought => thinking

3) [정답 및 해설] ⑤
develop => be developed

4) [정답 및 해설] ②
habitat => habit

5) [정답 및 해설] ⑤
interdependently => independently

6) [정답 및 해설] ③
similar => opposite

7) [정답 및 해설] ①
saw => sow

8) [정답 및 해설] ①
that => what

9) [정답 및 해설] ③
their => its

10) [정답 및 해설] ①
awareness => unawareness

11) [정답 및 해설] ④
arouses => arises

12) [정답 및 해설] ⑤
fixed => flexible

13) [정답 및 해설] ④
telling => to tell

14) [정답 및 해설] ③
competitive => competing

15) [정답 및 해설] ③
the other => other

16) [정답 및 해설] ③
interruptive => interpretive

17) [정답 및 해설] ③
impossible => possible

18) [정답 및 해설] ③
what => which

19) [정답 및 해설] ②
to match => match

20) [정답 및 해설] ③
consisted => consisting

21) [정답 및 해설] ①
recommend => remind

## quiz 3 Answers

1) [정답 및 해설] ④
ⓐ inquires => requires
ⓓ proved => approved
ⓔ needing => needs

2) [정답 및 해설] ②
ⓖ processed => proceeded
ⓗ thought => thinking
ⓘ been ruined => ruined

3) [정답 및 해설] ②
ⓐ literacy => literate
ⓕ conjunction => conjecture
ⓘ develop => be developed

4) [정답 및 해설] ④
ⓑ praiseworthy something => something praiseworthy
ⓓ satisfied => satisfying
ⓗ is => are

5) [정답 및 해설] ③
ⓔ resolves => involves
ⓕ where => which

6) [정답 및 해설] ③
ⓔ reliable => reliant
ⓚ miserably => miserable

7) [정답 및 해설] ②
ⓐ saw => sow
ⓗ careless => ceaseless

8) [정답 및 해설] ④
ⓗ given => been given
ⓘ been received => received

9) [정답 및 해설] ①
ⓓ willing => reluctant
ⓗ dessert => desert
ⓘ successful => successive

10) [정답 및 해설] ③
ⓑ impulsive => compulsory
ⓔ investment => investigation

11) [정답 및 해설] ②

ⓒ transferring => translating
ⓓ done => been done
ⓕ translating => being translated

12) [정답 및 해설] ⑤
ⓐ for => as
ⓒ are belonged => belong
ⓓ confining => defining

13) [정답 및 해설] ①
ⓐ inception => perception
ⓒ principal => principle
ⓕ is varied => varies

14) [정답 및 해설] ①
ⓒ expended => expanded
ⓓ competitive => competing
ⓔ decreasing => increasing

15) [정답 및 해설] ②
ⓐ reaching at => reaching
ⓓ independent => dependent
ⓚ seeking => seeks

16) [정답 및 해설] ④
ⓐ reveals => conceals
ⓗ interruptive => interpretive

17) [정답 및 해설] ③
ⓗ dissatisfy => dissatisfied
ⓘ encourages => discourages

18) [정답 및 해설] ②
ⓔ themselves => them
ⓕ is => are
ⓖ that => what

19) [정답 및 해설] ②
ⓒ excluded => included
ⓚ what => how

20) [정답 및 해설] ⑤
ⓐ circulate => accumulate
ⓑ different from => similar to
ⓒ alternatives => alterations

21) [정답 및 해설] ①
ⓐ satisfied => satisfying
ⓒ recommend => remind
ⓗ them => it

## quiz 4 Answers

1) [정답 및 해설]
② intermediate => immediate
④ proved => approved
⑤ needing => needs
⑥ been hired => hired
⑦ alterating => allocation

2) [정답 및 해설]
② conservation => reservation
④ thought => thinking
⑤ delightfully => deliberately
⑥ to appear => appearing
⑦ processed => proceeded

3) [정답 및 해설]
② critical => critically
④ informing => informed
⑥ conjunction => conjecture
⑨ do => be done
⑩ develop => be developed

4) [정답 및 해설]
⑥ habitat => habit
⑦ compulsory => impulse

⑧ is => are
⑨ what => how
⑩ possible => impossible

5) [정답 및 해설] ⑤
② the => a
④ very => much
⑤ resolves => involves
⑥ where => which
⑨ interdependently => independently

6) [정답 및 해설]
① that => which
③ that => which
⑤ reliable => reliant
⑨ to be => being
⑫ them => it

7) [정답 및 해설]
③ refined => confined
⑤ fascinated => fascinating
⑥ efficiency => efficacy
⑧ careless => ceaseless
⑨ is remained => remains

8) [정답 및 해설]
① that => what
④ easily => easy
⑥ appearing => appeared
⑦ unpleasantly => unpleasant
⑩ should want => wanted

9) [정답 및 해설]
② rise => raise
③ their => its
④ willing => reluctant
⑥ why => because
⑨ rise => raise

10) [정답 및 해설]
④ inferior => prior
⑥ assess => access
⑦ were required => required
⑧ application => applicable
⑩ change => changing

11) [정답 및 해설]
① who => whom
② reach => arrive
④ done => been done
⑥ translating => being translated
⑦ arouses => arises

12) [정답 및 해설]
④ confining => defining
⑤ determined => destined
⑥ lays => lies
⑨ were faced => faced
⑩ expensive => expansive

13) [정답 및 해설]
② should => might
⑤ that => which
⑥ is varied => varies
⑦ telling => to tell
⑧ more => much

14) [정답 및 해설]
① benefitted => benefiting
② be supported => support
③ expended => expanded
⑤ decreasing => increasing
⑧ it => itself

15) [정답 및 해설]
② offsets => is offset
③ reviving => retrieving
⑥ the other => other
⑧ that => what

⑨ serve => serves

16) [정답 및 해설]
① reveals => conceals
⑥ effectively => effective
⑦ analysis => analyzing
⑧ interruptive => interpretive
⑨ their => its

17) [정답 및 해설]
③ to => with
⑧ dissatisfy => dissatisfied
⑨ encourages => discourages
⑩ kin => keen
⑬ compulsion => revulsion

18) [정답 및 해설]
③ prescribes => describes
④ what => which
⑥ is => are
⑦ that => what
⑩ themselves => them

19) [정답 및 해설]
① influence on => influence
② depicting => depicted
④ made => were made
⑤ varied => varying
⑥ to match => match

20) [정답 및 해설]
③ alternatives => alterations
⑤ badly => worse
⑥ accelerated => accelerating
⑦ from => in
⑫ lays => lies

21) [정답 및 해설]
① satisfied => satisfying
⑤ to worry => worrying
⑥ ruin => be ruined
⑧ them => it
⑩ to feel => feel

quiz 5 **Answers**

1) 즉각적인 - immediate // 조정 - adjustments // 수정 - modifications //
   배당 - allocation

2) ⓐ
   been hired ⇨ hired
   as ⇨ than

3) 예상하지 못한 - unexpected // 의도적으로 - deliberately

4) (가) With a sense of ease,

5) 문해력 있는 - literate // 범교과적인 - interdisciplinary // 질적으로 -
   qualitatively // 변명 - excuse

6) ⓐ
   are ⇨ being

7) (가) teaching mathematics should be done in interaction with critical
   thinking along with a decision-making process.

8) 관대함 - generosity // 의심할 여지 없이 - Undoubtedly // 안정된 -
   stable // 충동 - impulse

9) ⓐ
   pleasing ⇨ pleased

10) (가) They are part of who you are, as they are part of how your
    character was formed.

11) 들어갈 연결어 - In other words // 중재되지 않은 - unmediated

12) ⓐ

measuring ⇨ measure
where ⇨ which

13) (가) Things get much more complicated if I want to know the mass
    of a distant star.

14) -를 추구하다 - strive for // 보상의 - compensatory // 잠재적인 -
    potential // 상응하여 - correspondingly

15) ⓐ
    hearing ⇨ heard

16) (가) She says that our attempts to escape being miserable are in
    fact making us even more miserable.

17) 적절성 - adequacy // 흐릿해지다 - blurs // 우선순위 - priorities // 끊
    임없는 - ceaseless // 매력 - temptation

18) ⓐ
    defined ⇨ confined

19) ⓑ
    aspects ⇨ aspect

20) ⓒ
    promise ⇨ promises

21) (가) What's fascinating, or perhaps disturbing, is the utter efficacy
    of this cycle in shaping our desires.

22) 연관시키다 - associate // 들어갈 연결어 - Conversely // 불쾌한 -
    unpleasant // 완화하다 - relieve

23) ⓐ
    defence ⇨ preference

24) ⓑ
    which ⇨ where
    spending ⇨ to spend
    what ⇨ that

25) (가) The two places are made obviously different to make it as easy
    as possible for the animal to associate each place with what
    happened to it there.

26) 적도 - equator // 촉발하다 - triggered // 번식의 - reproductive // 유
    목의 - nomadic // 유난히 - exceptionally

27) ⓐ
    combine ⇨ divide

28) (가) Most birds are not simply reluctant to breed at other times
    but they are also physically incapable of doing so.

29) 방해하다 - hinder // 필수적인 - compulsory // 수행하다 - conduct //
    대체 - alternative

30) ⓐ
    superior ⇨ prior
    inquired ⇨ required

31) (가) Often students are unable to identify the resources they need
    to perform the task required of them.
    (나) Even if some of the resources required for a task may not be
    available, identifying them in advance may help students' creativity.

32) 해석 - interpretations // 대화 - dialogue // 구두로 - orally

33) ⓐ
    transporting ⇨ translating
    refer ⇨ refer to

34) (가) All translators feel some pressure from the community of
    readers for whom they are doing their work.
    (나) his or her idea of the translation's purpose will be influenced by
    the expectations of the person or people it is for.

35) 생산적인 - productive // 유사성 - resemblances

36) ⓐ
    is ⇨ are
    quantifies ⇨ qualifies

37) ⓑ
worthy ⇨ worth
wish ⇨ wishing

38) (가) The more one tries to figure out where the border lies between reading and not-reading, the more edge cases will be found to stretch the term's flexible boundaries.
(나) The attempt moves toward an understanding of reading as a spectrum that is expansive enough to accommodate the distinct reading activities.

39) 감지 - perception // 그렇지 않았더라면 - otherwise

40) ⓐ
light ⇨ lit
where ⇨ which

41) ⓑ
strong ⇨ weak
very ⇨ barely

42) (가) Weber's law means that it is harder to distinguish between two samples when those samples are larger or stronger levels of the stimuli.

43) 교통량 - traffic // 들어갈 적절한 단어 본문 활용 - commons // 고립 - isolation // 들어갈 적절한 단어 본문 활용 - commons // 재생산하다 - regenerate

44) 수용력 - capacity // 상기하다 - retrieving // 지속적인 - consistent

45) ⓐ
independent ⇨ dependent
capturing ⇨ captured by
Similarly ⇨ Nevertheless

46) (가) The brain, being naturally against unnecessary effort, constantly seeks to simplify and generalize information to facilitate the cognitive process.

47) 예측가능한 - predictable // 감추다 - conceals // 연대기 - chronology // 분석하다 - analyzing // 무시하다 - neglect

48) (가) we can blind ourselves to the limitations of a given model and fail to note its potential for misunderstanding a situation to which it ill applies.

49) 권위 - authority // 불의 - injustice // 혐오감 - revulsion

50) ⓐ
idle ⇨ ideal
credited ⇨ been credited
satisfied ⇨ dissatisfied

51) (가) Theorists have maintained that literature encourages solitary reading and reflection as the way to engage with the world and thus counters the social and political activities that might produce social change.

52) 군주 권력 - sovereign power

53) ⓐ
with ⇨ without
believing ⇨ believes
that ⇨ what

54) (가) It is, rather, mutual fear of men's present and future that assembles them, since the cause of fear is a common drive among people in the state of nature.

55) 인지되는 - perceived // 상징적인 - symbolic

56) ⓐ
match ⇨ to match
were depicted ⇨ depicted

57) (가) Participants then had to match the figure to a background varying from dark to light red
(나) This implies that the cognitive association of objects to color influences how we perceive that color.

58) 중세의 - medieval // 들어갈 연결어 - Similarly // 동시에 - simultaneously // 계보 - lineage

59) ⓐ
copy ⇨ copying
copy ⇨ copying

60) (가) To make things worse, mutations may damage genes responsible for error checking and repair of genomes, further accelerating the introduction of mutations.
(나) If the mutation occurred early on in the lineage of the developing iris, then all cells in that patch have inherited that change.

61) 상기시키다 - remind // 급하게 2단어 - in haste // 만족감 - satisfaction // 예측 불가능한 - unpredictable

62) ⓐ
was ⇨ did
dressing ⇨ dressed

63) (가) Max furiously browsed through his planner without answering him, only to find the wrong date written in it.
(나) What matters is what we do when things get messy.